．．*．

for Jim,
a summer of
lost and found.
best
C. L. Rawlins

Broken Country

Also by C. L. Rawlins

Sky's Witness:
A Year in the Wind River Range

A Ceremony on Bare Ground
(Poems)

Broken Country

Mountains & Memory

C. L. Rawlins

A JOHN MACRAE BOOK

Henry Holt and Company
New York

Henry Holt and Company, Inc.
Publishers since 1866
115 West 18th Street
New York, New York 10011

Henry Holt® is a registered
trademark of Henry Holt and Company, Inc.

Library of Congress Cataloging-in-Publication Data
Rawlins, C. L. (Clem L.)
Broken country: mountains & memory / C. L. Rawlins.—1st ed.
p.   cm.
"A John Macrae book."
1. Natural history—West (U.S.)   2. Rawlins, C. L. (Clem L.)—
Journeys—West (U.S.)   3. West (U.S.)—Description and travel.
I. Title.
QH104.5.W4R36   1996   96-18048
508.78—dc20   CIP

ISBN 0-8050-3718-7

First Edition—1996

Designed by Betty Lew

Printed in the United States of America
All first editions are printed on acid-free paper. ∞

1   3   5   7   9   10   8   6   4   2

To Paul Shepard

Contents

Notes and Acknowledgments

Besides the Wyoming mountains and my memory, the source for this book is a journal that includes poems, sketches, rubbings, pressed plants, and grievous errors. I revised the poems where they needed it, by present standards, but kept their spirit (and cribs) intact. Where I was dead wrong (e.g., I logged sulfur paintbrush as *thermopsis*) I fixed it, but otherwise followed my original, rather wayward account.

The printed sources, then and now, are: *Horses, Hitches, and Rocky Trails,* by Joe Back (Sage Books, 1959); *Mountain Plants of Northeastern Utah,* by Berniece Andersen and Arthur Holmgren (Utah State University Extension, c. 1970); and *The World in Literature,* volume 1, compiled by Robert Warnock and George K. Anderson (Scott, Foresman, 1967). Passages quoted are from the last work, except for Robert Fitzgerald's fine verse translations of the *Iliad* (Anchor, 1974) and *Odyssey* (Anchor, 1963). Not being a literary scholar, I approach the canon much as a raven would a dead sheep: swoop in, snatch a tidbit, and flap off.

Though I didn't carry it, I had just read *Technicians of the Sacred: A Range of Poetries from Africa, America, Asia & Oceania,* by Jerome

Rothenberg (Anchor, 1969) and felt its influence. Henry Vaughan's letter in the prologue is quoted, with spelling amended, from Anne Cluysenaar's poem "Vaughan Variations" (*Poetry Wales* 31.2, 1995).

My good *compañero* Mitchell Black went on to herd sheep, guide pack trips, and patrol summer range. Now married to Susan Romyn, and master of Clear Creek Shoe and Leather in Buffalo, Wyoming, he read my first draft and nudged me toward his own high standard of truth. He also wrote that Royal Preston was firmly against the Vietnam War, which I didn't know, and had thus set himself apart (for reasons near my own) from his lifelong ranching community.

Roger Preston is now a veterinarian in California and a rancher in Wyoming. He grazed sheep in Murphy Creek until 1993, when he switched the permit to cattle. Since cows prefer canyon bottoms, much of the high country is no longer grazed by livestock, and in 1994 some of the herding trails were overgrown.

My brother Chris Rawlins lived in Santa Fe, New Mexico, for many years and worked as a librarian; he is recently in Seattle: I expect a letter soon.

"Cassandra Massey" is a name I chose, with changes in details, to guard the privacy of a woman I no longer know. Some aspects of our life together were condensed to fit this limited frame, and she would tell it differently, perhaps.

Linda Baker Rawlins accompanied me on the first trip back, endured my spells and trances, and helped withal, more than she knows. I'm deeply grateful to Paul Shepard for *Nature and Madness,* and all his work, and to the late Sherman Paul for our lively exchange of letters as this book took shape. I'm also grateful to literary agent Carl Brandt for encouragement, and to my editor, John Macrae, for his sense of style. Likewise, my thanks to Susan Marsh, shy essayist, for out-of-print maps, and to novelist Liz Arthur for her icy and compassionate perspective.

Between 1973 and 1993, Murphy Creek received new bridges, more clearcuts, and exploration for oil and gas. The most visible scar is a barren rectangle, roughly a half-mile long by a quarter wide, just above Ray's Knob, where two wildcat holes were drilled in the 1980s. The big spruces and firs were clearcut, and the ground was scraped into well pads. Afterward, it was shoved back and seeded with grasses, none of which seems to be doing very well. Out of this willful desolation are thrust two black drill pipes, which may someday be seen as historic or valuable, unlike the forest and animals they displaced.

And finally, this is not a guidebook, so be prepared to find your own way.

Eyes bright! Cinches tight!

Go.

C.L.R. (*in partibus infidelium*) 1996

Prologue

In July 1973, mostly by chance, I went to the Salt River Mountains with Mitchell Black, three dogs, a string of horses, and a herd of sheep. When we came down in September with the snow, I'd lost part of myself. But what I found, or recovered, there has made all the difference.

I grew up in the dry valleys of the western interior with mountains always in sight. They were closer than the sky, and streams flowed from them, and they were cool when the valley was hot, and green when it was dry: sanctuary in times of trouble.

And I grew up in a time of war. Some of my friends died in Vietnam, and others bear the marks, and I honor them now, as I did then. But I realized that war was not something in which I could take a willing part. The power I'd taken for granted, steel and fire, was suddenly ranged against me. And I also sensed a rage that swelled, with no reason but to see its own will done.

No is a short word, but when I spoke it you could almost hear the crack. It opened a rift I could never cross again, between me and my family, me and my heritage. My father's values were forged in the ond World War, but they came from western livestock ranching, and my mother grew up in mining camps. Our myth was the frontier, and that vast and violent taking was the legacy on which my life was built.

Having refused its central rite, I set myself apart. So I went to the mountains not as a pioneer, to take up land, nor as a pilgrim, to confirm my faith, but by chance, and in disarray. To be found you must be lost, or lose yourself in some way, not necessarily geographic. To be healed, you must court wounds, or even death. And to be whole, you must know that you are, or can be, or will be, broken.

The place of understanding is not necessarily kind. Heaven and earth meet there, and they will crush you if you do not hold them apart, so you need resolute strength, like the hardness of old cowboys. But such strength, unrelieved, will crush you, so you also need lightness and trickery and music.

Edward O. Wilson writes: "The green prehuman earth is the mystery we were chosen to solve." And just as we've built cities we can't inhabit, we may also have devised lives we cannot live. In this pass, wisdom may consist not so much of learning bright new tricks as in keeping our old ones intact. And in *Nature and Madness* (1982, pp. 11–17), Paul Shepard writes:

> Western civilized cultures . . . have largely abandoned the ceremonies of adolescent initiation that affirm the metaphoric, mysterious, and poetic quality of nature. . . . But our human developmental program requires external modes of order—if not a community of plants and animals, then words in a book or the ranks and professions of society, or the machine. . . .
>
> The person himself is, of course, caught between his inner calendar and the surgeries of society. His momentum for further growth may be twisted or amputated, according to the hostilities, fears, and fantasies required of him, as his retardation is silently engineered to domesticate his integrity or to allow him to share in the collective dream of mastery. . . .
>
> The individual growth curve . . . is a biological heritage of the deep past. It is everyman's tree of life, now pruned by civic

gardeners as the outer branches and twigs become incompatible with the landscaped order. The reader may extend that metaphor as he wishes, but I shall move to an animal image to suggest that the only society more frightful than one run by children, as in Golding's *Lord of the Flies,* might be one run by childish adults.

Reading this, I felt a surge of recognition. And I dug for the old black journal, which had gathered dust. And it confirmed what I felt: in 1973, in the Salt River Mountains, I learned to live in a world that I could love and also trust.

My going to mountains and returning with a gift (or fury) for words is not unique. As I was finishing this book, I saw this account in the journal *Poetry Wales*:

There in summer time following the sheep & looking to their lambs, he fell into a deep sleep; In which he dreamt, that he saw a beautiful young man with a garland of green leaves upon his head, & a hawk upon his fist, with a quiver full of Arrows at his back, coming towards him (whistling several measures or tunes all the way) & at last let the hawk fly at him, which (he dreamt) got into his mouth and inward parts, & suddenly awaked in a great fear & consternation, but possessed with such a vein, or gift of poetry, that he left the sheep and went about the country, making songs upon all occasions . . .

Henry Vaughan, in a letter, 1694

I started by transcribing my journal, but it was too sparse at some points and too rapt (or foolish) at others. So, to refresh my sense of the landscape, I returned to the Salt River Range for one week in 1993, and four week-long trips, July through October 1994, and the descriptions are as faithful to the place as I could make them.

Life, being a landscape we traverse but once, is more difficult to reconstruct. Yet when I found our old camps and trails, I also found unlooked-for recollection: I was flooded with circumstance, so vivid and in such quantity that each trip was like a walking dream. Never before have I known how much my thoughts and memories are not simply *about* the land but *of* it.

My articulation of these events is present, not past: the combined work of two different selves, twenty years apart. We write about the past not so much to recover it as to absolve or free ourselves. And often I felt the urge to render myself as the hero I was not. So I've tried likewise to recall anger, selfishness, and fear, which I hope you will forgive.

Through countless moves and spring cleanings, I kept the books I carried into the Salt River Range: a horse packer's bible, a guide to mountain plants, and a classics text. When I took them to the mountains once again, I heard familiar voices.

And just as the voices we hear in songs and poems and books live in our imagination, so must our lives be risked, at times, in imaginary terrain.

So let us go into the dark country. Let these pages be your fire. Watch the flames and follow the map of shadow they cast. Earth's night will pass; so will fear. And you may see your landmark in the rising light, wherever you find yourself: in the mountains of memory, in the forest of contradiction, or in the broken country of the heart.

So was I then / if that was I and not a dream. . . .

Iliad (XI: 729–30)

1 ~
Star Valley

We drove them up the mountain in the rain. The ewes bellowed and the lambs cried back in their wavering voices as they moved in a circulating mass, their dirty wool mounded like foam. Around us the grass bowed down and the dark leaves of chokecherry gleamed, and as it rained, the red of the soil deepened. Tiny pools formed and spilled, turning the trail from mud to grease, and our horses slid and struck.

Mitch rode close and flung his arm toward the crest. "Another week, we'll be right on top," he said. "Two months. We won't come back this way."

I could feel the rain's weight, slipping off the brim of my hat down my yellow slicker, onto my denim thighs, cold. We split up, crowding the sheep, cursing them, inciting the dogs. The herd surged east, like a flood returning to its source, and we followed, climbing in long jags through thickets of serviceberry, each horse track a muddy cup for the rain to fill.

That last night at the ranch I lay awake, staring at a patch of moonlight. The upstairs room had one window and one door, and the four walls belonged to someone else, and the sheets and the musty blankets. All I owned was the dark. The coming day would be hard, and each hour without sleep promised to make it harder, but sleep wouldn't come: I felt like a boulder, heavy and perfectly round, balanced on a bare hill. Given a push, I could roll to any point of the compass, and I would roll for a long way, and for a very long time.

Another year in school had passed, without a proper ending. My family hoped that June would see my graduation, but I was many credits short, with thirty failed hours. In the middle of spring term, I'd spent a day examining another wall, then filled a pack once more and hitched south to the canyons, to find red rocks and quiet sand.

Is there a word for the color of moonlight? On the papered wall of the room, the moon laid its moving pattern over the faded flowers, shadowing the cottonwood leaves that rattled faintly through the open window. My clothes hung from a hook on the door, and my boots gaped by the bed like two open mouths. There were still long hours to wait. "It's not your fault," Cassandra had said the week before as we huddled in a sleeping bag, under the rush of the creek. The question was how to live. She had plans and I hadn't, except for this. She wanted things and I wanted out. Something had snapped, between me and all else.

I had been told too many times how I should feel, too many times what I should do. On television, the old men stood between us and the flag, hiding its stripes with their dark suits and pressed uniforms, their heads a moving blot against the field of stars, with lies falling from their lips. Defense? Did they believe that skinny, black-clad troops, from a poor country across the world's widest sea, would overrun San Francisco on bamboo rafts one rainy night?

This country is ours, earned with our blood. Always that. The blood-marked valleys under these high ranges, the Salt Rivers, the Bear Rivers, and the Wasatch, were my home, if I had one. My great-grandfather once had a ranch in this valley. My father was born not far away. But how could I earn the right to live in this place? By killing someone I'd never seen, in his own land, on the other side of the earth?

I couldn't make sense of that: our deeds never cancel out. The wrong stays close to the right, twisted like strands in a rope.

A peace treaty had been signed in Paris in January, and that same month the military draft had been ended, but I was still on the hook, my case pending. There'd been a siege at Wounded Knee, dissident Indians with rifles hemmed in by FBI agents and federal marshals with machine guns, armored vehicles, and helicopters. The Watergate hearings were underway, and Senator Sam Ervin was digging for President Nixon's tapes, and Nixon had ordered the Secret Service not to testify. There was no end to it. Our soldiers had been called home, but the war would go on inside us. I could see those heavy-bodied old men, chins thrust out. *All countries are ours.*

I had to find one that wasn't.

In a high valley on the far western edge of Wyoming, the Preston ranch house stood alone, cornered by lanes of rutted dirt. The house was nearly a cube, and the direction it faced was uncertain. The front door, clean and unused, opened west. On the south, a cottonwood old as the house loomed over a sidewalk cracked by roots, and the south door had a tire-tread mat and bore signs of use. But the real entrance lay on the east, where a streak of muddy prints led up to a boot-marked door. The east door opened on the sprawl of corrals and sheds, and the white barn, and the mountains, which rose up blue and close beyond.

Mitch, my skiing partner, had tended camp the year before for Prestons' regular herder. The herder was named Alfonso Gonzales and was called Pancho. He stayed in a tiny trailer by the barns, going to Thayne or Afton to drink, fight, and hunt a bedmate. He would return in a fine, high glow to sing, curse, challenge, and scandalize the Mormon ranch. Eventually, sometimes with help from Royal or Roger, he would burrow into his quilts.

The trailer had a propane heater, and in late spring 1973, during lambing season, the heater exploded. Pancho was burned on his face, arms, shoulders, and chest. Roger called Mitch, who had been his college roommate. "Pancho's hurt, his trailer blew up. Can you herd instead? Okay? Good deal. Can you get a campjack in Logan?"

"The tall guy? Rawlins? He *might* work out."

∾

At first light we started the sheep from the pasture north of the house and drove them up the long fenced lanes that followed section lines as rain swept in on a blue front. Roger rode ahead on a gelded palomino named—rancher's joke—the Black Stallion. I rode a sorrel named Red, and Mitch rode a young black horse called Tony. We stayed behind the sheep, and I could see the rain dripping from Mitch's hat into his black beard, and his teeth flashing as he yelled.

Uncle Warren, crippled by a stroke and near blind, pushed the center, his yells emerging as gargles and coughs. His white horse, Tom, spun and trotted as Warren hung on and let the old gelding work, his bony knees clinging to the ribby flanks.

It rained in pulses all morning, clouds dropping almost to the ground, then lifting to admit the sun. The oatmeal and boiled rhubarb made a fist in my guts. When I yelled at the balky sheep, I also cursed Mitch and Roger, who yelled back, red faced, with equal fervor.

"Goddam, goddam, goddam—*booooooorrega! Yiiip-yiii-owwww!*"

Twice an hour, a ranch truck would come to a halt as the sheep eddied around it. The hay harvest was rained out, and the drivers, sunburnt men with tension in their jaws, spoke to Roger while eyeing me and Mitch. "New herders? How's Pancho? My damn baler's broke and the part just got in. Clear up tomorrow, they say. So . . ."

Mitch didn't resemble the men who drove the pickups. They were broad faced, like Herefords, with the solid presence that came of living where they were born. Mitch was fine boned and lightly knit, with black eyes and a ponytail sprouting under his slouch hat. He looked more like a gypsy fiddler than a livestock hand.

Roger, even with his rimless glasses and a collar awash in blond curls, was at home here too. But Mitch was self-conscious in the way he sat his horse, and held the reins, and yelled at the herd. He watched Roger for cues, furtively, while I watched him openly, not taking chances. Having grandly overstated my knowledge of livestock, I wanted to get into the hills and out of sight.

We nooned at the canyon's mouth: Louise's white-bread sandwiches, canned beans, and boiled rhubarb in a plastic bowl with just one spoon. While one of us ate, the others herded, keeping them out of the green alfalfa, heading them off a field of ripening wheat, and turning them back from the freshly graveled road with its sign: PUT YOUR BRAND ON A HUNK OF LAND!

"Seems like a guy could have a seat," said Roger, apologetic, as I spelled him off, "but they won't settle down. Sooo . . ."

Warren trotted by, his brown baseball cap soaked black, sputtering like a percolator at the herd: "Mother up. Mother up. Mother up."

The sheep struggled and blatted, fighting up the incline through wet brush. The canyon's mouth yawned under us, and above us the mountain disappeared, green and rocky, into cloud. When the rain slackened mosquitos rose, stirred into the air by the horses as we brushed by, boring in on our faces and necks and wrists, seeking our heat and breath.

"*Andale! Yow!* Stinking devilbastard rotten scum of hell."

Coursing between rock outcrops, milling in the meadows, traversing loose side slopes, the sheep moved in parallel, complaining lines. The lambs, cold and slow, tried to huddle in the shelter of each dripping bush. Here and there, a ewe would cry out and turn to locate her lost one, so the herd traveled like a cyclone, circling for the lambs in its heart, churning the slope with its revolutions.

"*Borrega! Booooooorrega! Yiii-yip-yowwww!*"

Warren's gelding lunged and dug, with the old man holding to the saddle horn like life itself. The sheepdogs darted, with Ansel, the gray mama, leading as her pup Tiger dashed in on her heels to undo her work, while Roger yelled: "Ansel! Tiger! Damn you! Get *back*!" Pookie, my dog, a shepherd-collie cross, dodged hooves and whined excitedly and made sporadic dashes.

"Git-git-git, *yeeeeeeeeee—owwww!*"

My boot soles squeaked in wet stirrups. My thighs were raw in my jeans, and I hated everything in sight: ewes, lambs, dogs, horses, mud, and men. Finally we let the sheep settle around the bases of pines and assort themselves in pairs, ewes bawling even as their lambs began to suck. Two hours after most people in Star Valley sat down to eat, we splashed through runoff braiding down a rough dirt road and fetched up on a foggy bench. There was an unfinished summerhouse, its plywood sides warping in the rain, and our camp was the covered porch. We tied the horses and, too starved to make a fire, we dug in a sack for cans.

Dinner was sardines, soda crackers, and cookies. Warren ate fitfully and then limped around the hill to check on the herd. Roger got up to follow him, reluctant to leave the food. I didn't think the sheep would go anywhere, if they were as tired as I was. I was so exhausted that when I looked at anything, I would stop chewing, so I had to close my eyes and command my jaw to work. Maybe I dozed off. When I opened my eyes again, Mitch was gone.

The west cleared, and a thin curtain of rain gleamed in the slanting light. Roger and Warren rode by and Roger waved. "Tomorrow, early," he yelled, as they went sledding down the access road, their horses' forelegs thrust stiffly out, carrying them out of sight.

A month past the solstice, the dark holds high. Mitch rode up, tied his horse, and dumped his saddle on the planks before rolling out his bag under the locked front door. "Roger and I have to move the sheep up tomorrow. Royal's bringing the rest of the horses up, with all the gear. Think you can get 'em packed?"

"I've got my little book. So, yeah. As long as I know where to go."

"There's a trail. Steep, but not too rough."

The green reach of Star Valley appeared, bright and close, then was gone under a cloud. The sky rolled its blue darkness at us, hiding the sunlit west, and we sat on the porch under the eave and listened to the renewed beat of the rain. The dogs crunched their food, growling softly at each other, then subsiding into groans. And the distances grew between our few words as the rain and the night cut us off from the roads, the ranches, the lights, and from the life I knew.

JULY 22

Across the valley the ridges went from transparent black to the darkest green, then flamed muddy red as the sunrise took them. Bright runs of aspen gleamed, their leaves like tiny mirrors under the shaggy pines that showed a sooty green to the first clear light.

We left our gear piled on the porch and walked through the wet grass to bring our horses in. They flung their heads up, snorted, and then relaxed. Red shifted but stayed put as I draped the rope over his neck, dipping his long head to accept the halter and relaxing as I caught the loop. I worked at the wet picket rope knotted around his foot until the bowline loosened, conscious of his weight balanced above me, feeling his breath as he sniffed the back of my neck.

"We'll ride around the sheep. Roger should be here soon. Then you ride down and wait for Royal with the rest of the horses and the packs. Don't forget the book."

I'd found a book called *Horses, Hitches, and Rocky Trails* by a man whose name seemed to have too few syllables: Joe Back. It had an olive green cover with the title in black and a drawing printed in red of a packhorse, picking its way down a steep slope. Inside were diagrams of a forbidding array of saddles, knots, buckles, and ropes, with drawings of horses in steep, rocky country: the horse packer's arcana. I'd been playing with furry scraps of rope for days, throwing hitches over the propane tank at the ranch and looping bowlines around the legs of the workbench as I patched and riveted the ancient packsaddles back together. Some of the leather straps had been broken so regularly that little original leather was left: one britchen strap, which ran around the hindquarters to keep the pack from sliding forward, was composed of seven pieces, variously aged and punctuated by copper rivets.

Mitch and Roger didn't offer me help unless I asked: they acted as if all this was self-evident, like tying my bootlaces. While I was western in birth and heritage, none of the specifics came with the genes. So when Royal had asked me if I knew how to pack horses, I lied. He caught on to me the first morning, when he told me to catch Tony, a black gelding he said was "a little green," and I came back leading a twenty-one-year-old mare named Tubby. There were two black horses in the big pasture, and she was the one I could catch. He'd looked at me hard but hadn't said a word, since aspiring campjacks weren't exactly thronging the ranch gate.

My questions had been met with blank looks, *western* looks, so I decided that I'd keep them under my newly acquired cowboy hat. Instead, I pored over the book. Joe Back's drawings were obsessively detailed, rendering the grain of the wood in the saddle bars and the twist of fibers in each rope, but they didn't take at first: rope in hand, I immediately forgot what I'd seen.

So I watched Mitch as we led the horses to the porch and put the saddles on. With my extra height and long arms, I managed to get Red's cinch too tight, and he snorted and fidgeted.

"Loosen up that *cincha*," Mitch said. "Can't slip your hand along his ribs, it's too snug. Pull it up, then lead him a few steps and check it. They blow up." He made a horsey face and puffed his stomach out. So I loosened the cinch, watching how he rolled his yellow slicker and bound it with the saddle strings, and I did that too. Then I led the gelding in a circle, tightened the cinch, led him around again, loosened it, and was starting on a third circuit when Mitch laughed.

"Hah! You'll tucker him out before you get on. Let's check the sheep before they get away from us." We rode into the sun, and I tipped my hat to break the glare. The ewes were spreading up the slope, giving soft moans and grunts as they fed, each followed by a lamb or twins. Yesterday had been hard for them, driven from the ranch along fenced roads, then shoved up the steep foreslope, and they were hungry, sorting the grass and leaves with their lips, nipping the best, taking a step, and nipping again.

We were taking them up to the high meadows that had just melted out of deep snow, where mountain plants ripened fast, throwing up leaves with the urgency of alpine summer, two brief months before the snow. With the sheep on the mountain, hayfields could be irrigated and cut, and the hay stacked for winter. But hay was poor food for sheep compared to the leafy mountain plants. And the lambs would come down from the mountain fat, ready to be sold.

The front line of sheep took the flower tops and tenderest leaves. The second wave took the best of what was left. Each successive rank found less and took the best of that. Stragglers got stems, the toughest leaves, and overwintered stuff. The larger the band, the harder the range was browsed. The Prestons grazed 750 ewes, small as commercial bands go. Some summer bands numbered 2,500 ewes, each with at least one lamb. Successful birth was the prerequisite for continued life: it wasn't worth keeping a barren ewe around just for the wool clip, and full-grown mutton is not much desired in America.

One night at the ranch table, Warren gave me a lecture on sheep husbandry, much of it unintelligible, but out of respect I nodded as if it were clear. Given the root equation of ranching, a ewe that bears healthy twins is worth more than one with single births, even if she doesn't live as long, so the twins—or one of the pair—are kept in the herd.

The sheep waddled in clots of ten or twenty, working up the slope. We rode around, careful not to push them, and then rode the north flank. Mitch swept his hand in a circle. "Keep 'em loose and don't bunch 'em up. We want 'em to move easy. They like to spread out and climb, and the fast ones break off. If you lose sheep, always look high."

We called the dogs back, but their blood was up and they were hard to restrain. Tiger, the pup, was the worst. Mitch called him "Tikki-Lo," which was easier to yell. It took an hour to circle the sheep, and then Mitch pointed me down the hill.

"Ride down to the end of that road in the quakies and meet Royal."

"What then?"

"Then you pack up."

"What then?"

"Lead the pack string up to the cabin and pack the sleeping bags and the food sack." He pointed to a higher bench, where aspens ruffled in the dawn wind. "Then head for that. You can see where the tent goes, and there're some big rocks to set the stove on. Roger should be here soon and we'll take 'em across, then drop 'em off north so they work upslope. After we get 'em bedded we'll show up for lunch."

I rode off, Pookie first tailing my horse, then yearning back toward the sheep: she'd discovered a new doggish endeavor and liked it. The steep road had firmed up in the sun, and Red slipped in only a few spots. I grabbed the horn and looked guiltily around, but there was no one to see.

It was still moist and cool under the aspens. Royal and the red stock truck were nowhere in sight. I listened for the sound of an engine, then relaxed. I tied Red to an aspen and took a leisurely piss on the base of another. A few mosquitos bounced under the brim of my hat. I checked my saddlebag for the packer's bible, then looked up. In full sun, the ridges were faintly hazed by evaporation, summer green softening their rocky bones.

The Salt River Range follows a crack in the continent where layers of sediment folded and rode up on the backs of other layers to form a series of parallel ridges called the Overthrust Belt. The rocks that shifted under the hooves of the sheep were silt-brown and gray, limestones and dolomites laid in the beds of the sea. To the east, the hardest rocks formed a single high spine above Star Valley and the Salt River. Cut by glaciers into cirques, deep bays in the ocean of air, the ridge walled off a narrow valley to the east, centered on Greys River. I knew this from my single geology class, and the map, but it was country I'd never seen.

The rust-spotted truck nosed into the glade. Red whinnied, and I stood up and tried to look competently western. Royal Preston slid from the seat, his white hair brilliant in the sun. He was a small man, fierce-faced and handsome. He spoke gently, the family tenor aged in his throat. "I'll unload the horses. You pack up."

He backed the truck against a bank, and we jumped the horses out: Tubby, the old black mare; Elhon, a young mare crossed from a Belgian dam and an Arab stud; Pronto, dark and shapely, and her foal, that skated on the wet manure covering the floorboards, squealed, and then ran head down out of the truckbed and crashed in a glossy heap. The foal bounced up, unharmed, and kicked, then trotted to the mare. "No name for that one yet," Royal said, "but he's sure a pistol. C'mon, old bud. Tom. Hup!" He whacked the side of the truck, and Tom lumbered to the gate and eased out, grunting and shaking his mane.

With the horses tied to trees, Royal hefted the gear down to me: the panniers Mitch and I had packed up at the ranch, the kitchen boxes, the packsaddles tangled in their straps, the stacks of hair pads and pack pads, manties of canvas, coils of rope, and woven cinches dangling their heavy brass hooks. One hook swung and caught me on the knee. I gritted my teeth but didn't swear; Royal's dignity made me self-conscious.

He heaved out fifty-pound sacks of sheep salt, coarse crystals that crunched as I took them on my shoulder. "That's it." I looked at the disorganized heap, thinking that it would never fit on four horses, even if I had known what I was doing. The truck's starter ground and Royal clunked it into gear. "Put that salt on Elhon. She acts up." Then he was gone.

I propped the book open in the crotch of a limb and started on Tom, who seemed to be asleep. The packsaddles were called sawbucks, curved wooden bars that fit the horse's back, connected by crossed pieces of oak. Wrapped around the joint of the oak bucks were straps of latigo that were screwed to the bars and ended in rings and buckles and woven cinches, a bewildering tangle. The saddles were old and beat-up: some of the bars were cracked along their length, the oak bucks were loose at the joints, and the leather straps for the breasts and britchens were glazed and cracked.

Consulting the book, I started with a felt hair pad and covered it with a canvas pack pad, then set the sawbuck on and cinched it, front and rear. Okay. There were two kinds of panniers: soft ones that looked like giant leather-bound L. L. Bean tote bags, and hard ones that were wooden boxes with one side of sheet metal, curved to fit the horse. They had loops of heavy stitched leather that went over the tops of the bucks. Good. With the panniers on, I set the box stove across as a top pack. "Joe Back, Top pack." Pretty simple, so far.

I picked up a manty, a six-foot square of canvas, and flung it over the load, and Tom woke up rather suddenly and spilled the box stove off with a clang, raising a cloud of soot. So I put the stove back on. Then I let him sniff the manty, which he did in a grudging fashion, and draped it over the load in what I hoped was a comforting way. Check. I tucked the corners in and then came the hard part: the hitch. According to Mitch, the hitch was the most important element.

I picked up a lash rope, about thirty-odd feet of stout hemp braided into the ring of a lash cinch, which was a woven band about three feet long with a hook on the other end. The cinch went under the belly, and the rope went over the load and through the hook, and after that things got complicated. There were single diamonds, double diamonds, and Decker slings, all of which looked like games of cat's cradle played by mental patients, and *aha!* with box panniers and a box stove, I could use a *box hitch.*

It only took a half hour, and Tom went back to sleep. I worked my magic on the other horses, remembering to let them sniff the manties, and tied each hitch once, then twice, checked, and finally stood back with a nudge of pride. Only Elhon stood without a load. I let her sniff the panniers, and she stood unmoved, so I hung them on the saddlebucks. Good. I lifted a sack of salt and flopped it down, as she dodged. It landed on my foot, and I swore, and Elhon bucked the empty panniers off, nearly uprooting the aspen to which she was tied.

I moved her to a thicker tree. A long half hour ensued, of snorts and flounders and my dances with a heavy sack balanced, before I got the five bags of salt on, two hundred and fifty pounds: two per side and one for the *top pack.*

"Break *that,* you big . . ."

The gold horse looked at me with a murderous eye as Tom, packed and standing for two hours, coughed. "Don't die," I pleaded, "yet."

When we reached the cabin I realized that I had to untie the hitches on two of them to get the food bag and bedding packed, which ate up another half hour. I imagined Mitch and Roger waiting for me and, more to the point, for their lunch. When we finally set out it was hot, and the flies made the horses twitch and huff.

The trail was steep, but at least it had dried up. I led the line of horses, digging and blowing on the steeps. Angling up the slopes to the bench, I found the camp. It sat in scattered fir and aspen, poles stacked and wet on the undersides with the rain, and two big blocks of limestone for the stove. I'd pictured Mitch and Roger waiting, but I'd beaten them here. Good. I unroped the horses, fought my hitches loose, and plumped the panniers in workmanlike stacks. Then I unsaddled the horses, their hair sweat-streaked under the pads, and made a pile of the saddles. Finding the food sack, I filched a cookie and let it dissolve in my mouth, eyes closed. Grace. I heard the breaths of the horses, the soft thumps of their hooves, and the panting of my dog.

Mitch and Roger rode up, and we unrolled the tent and staked it tight. It was heavy canvas, eight feet by ten, and well worn. Mitch showed me how to set up the box stove, resting it on stacked rocks. The stovepipe was telescoped inside the firebox, gritty with rust. Mitch fitted the sections and thrust the tapering pipe up through the steel-thimbled hole in the tent.

I dragged in the box panniers, plywood with rawhide shrunken over it, red-and-white hair still on, and he set the kitchen boxes on them, across from the stove. He drove two long stakes, to let the front flaps swing down as tables. In the back of the tent he cleared pinecones and sticks, and laid out canvas pack pads for a mattress, leaving me a space at the rear.

We made sandwiches: one for Mitch, two for me, three for Roger. Then we ate in a patch of shade. Roger finished first and stood up. "I'd better get back and move sprinkler pipe," he said. Mitch walked him out to his horse and they conferred, with Roger waving his hands to illustrate—something. But I couldn't hear what they said.

Roger rode out of sight and Mitch came back. "It's a home," he said. "You can do the rest. Turn the horses loose. And tie up that damn Tikki-Lo. I'll go watch the *borregas*. I'll be back around dark. Let's eat light—open some soup or something."

I turned the horses loose and they thundered north, out of sight. Then I moved things about, stacking them in one spot, then shifting them to another that seemed more functional. I strode out with the axe and came back with an armful of wood, mostly aspen that would burn quickly, giving little heat. Tiger whined and tested the dog chain. Pookie claimed Mitch's bedroll, and I shooed her off and brushed away the prints.

Clouds rose from the Caribou Range and advanced over the valley, and a brief rain swept up the slope. I could see the raindrops land on the tent, each making a shadowy circle and a little slap on the cloth, then gathering and running off in blue braids. When the rain stopped, I laid a pole at the back of the tent and rolled it in the canvas, weighting it with rocks, to stop the draft.

The stove inspired my reverence, such an odd and perfect artifact. One door, in front, was for the wood and the other, on the right side at the rear under the stovepipe, opened on a tiny oven. I scrounged more wood, moist rather than soaked, from under the brush and laid an experimental fire. A quick draft roared up the pipe, and the stove radiated instant heat. I opened the kitchen boxes and admired the tidy counters. Inside were jars of syrup and salt, cans of beans and corn, cotton dishtowels and pots. Underneath, the cowhide-covered panniers held sacks of flour, cornmeal, and beans.

The stove got so hot that I shut the damper and tied back the door flaps of the tent. I went down and filled a canvas water bag at a tiny spring and poured the coffeepot full, setting it on the stove with a satisfying clank. It works, I thought. It's a perfect little home you can take anyplace. Another wave of rain came and I closed the flaps. The water began to boil as I sat by the stove and luxuriated, out of the wet.

"Where are the horses?" Under a dripping felt hat, Mitch's face poked between the flaps of the tent.

"They're around, I guess. Ready for some coffee?"

"They're *gone*." He spoke with exasperation and a touch of scorn. "You didn't picket one?"

The notion that the horses might leave was new to me. I thought of a horse as a hairy motorbike—park it and it stays. Mitch disabused me: "In this rain, they might head back to the ranch. We'd never hear the end of *that*." His black brows met.

"I'll go look while you dry off." Taking a bucket of oats, I wandered the slopes, up and down, squinting into the rain, boots squelching in the mud. I tried calling: "Tom! Pronto! Tubby, Red, Tony, *Elhon*. Yoo-hoo? Oats! Goddam!" Nothing. I wandered back.

"Did you find their tracks?" Mitch asked.

"Tracks," I repeated gravely. "Tracks. Well. No."

"Horses leave them," he snapped, and stomped out into the rain.

JULY 23

The door on the stove squeaked; I heard paper rustle and smelled pitchy smoke as the kindling took fire. Mitch's face appeared, lit by flame, and the tent grew walls at his back. He carefully laid more sticks on the fire and shut the door. As he slid the damper back, the draft began to hum. He lit a candle and set it in an upturned lid. I felt safe in my sleeping bag. Why get up, to aches, hard work, and embarrassment?

Mitch was dressed, his wool coat buttoned, though his boots were still unlaced. He'd found the horses yesterday after an hour in the rain, and wrangled them close to camp. "Better ribs than tracks," he said. It took me a while to figure that out. He'd caught Tubby while I drove a green stake, and he tethered her by a front foot.

He filled the coffeepot from the water bag and peered in my direction. Then he made a raven squawk: *"Awwrrrkkkk*—I see your eyes. Roll out. The campjack starts the stove, while the herder stays in his quilts and waits for hot *café."*

Four-thirty, said the clock: dawn was still far under the earth's curve, and beyond it stretched the day. In camp, the hardest moments come as you leave the comfortable heat of your bag, feel the cold air, know the weight of your body again, and take on your pains and your name. I warmed at the stove, retied my boots, and wondered if I dared eat a cookie, coveting the sandy crunch and melting chocolate bits. But I kept my hands easy and waited for the coffee to boil.

"We have to get up before the sheep, so we can be there when they start to move. We can trade off starting the fire. I don't eat much. Just cowboy coffee and toast on the stovetop. The big meal's at noon, when the sheep bed down."

We checked the horses in the dark—black hulks with gleaming eyes: they snorted as Mitch counted heads. The sheep were close, he said, so we didn't need to ride. We hiked out to the herd in the dark, stopping where we heard the muffled bleats and saw wooly forms bound up, snapping sticks as they fled. "Give 'em room," said Mitch. So we waited until light began to show, and then we walked around the herd.

"Sheep go up," Mitch declared, "and cows go down."

"What about horses?"

"Hah! Back to the ranch. Then we're afoot and lonesome." The sun cleared the ridge and swam up into stark, even blue. Mitch sat on a boulder and smoked his pipe as I walked to camp.

I mixed starter from the sourdough crock with flour and water, and kneaded the mess into rubbery form. While the loaf plumped up behind the stove, I dug a pit and greased the dutch oven. I consulted *Sourdough Chuckwagon Cooking,* the sort of paperback you find in roadside diners in the West. Helen, my mother, sent it when I'd written home about finding summer work, and it was my only reference. A pot of split peas bubbled. The tent was hot.

Our bedding hung from the tent ropes in the morning sun, the white canvas of Mitch's cowboy roll and my blue sleeping bag. Horse pads and blankets festooned the pines. A heap of packsaddles steamed, pine bars and oak bucks gleaming.

I gently poked the rising loaf, then stepped out into cool air. The horses grazed, their bells chiming softly as they fed. Tubby was picketed by a fat hemp rope to a freshly hewn stake. Pronto's colt danced into camp, sniffed the tips of my fingers, and spun off with a whistle.

This is the world my granddad knew, I thought, and it's good.

July 24

In Utah it was Pioneer Day, my ancestral holiday, if I had one. But I was in Wyoming, and not being much of a pioneer I failed to wake on time, so Mitch crawled to the stove and laid a fire. Then I got up and, in further defiance of my Mormon heritage, started a pot of strong coffee. (Recipe: Fill the pot with cold water—at 4:30 A.M. in the mountains there's no other kind—and tip in a heaping half cup of coarse ground. When it turns, just before boiling, dash cold water in to settle the grounds.)

Mitch rode the picket horse bareback to wrangle the others in, their bells pealing above the drum of their hooves. We saddled up and then came back to the tent. I'd burned the bread, but we sliced off the carbonized crust and ate it anyway. The coffee was hot and bottomless;

my teeth found suspended grains, and I chewed them, bitter stars, to wake me up. Two cups each, and we rode out.

Mitch took Red, with me on Tubby, the barrel-shaped mare: a kid horse, I thought. I beat a tattoo on her ribs with my Red Wing boots. She tolerated it without changing her gait, a careful, belly-swaying walk, so I let my boots rest in the stirrups. Mitch halted, took out his field glasses, and scanned the slope, counting with his lips. "Eight markers," he said.

"Markers?"

"The black ewes are the markers. There's nine in the herd, and I can see eight, so we're probably okay. The other one's probably behind a bush or lying down. If I only counted four, then we'd hunt for lost sheep. It's pretty simple to herd this west face. Once we go over the pass it's tougher, in those steep canyons and fir jungles." He gave his raven squawk.

The herd ranged the slope in small bands, eight here, twelve there. I liked the horses and the camp, but the sheep didn't interest me at all. In fact, even though they were the reason I was there, I wanted to avoid them.

Eight days before, Roger, Mitch, and I had sorted out the ewes with hoof rot and hazed them into small pens. The wet lambing pasture was puddled with snowmelt, and the crowded pens all spread the rot. But the sheep would heal fast on dry hillsides, up in the rocks, where their feet stayed clean. Mitch and I took turns catching them and tossing them on their tails—balance a sheep on the point of its spine so its legs are in the air, and it goes limp. Roger did the cutting. The rot had an amazing stench, as each diseased hoof was pared deeply to a clean, white edge, a process that often drew blood.

The doctoring was gruesome, but the alternative, Roger said, was death: if they were too crippled for summer range, they'd be slaughtered. The trimmed hoof was daubed with a sticky purple antiseptic, and the sheep was flipped up and turned out, stunned and limping.

Among the huddles, one lamb was falling, reeling, spinning, stumbling: a broken toy. I asked Roger about it. "Something wrong with its nervous system. It'll never get any better," he said. I watched it butt the ewe and start to nurse, then tumble on its side and lie in spasm. Then it leapt up and shook its head. I wanted to catch the lamb and help it, but there was no help I could give. I looked at my hands, black with blood and dust from the pens, blackness greased into the pores with wool-fat. I turned away, caught another ewe, and tried to close my ears to the cacophony, breathing through my mouth and watching as Roger gripped a hoof and cut deep.

At sunset I held a ewe, mother to the crippled lamb, down on the tailgate of a pickup while Royal, the eagle-headed rancher, shot it in the brain with a .22 rifle. She made one hard thrash in my arms, and shuddered and kicked as he set the rifle in the truck and then slit her throat with a pocketknife. Purple venous blood ran in thick streams over her eyes into a steel bucket. My forearm was over her heart, which beat faster, trying to pump blood to the shattered brain, then fluttered, like a moth, and stopped. When blood no longer flowed, Royal rolled her into the pickup bed.

Our other victim was her defective lamb. He'd forgotten to pocket another bullet, so he simply bent and cut the lamb's throat. An artery beat bright scarlet into the thin wool. As the lamb breathed its own blood, it made a bubbling gurgle and fought. The blood fell and mixed with the dark blood in the rusty pail. The lamb weakened, went slack. I wanted to stop everything for a moment, to look into the sky. Royal turned and walked to the faucet, and rinsed his pocketknife.

I was blooded: it was under my nails, lined into the weather cracks on the backs of my hands, spotted on my cuffs. How many times in a working life will a rancher perform this unceremonious killing? There are the fat, the ripe, the destined, and also the suffering, the damaged, the lame, the old. A rancher, like a hunter, must kill to live. If there is a sin in that, it occurs in the instant that such killing becomes casual, when there is no longer mystery or dread, when the animal's soul is not attended by some measure of shared pain, of a common longing against death.

I couldn't tell what Royal felt, but his features were set in an expression I'd seen before: jaw tight, eyes front, no opening. Too many sheep, and too many deaths: repeated, this brief hardening eventually hardens a man against the whole of life. With a handful of sand, I scrubbed in cold water at the tap by the trough. He carried the rifle to a shed, returned, and slammed the tailgate on the ewe. One limp leg flew up, and the hoof struck the pickup bed with a hollow bang.

"I'll run over to the locker plant." He got into the truck.

Tiny and gaunt, the lamb sprawled on the ground next to the bucket. "What do I do with this?" I asked.

"The pigpen," Royal said, and drove away.

JULY 25

I didn't like sleeping in the back of the tent, fenced in by Mitch. So I tried sleeping outside with the dogs. Mitch was dubious. "I think I saw a bear," he said. "If it comes around at night, the horses will spook. You might get trompled."

What? Mitch and I had both grown up in the suburbs. We met at college and went three-pin skiing together, and lived for a few months in the same ramshackle farmhouse, a spot abandoned to all but the willing poor. And he didn't talk this way, then. I knew he loved acting western, but *trompled?* I sang a foolish hymn: "Tromple me not on the lone prairie, Where the coyotes hooooowl and the wind blows free." He tucked his chin and looked away.

And I slept out, with Pookie curled next to my head. The mountain slope was quiet and open to the sky. I lay on my back with my glasses on, to watch the stars. Distance made them safe: the roaring of those white fires could be imagined but not heard. We didn't have a radio, and that was a relief too, not to hear that metallic yammer or the bad news that invaded my sleep. I took the small night sounds as articles of faith: the breathing of my dog, the brush of aspen leaves, the sigh of a horse, and a gentle bell.

I thought about the war. Some of my friends had gone early. Lawson, my den chief in scouts, was the neighborhood's favorite son. His family lived across the street and he was their center. After he was killed by stepping on a mine, the family fell apart. His father drank hard, and his mother went gray, and his younger sister, who had smooth skin that darkened every summer and eyes with tiny fires in them, grew distant with drugs. He died, and they suffered.

On television I'd seen the big demonstrations. In the cities they were news, but here that news was distant. In the heart of the West, on the campus of Utah State, a big demonstration was fifty scared-looking people, surrounded by cowboy-hatted Ag majors and football players. There were ugly moments: I didn't like being called a coward. When someone sneered and said that belief had nothing to do with it, said something like *You're just afraid to die,* I wanted to say *You're not?*

Of course I was afraid to die. But I was more afraid to give up my sense of right and wrong to a power that was not higher but only more terrible, a power that had grown great not on wisdom or mercy, but had fattened on fear and lies. And seeing those faces, red and cursing, I wanted to hit them. Sometimes I even wanted to kill them.

Most of the people who helped me preached nonviolence, and I was ashamed of the smoldering fury that inhabited me. But I knew that it did: I was not innocent. Each time I wanted to punch some rude-mouthed jock, and figured which foot to lead and which fist to use, and then made the choice not to throw that punch, it was a step away from the war.

Just three generations from the western frontier, I was the spawn of invasion, murder, and the theft of entire landscapes. My history was violent, my heritage was violent, and so was I. But for me, the son of a rancher turned engineer, to accept as my natural enemy a Buddhist rice farmer halfway around the world, on the assurances of postcolonial Catholic aristocrats that he was dangerous, and then, on the orders of corrupt politicians in Washington, a city I'd never seen, to kill that farmer and his family: that was too long a stretch.

I was willing to empty bedpans in VA hospitals, wipe up the drool of the mad, clean bus stations, or perform any service that didn't support the killing, or enlarge it, or prolong it. But to do that under the law, I had to belong to a religion, like the Quakers or Brethren, which held such beliefs. The ex-marine colonel who headed my draft board was

Mormon, and he told me that no Mormon could in conscience and belief, refuse to serve in this war. That is, in a nation where personal freedom and responsibility were supposedly the root of public morals, I could make no decision on whether to kill another human being.

You're afraid to die for your country. But what was my country? Was it a known landscape and the people who lived in it? Or had it become the worship of power, a deadly accumulation of force? I would defend my country, but what we had done in Vietnam was not defense.

You're afraid. True. But death could happen anyplace. During high school I worked nights in a gas station. One night in summer, on graveyard shift, I noticed a dark blue car parked across the street, a shadow in the driver's place. He never moved, but I felt his gaze.

I was afraid, but I wasn't paralyzed. Why didn't I call the police? I don't know. I hefted the biggest open-end wrench, long as my forearm, and carried it out under the fluorescent lights, and flipped it and caught it, so it snapped the glare back. The car started and my spine went cold, but he turned north. But he waited half a block to turn his headlights on.

In the station worked a young man named Frank, newly discharged from the marines, whose younger brother was in my class. Some nights he'd ride in drunk on his black Harley, an hour late. And he'd circle the station, hooting and yelling out "Fuckin' A, Fuckin' A"—his all-purpose phrase—and park the bike, and then he'd pass out on the Firestone tire display, a giant set of white plywood steps.

I knew he'd get fired for showing up drunk, so I tried to talk him into crawling to the office, which was out of sight and had a carpet, but after the first time he hit me—a direct shot to the gut, launched from an apparently helpless sprawl—I never tried to drag him there again.

But I didn't turn him in. I worked his shift more than once, midnight until dawn, and he took me under his ragged wing and bought me six-packs and told me war stories: "Nam sucks, bigtime. Like swimmin' in a lake of shit. You don't give a fuck about nothin', man. Except fuckin' firepower. I even quit fuckin' eatin', man. Couldn't remember if I ate or not. Drink some beers, smoke dope, and pop caps. We fuckin' wasted every motherfuckin' thing that moved."

That was real: a blind, absolute violence that couldn't be forgotten or outrun. Drunk, he said that if his younger brother tried to enlist he'd stop him any way he could—break his trigger finger or shoot off his toe. I heard, from Frank and others, about horror and cruelty and sacrifice. What I never heard, from any combat veteran, was that much good had been done.

I had to get away from that murderous power, out of the doubled lock of guilt and obligation. I'd come to the mountains by chance, but that night it seemed part of a design. I'd found a way to hide in my country's heart. The starry desolation held no answers, so I went on looking at it without expecting one. It was quiet. That was enough.

JULY 26

I heard the alarm clock even through the tent, and went in and lit a candle and started the fire. Mitch opened his eyes as I made the coffee. I went out and brought a fresh horse in, and turned the night horse loose. When the coffee turned, he got out of his bedroll and pleased me by not saying anything out of the ordinary.

Mitch was conscientious: a good shepherd in the flesh. He rose without fail, gulped a cup or two of coffee and nibbled a biscuit, and then went out to the herd. And loose herding was his gospel. He explained that the band should travel in a natural, easy way. "That's why we have to get out before it comes light. Sheep start to move before dawn and try to fill their bellies before the day's heat. Once they fill up, they move. If they get away and scatter, you have to bunch 'em and push 'em, and that's what raises hell. If you're lazy, it's harder work."

The traditional way was to bed the sheep every night on the same ground near camp—his hands sketched a hub and spokes in the air— and then drive them out to feed. The bed-grounds were quickly demolished, as were the trails leading from each camp. When the daily drive got too long, you moved the camp and bed-ground.

"The idea was that the herder and the dogs would keep coyotes away. But it tears things up, plus the *borregas* travel farther to get the same feed. Loose herding's better for the sheep and the country, but it's more work. You bed in a different spot each night. You worry about coyotes, but your lambs gain more weight. Hah! The sheep get fat, and the herder gets skinny."

In good spirits, he packed his lunch and rode off alone. Some mornings he asked for help. Usually, after a circuit of the herd at sunrise, I would return to camp. In my round of chores the horses came first. I'd check the picket horse and move the stake to fresh grass, then find the horse band and push them closer to camp if they showed signs of straying. I'd check the hobbled horses for lameness and maybe take their hobbles off for the day. And I was expected, at any time of day or night, to know exactly where the horses were.

Water was next: I'd catch Tom or Tubby, put a saddle on, and fill the two five-gallon canvas bags by laying them flat in a stream or by dipping from a spring with a cookpot, which took a while. Then I'd lead the horse, *ka-slosh, ka-slosh,* back to camp.

Next came cooking. Since we had mostly staples like flour, molasses, and cornmeal, everything had to be prepared at length, biscuits mixed and dropped, beans boiled for half a day, and sourdough bread kneaded and left to rise while I kept a fire going to build coals for the dutch oven. I'd start in midmorning, poring over the little cookbook my mother had sent for answers to the riddles of sourdough flapjacks and cowboy beans. I knew how to heat food but not how to cook it. At college, I'd lived on sandwiches and canned soup, with carrots and apples.

My cooking trials produced the predictable messes—burnt bread, beans so salty that we gagged, pancakes like round shingles. Traditionally, camp cooks are monsters of temper. I had tendencies in that direction even before I took up cooking, so at first Mitch gave me gentle suggestions rather than complaints. Surveying my first loaf of dutch oven bread, which looked like a giant charcoal briquet, he said, "The outside's *maybe* a little crisp."

Early afternoon, when the sheep were bedded, was the time to read a book in the shade, or take an exploratory hike, or enjoy a reverie in a nest of rocks. Besides the packer's bible and the cookbook, I'd brought the fat, dull green text from a class I'd nearly failed—World Lit to 1650—having vowed to read every word. Close to the start, I found:

A Summer Day

Naked I lie in the green forest of summer . . .
Too lazy to wave my white feathered fan.
I hang my cap on a crag,
And bare my head to the wind that comes
Blowing through the pine trees.

Li Po (A.D. 701–762)

I took off my hat, and the breeze ran cool fingers through my hair. I
liked old Chinese poems more than all the high-minded, jog-trotting
Tennyson and Longfellow I'd been forced to memorize. Li Po seemed
right for this place. Between poems I closed the book and rested, listening to the breeze and the horse bells.

Besides my penitential dabble with classics, I was determined to
learn the wildflowers. I'd brought a guidebook, *Mountain Plants of
Northeastern Utah,* with clean, exact line drawings. Northeastern Utah
wasn't far, and the Salt Rivers were the same limestone and dolomite,
so I thought it would be close enough.

My method on finding an interesting plant was to page through the
entire book to identify it, or at least one that resembled it. The advan-
tage of this was that I began to recognize the features that gave each
plant identity: leaf shape and margin, the configuration of stems and
leaves, the number and arrangement of petals, and the presence of
things like bracts.

I love the word *bract.* I'll always remember twinberry, a wild honeysuckle, by its "doubled, shiny-black fruit, circled by *rose-colored invo-
lucral bracts.*" That was poetry, too, and verged on erotic fantasy.

While Mitch napped, I would choose a patch of blossoming un-
knowns and traverse the book again and again. On the slopes around
the camp I met with blue flax, fleabane daisy, Richardson's pink geranium, tall larkspur, fireweed, spurred lupine, northern sweet broom,
hawksbeard daisy, cow parsnip, wild rose, showy gentian, harebell,
mountain bluebell, monkeyflower, snowberry, sego lily, shrubby
cinquefoil, yarrow, arnica, columbine, penstemon, scarlet gilia, and

spearmint. And there were others, like bright faces in a crowd, that I wanted to know.

Mitch roused himself and circled the camp in a yawning daze, then saddled a horse, and rode off to the sheep. Left to myself, I topped off the woodpile and heated a basin of water. Then I took off my clothes for a bath, with all the flowers watching, first kneeling to wash my hair and then squatting over the dishpan to soap and rinse. It was a strange luxury to be naked in the middle of the afternoon, in the open air above the valley, in the warm sun, and to see my long limbs gleaming wet, and to feel my balls swing free like church bells in the wind.

July 27

Disgrace. Burned a second loaf of bread and lost the horses. We had to scramble all over the mountainside to find them. After that, Mitch was monosyllabic, so I wrote a letter to Joe Back, praising his book and mentioning that the publisher had left out twenty pages in the middle, and before sealing it I folded some yarrow in.

A thunderhead rose over the hot, green valley, a dark blue circulation at its base, and swelled into the upper air, rearing up with a brilliance beyond white to shadow the camp. Then came a wall of wind, and big shuddering crashes, as whole blocks of atmosphere toppled and split, and then lightning so close it sounded like tearing cloth, and then a barrage of hail. I dodged into the tent for cover, like a mouse hiding under the drum at a powwow, as the canvas boomed and sagged under the plummeting white. Hailstones the size of buckshot tore leaves, caromed off limbs, and covered up the smallest plants. I thought of the birds—how a nestling would shiver and strain at each cold impact, how unprotected nests would fill up with white stones. Then I thought of Mitch exposed on the mountainside; he would huddle, I hoped, under a tree or ledge, grumbling as the sheep scattered in fright.

The storm passed quickly. I found the horses, wet but seemingly content. As I hiked toward the herd, drifts of hail melted in the brassy afternoon sun.

Mitch was soaked but otherwise fine: "Hell, I never even buttoned

my cuffs," he claimed, in the voice of a creaky old-timer. Then he
thanked me in his normal voice for coming out to check. "Better locate
the horses."

"I kicked 'em up above camp."

"Now you're thinkin'. There's an old ewe we'd better plug," he said.
"Let's go get what we need." The victim of hoof rot and Roger's knife,
she wouldn't climb the hill. "Old bugger can hardly walk," Mitch said.
He explained that the orphan lambs—bums—would stay with her, to
be lost or killed by coyotes.

"Fresh meat," he said, "even if it's old mutton." We sharpened our
sheath knives on the stone we kept in the kitchen box, Old Timers with
five-inch blades and fake stag handles. Good steel, Mitch said, and I'd
bought one like his.

But I remembered the dead lamb in the mud and then the bucket.
When I put my hand under to tip the blood into the pigs' trough, the
steel bucket was warm.

"Let's go and do it," Mitch said. "Catch Tom—he won't spook."

I haltered the horse and cinched up a packsaddle. Mitch rolled
up a canvas manty, and we filled a pail at the little spring. I led the
horse. "I'll go first," he said, and started around the belly of the
slope.

"I can handle it." I wasn't sure but I followed, pulling the old horse.

"Not you. The horse. The shot? Sometimes they go crazy."

"Okay." I stood there as he spoke over his shoulder.

"When you hear the shot, bring the horse."

I waited, and heard a muffled bang. The horse didn't even flinch.

He'd cut the ewe's throat and turned her down the hill for the
blood to drain. The dogs quivered, and Tiger crept toward the puddle
of sticky blood, his tongue lapping the air. "*No,*" shouted Mitch,
"Tikki-*Lo!*"

"Don't let 'em eat fresh kill," he said, "or they start killing on their
own." I walked over to the dead ewe. "Ever done this?" He gave me
his measuring look.

"Deer hunting. I don't remember much." It was a lie: I'd never
gutted a deer.

The dogs sat in a half circle, whining and shifting in the dirt as I butchered my first sheep. Mitch told me where to cut, as I slit the thin belly hide, cut the anus loose and then the throat, split the pelvic bone with the axe, and then tipped the guts onto the dirt. I could feel moist heat escaping from the cavity.

The gut pile made a liquid slosh downhill, dirt sticking to its milky colors, and then settled, flies clouding it, one, two, ten, a hundred. The dogs keened and Tiger made another dash. *"No.* Tikki-Lo, get *back!"* Mitch shouted. I could taste the simmer of my own insides.

"The Bascos eat the head first," Mitch said, "but I'm not man enough for that." He bent over and sliced at the muscles and tendons of the neck, then twisted it completely around and cut until the head came free. I had to look away, jaw clamped shut, and breathe through my nose, look at high clouds and the perfect blue around them. I imagined that I could inhale that blue, that it was a rare fluid, a solvent for the blood, the dirt, the whining hunger of the dogs, and the chorus of flies.

"We'll skin her out over here: don't want offal around the camp to draw bears." I rinsed my knife, gripped the spongy white edge of the hide, and began to make small cuts. "Too slow," said Mitch. "Sheep have loose hides. Just shove your hand as far as you can. Don't have to use a knife much." I tensed my hand and forced it between the skin and fat. And it was easy. I wasn't numb or sickened then. The thing was food, and I pried and pulled until the hide was loose. Then we wrapped the carcass in canvas and slung it over the saddle.

At camp we unwrapped it and hung it in the shade to cool. We fed the dogs on scraps, and they gorged and slept. I fed a fire in a pit, watching the flames go from wavering transparency in the sun to shifting yellows and blues in the dusk.

Fresh kill and a smoky fire. Over a deep bed of coals, I broiled the ribs, one rack for each, and we feasted. Mitch told me that an Indian band—he couldn't remember the tribe—called themselves "Greasy Chins," such skilled hunters that they ate only the fattest meat.

I was both uneasy and exhilarated at the ancient, half-charred snack, but there it was. And I liked the taste. We gnawed, gulped, reveled, groaned, rested, and ate again. The dogs jostled for scraps, growled and retired, and then slept again, bellies turned up to heaven.

"The Bascos always have red wine," Mitch said. "A big, fat *bota* hanging from a limb." Across the fire, he was darkly intent, a mutton rib spanning his beard. "*Hah!* These damn *Mormóns* don't know what's good."

"Maybe Roger will bring us wine. He drinks."

"*Rogelio?* He's different close to home. He may sneak a few cans of beer up sometime, but if we ask him he won't."

A wind breathed out of the dark, and the coals glowed and tumbled into ash. A gust flailed the aspens, and the dogs groaned and changed their beds, finding shelter under the pile of saddles and in the lee of the tent.

I finished washing up and crept into the tent and unlaced my boots. The candle, set in the upturned lid of a jar, flickered. Mitch stepped out, and the wind came through the flap and snuffed the flame.

JULY 28

I rode Pronto and led Elhon and Tubby with empty packs down the slope and into the canyon. Roger was driving up with supplies to Star Valley Ranch, which seemed not so much a ranch as a scheme. It had been inherited and then subdivided by a band of Stewarts from Las Vegas. I'd been friends with one of the sons, Dale.

Riding in I looked with new eyes at the badly built log fences, the half-rotted wagon wheels, and the plywood "lodge" festooned with elk antlers and pieces of rusty junk. It was supposed to look western, but instead it looked like a dump for some alien culture.

Roger hadn't arrived, so I tied the horses and went to the back door. Dale's mother didn't remember me, and introduced herself as Mrs. Harold Stewart. Her eyes were a shiny black, like windows set in a thick wall. When I said I knew Dale, she gave me a glance as if expecting me to follow with a claim. Suddenly aware of my wind-brushed hair, sapling beard, and dusty jeans, I fidgeted my way back outside, a relief to both of us.

Another woman came out, with flour on her hands and welcome in her face. She introduced herself: Mrs. Dana, the cook. The guests would eat soon; would I like to join them in a meal? I'd left my wallet at the Preston Ranch, and said so. She smiled. "No charge, but if anyone asks, just say the Prestons are covering it."

In back of the lodge were plank tables and a decrepit freight wagon painted barn red with white wheels. Men in golf clothes and women in flowered dresses filtered in and took seats. I felt sweaty and disreputable, but I was hungry so I sat tight. An old man in cowboy dress shambled out and eased onto the seat of the wagon. The springs creaked as he lifted a guitar from its case, tuned it briefly—too briefly—and then bawled out a song:

> The eyes of my bronco are flashing,
>   Impatient he pulls at the reins,
> And off round the herd I go dashing,
>   A reckless cowboy of the plains.

> Roll on, roll on, roll on little dogies, roll on, roll on.
> Roll on, roll on, roll on little dogies, roll on.

He mugged and tilted his head, his grin making its way from one table to the next.

> The trail to that great mystic region
>   Is narrow and dim so they say,
> While the one that leads down to perdition
>   Is posted and blazed all the way.

With real estate signs, I thought. I ate with my head down, trying to shut out the song and the tourists, one of whom made a show of conducting with a fork on which a dripping piece of steak was impaled. Later, as the couples wandered away, sales brochures in hand, the singer told me that he'd played that guitar for forty-one years. The frets were scalloped, worn flat in spots, from which I could guess his favorite chords: C, F, and G.

It was a relief when Roger drove up, tanned, in old work clothes. It occurred to me that I'd never seen him in a cowboy hat. He let me pack up, and made a few tucks but generally seemed to approve. As I rode away, I saw him talking to Mrs. Dana. She held the door of the kitchen half open and she waved. I lifted my hat: good-bye, America.

2 ~

The Pass

Before dawn, Mitch and I wrangled the horses and tied them to trees. Roger rode up at first light. Mitch looked past him and then spoke. "I thought Warren would be up."

"He's got a cold or something. Besides, I'm camping with you guys tonight so we can get the herd over the pass. Warren would have had to ride out alone."

Our first big move was to shift camp to the head of the canyon and to gather the herd to a high bowl under the pass. First, we had to push the sheep south, into the canyon, and then drive them up through a rocky narrows. They protested the move, blatting and circling, carving trails into the brush before they formed lines and began to march.

Roger kept them moving with the dogs, the dust rising and forming a gray wake in the air, while Mitch and I rode back to break the camp. It was quick, with two of us, and I liked how the stovepipe telescoped and fit inside the stove, and how the tent could be reduced to a bundle, the way our material lives could fit inside eight panniers, ready to be moved. And I liked how the scuffed opening under the trees seemed to belong to the mountain again.

The sun was high and bright enough to make us sweat. I left the packer's bible in my saddlebag, my moral first-aid kit, and tried to thread the ropes and jerk the knots from memory. Mitch checked my hitches and retied one that was loose. "Never give up slack," he said as he jerked on the lash rope and half-hitched the end to the ring on the *cincha.*

It went easily, except for Elhon, who reared back to the length of her rope and sat down in the dirt, hooves flashing in the air. "Salt and bedrolls," Mitch said, "nothing she can break."

We each led two packhorses. They grunted under their loads as we slid down the steep trails loosened by the sheep. We rode into the canyon, each with our own attentive cloud of mosquitos and flies. The horses twitched, snorted, and jigged their heads. Mitch slitted his eyes and bore it. I cursed and swatted. I inhaled a brace of mosquitos and spat them out with a roar.

"That's what you get for complaining," he said.

Ahead, we saw sheep meandering along the north slope and clotting in the trail, half hidden by dust. We heard Ansel's bark and Tiger's answering yip. Roger emerged, red-faced and bareheaded from the brush, leading the Black Stallion.

"Hot," he said. "They're slowing down. We'll noon a little farther on, where it gets steep."

"Si, Señor Rogelio." Mitch bobbed his head.

"Dammit, Mitch. Talk English."

"I'm studying to be a wetback."

"Pancho's legal—crispy around the edges," Roger said, "but he's got his papers."

"I'd trade my papers for a beer. *Cerveza."* My contribution.

"Didn't bring any. Dad doesn't like liquor in the camp."

"Jeez, Roger," I said. "Beer's not liquor. It's wholesome, like orange juice. And I'll pay."

Roger looked up with a squint. "Beer's expensive, plus I'd have to charge for shipping. How much have you got?"

"Nothing here. My wallet's in my blue trunk at the ranch."

"Qué lastima," Mitch exclaimed. "We'll both end up good little *Mor-móns."*

Roger chuckled: "Brother Rawlins and Brother Black."

"Does that mean we get Sundays off?" Mitch tried to look innocent.

Roger hooted. "You will when *I* do." He swung into the saddle and plunged through the brush to the tail of the herd. The canyon narrowed between outcrops of limestone, and the trail thinned from a jeep track to a single thread. Mitch tied the packhorses he led to my pair. "See that green slope? There's only one patch of trees above, and that's camp. Go ahead and set up."

I forded the creek with the pack string, the hooves sounding hollow and the rush of water changing in pitch as we parted it. On the south side I halted and watched water drip from the horses onto the dry ground, raising puffs of dust.

The trail was loose in spots, rocky in others, and everywhere steep. I stopped when the horses began to blow, and stood in the stirrups and peeled my jeans away from my thighs. The bowl was a rocky funnel, and the camp was easy to find: the only level spot, set in a solitary patch of spruce and fir. There was a stack of weathered poles with dead needles pasted to them by the snowpack, and two stones for the stove.

I was sore and tired, my forehead lumpy with fly bites, but I got the horses unpacked and the camp set up. Roger and Mitch rode up laughing and hungry. Mitch tightened one of the tent ropes, but that was all. Roger ate more than Mitch and me together, and Mitch rolled his eyes but kept his thoughts to himself.

They walked to their horses. "We're going up to scout the pass," Roger said. I nodded and looked up. The trail looked like a slanting stain on a cracked wall: nothing I'd want to ride a horse up. "We may have to dig out a snowbank," he said. "Make sure the sheep don't drop back down." I wandered down until I ran out of sheep to curse, then searched the country below: it was tracked and beaten and empty. Above, the sheep were bedded and quiet, so I tipped my hat over my face and slept.

I woke to a shot, and another, its echo chasing the first into nowhere. Then I heard the panicked bellow of the herd. The sun was low. In a guilty rush, I ran toward the noise, rounding the north slope into shade.

In the V of a tiny stream, in dark green sunflowers, Roger and Mitch were bent over a body. A heavy rank of spruce and fir rose like a palisade behind, darker than the open slope, deepening the foreground colors.

"A bear killed a lamb and Roger shot it." Mitch looked shaken but determined not to be. I could see the tightness in his jaw and neck.

"Jesus. I guess it's . . . dead," I said. Roger looked up, the Roger I knew, and then his face changed. Roger the sheepman, I thought.

"A guy hates to do it, but it was in the herd with a lamb down. Then it saw us and ran down the hill. I grabbed the .30-.30 and that was all she wrote."

"Dammit," I said. Mitch looked at me, his face blank. I looked away, up at the canyon rim, and felt tears in my eyes.

I walked away, up the drainage, and sat on a rock, dabbing furtively at my eyes. "Jesus." I sat on the rock and tried to recover my breath and compose my face.

I stood up and went back. Roger had started to skin the bear, and the red carcass lay exposed. My first thought was that it was a young boy, the way the limbs articulated, and the image frightened me: murder in the mountains. The inner surface of the pelt looked like white satin, like a blanket with a black fringe. I could hear the snick of his knife as he cut carefully along the spine.

Roger glanced up and saw, I suppose, my look of horror, and turned away. "Roger has a right to protect his sheep," Mitch said. What I felt didn't fit into words, so I didn't speak. Roger dragged the carcass up the hill into the edge of the woods, then returned and scattered stock salt on the hide and rolled it. He looked up with an embarrassed smile, but I looked away. "Young sow," he said. "Too bad. Wrong place, wrong time."

I wanted to hit him. Mitch tossed a piece of nylon cord over a limb, and Roger hung the rolled pelt. "It'll stay cool. I can get it when I ride back tomorrow."

Mitch looked up at the hanging black parcel of hair. The moisture drawn by the salt began to drip from the end of the roll to the ground. "Are you going to tan it?" he asked.

"Try. I'll stick it in the freezer for now. We'd better see if there're any wounded sheep. Flies'll get 'em if we don't treat the cuts." They went back to the herd, leaving me alone, listening to the drip from the rolled hide.

The carcass lay still on its slanting bed of duff, needles stuck to the glazing red flesh. There was nothing I could do, and I couldn't shake the feeling of doom, so I walked away.

I hiked back to camp, and washed my hands, and then cried into the basin of soapy water. Fool. To be here at all. Spreading death. I washed my face and set my jaw. I got the stove going and set the coffeepot on it. Fix dinner. But I didn't feel like cooking. Fuck it. Fuck Roger and his stinking sheep.

I thought about rolling my gear and hiking out. But they were below me in the canyon's darkening V, and I'd have to explain, and I couldn't talk to them.

I was cut off from the valley. I tied the flaps tight and fled up the canyon. Soon I turned south, away from the trail, and climbed an un-marked slope until I reached the snow. I kicked steps into the surface melt, toeing into the hard layers below, and climbed fast up to the rim of the bowl, working my way onto a long knife ridge. I followed it higher, skirting broken blocks and drops, to the top, where the world gaped open at my feet. Below, I could see the trail straggling up to the north, slipping over the pass and disappearing into a bank of snow.

I bellied down on a gray block where the ridge fell sheer to the east, and looked into a cirque that was filled with blue shadow, still lost in snow. I couldn't get away. I knew that suddenly. I couldn't forget. I could only live with what I knew.

I hadn't lied to escape being drafted, though it would have been easier. The group of resisters I joined at school quickly dwindled: three joined the Guard, two were bought out with the help of family doctors. One convinced his draft board he was queer, though he wasn't. An-other, from Boston, claimed to be a Mahayana Buddhist, and his board gave him a C.O. to work at the Harvard Medical Center. Two just peeled off without a word; I saw them around, but they'd stopped talking.

The hardest part was telling the chairman of the draft board—the ex-marine colonel, father of one of my best friends, and my former scout leader—that I wouldn't go. I didn't say my piece with dignity. I choked up. And on my C.O. application I got a unanimous denial.

So I took the physical exam and the written test. I passed both. But I filed an appeal on my C.O. claim. They held out officer candidate school and stateside duty, in exchange for my name in ink, and I realized something else. They didn't need me to fight. They had plenty of cannon fodder. But they were frightened by the enormity of the war, and by the awful waste of life it had caused, even as they defended it and served not the country but the lie.

I felt, then, how the lying thing drew you into itself; I felt its black gravity without touching any core of truth. I sensed fear in the cities where I slept on basement floors, and in the hospitals and counseling centers where I looked for C.O. jobs, and in strained talk with friends, and in long arguments with my father that ended in mutual despair.

On the ridge the wind was cold, and the world was quite empty. "Roger killed . . . *we* killed that bear." I said it.

Nothing answered, nothing cared. "The bear is dead." The black bear had seen the world through its dark eyes, smelled the air, stood firm on four feet, belonged here. The mountain was its home and its country. We came into its country, into its mountain house with our bawling disorder, and then killed it. It was dead. "Dead."

I pictured the exposed teeth, the red muscles tipped with white sinew, the joining of the limbs so strangely like my own. Death was a horror I couldn't transform.

I tried to make up a prayer but couldn't, so I howled until I ran out of breath. Facing into the wind, away from the valley and the camp, I thought I wanted to be dead. The shattered limestone was sharp, so sharp. I found a piece that looked like a broken shell, with a curved, keen edge and a point, and I cut myself. The blood dripped onto a rippled gray stone: *one bear, two bears, three bears.* There were fossils in the rock, closed eyelids, little curls of smoke.

The blood stopped: it was only a deep, stinging scratch, between my wrist and thumb.

The wind swept across the broken comb of the ridge, sighing in the cracks, buzzing in the thorns of the bushy currants. I looked east, at my shadow falling off, diving into the country where we would go, at the shadow pooling in a long cirque just emerging from late drifts, and the heaps of sharp stone that bunched and flowed toward a drop, into the submerged blue of the canyon itself.

It looked like a place in which the decisions would be few: up or down, left or right, yes or no. The trail looked dangerous, coming out under corniced snow, a thin line sketched along a bad slope, disappearing around a toothed point. How would this end?

Something flashed in the air, not far from me, and was lost. I stared but it was gone. Then it flicked into sight again—a small bird. And then there were four, six, twelve, a multitude of birds, diving in and out of the mountain's shadow.

Swifts. They rode the turbulent air that broke like surf from the ridgetop, flaring their long wings to catch the upward burst and riding it so near the broken edge that I could see the sun reflected in their tiny eyes, could almost cup them in my hands, a gleaming pale gold. Then they sheathed their wings and dropped, falling through the shadow plane, seeming to disappear as they skimmed the shattered cirque, the country of stone knives. Then they thrust out their wings, slim and strong, to breast the updraft, and burst up again, birds of darkness, birds of light.

It was almost dark when I got to camp. Mitch had cooked some of the bear's liver. I tasted it. It was heavy and rich. We ate it with slices of bread and canned pears by the light of a candle, while Roger finished a can of corned beef hash. I tried to imagine some of the bear's spirit in my throat, the bear's life inhabiting the weight in my stomach. But what I felt, more than anything I could imagine, was the night like a huge, unblinking animal outside the tent.

I prepared my bed outside, at the edge of the trees, but I couldn't sleep. Instead, I listened to my breath, and caught my tongue between my teeth, and stretched out my cut hand to touch the dog sleeping next to me, to feel her breath and heartbeat under coarse hair, the heart under the rise of her ribs, to touch the thing that we call life.

There was cold perched in my bones, the cold of no wind and no storm, a cold that no winter ever knew. There was a shadow opening at my feet, a darkness that had nothing to do with the casting of light or with the sun's rising or the moon's. And when I slept, I fell forward into the ponded black.

First, I dreamed about the bear, which became my brother lying dead, abandoned in the leaves. But instead of seeing his body, I could see only the sunflowers around it: the striated, brilliant yellow tongues, radiating from their velvet centers, each blossom a corn-colored star waxing huge in a green sky.

It took time, as I watched real stars appear over the black ridge, for the image to pass.

When I slept again I was the bear, covered in my black fur that gleamed as I moved, feeling the sun on my back, crossing a field of sunflowers, and then I was surrounded by scudding ewes and lambs that streamed by like low clouds, and I smelled hot metal, and heard the shot that killed me.

I woke again, stroked the sleeping dog, and tasted night's moisture in my breath.

At last, I dreamed that I was the one dead. And the bear was alive, and it circled me, walking in my spilled blood. With every circle the bear grew larger as my blood stained its feet. And then the snow fell.

And I had no body: I lay coiled like smoke in the earth, under the buried rocks and the fallen trees; under the snow I lay hungry and empty, making green shapes of the dark.

3 ～

Head of Murphy Creek

I built a fire and started coffee and wrangled the horses in before the alarm sounded. Mitch seemed subdued, while Roger talked as if all things were the same, and for him perhaps they were. I took refuge in silence. I licked the cut on my hand. My dreams and a corresponding lack of sleep had filled me with dread: by killing the bear we had upset things, and they would rebound. We would get hurt.

But the day dawned clear and calm, without apparent blemish. We packed the camp and lashed it to the backs of the horses, and they cooperated, even Elhon. As Mitchell and Roger started the sheep with shouts, I got underway with the pack string. The sheep moved in clots and clabbers through the morning shadow that lay in the bowl under the pass.

Etched into the mountainside, the trail was steep and narrow, lacking a solid edge. I rode Tubby, slow and surefooted but fat. I heard shouts and the frenzied yips of the dogs as Roger and Mitch came behind, awash in the herd, holding them tight and shoving them up. The sheep overflowed the trail, dodging and blatting, loose rocks clattering from under the hooves of one to roll under the hooves of the next. The clamor rose almost visibly, disarranging the morning air.

I wasn't used to sitting so far off the ground, above such a drop. My boot stuck out at a sharp angle into space, the oiled leather brick red, the laces yellow, and the sole a creamy white. When my eyes shifted from the toe of my boot to the distant floor of the cirque, the leap in focus made me feel faintly sick.

So I stopped looking down. Enough of perspective, irony, all that. I was closer to the ridge now and I could see the big snowdrift, light blue in shadow with a dark blue edge that seemed to vibrate against the rising sun. I stopped to let the horses blow, hearing the air catch and grate in their throats, the grind of iron shoes against rock as they adjusted the weight of their loads.

At last I led them onto the pass. It was a bare swoop not much wider than the horses themselves, and I got off to breathe and gaze, glad to have my feet out of the air. The snowdrift, which lapped over the bare rock and dirt of the ridge, was frozen hard. I could see the sets of tracks where Mitch and Roger had scouted, postholed into the snow in the day's heat. I stepped on the margin of it, and it crunched as my boots sank two inches. There were veins of dirt and broad reddish stains, like dried blood, which I knew to be algae. The drift curved out of sight to the east, and I could see the horse tracks disappearing. Following them to the lip, I looked into the cirque below.

The high basin was a long oval hemmed to the south by fractured walls and shaky towers, which threw long shadows toward the pass. To the north, the ridge was a bright golden curve, snowless and browed with neanderthal outcrops. A black cave-mouth yawned under a castellated point, and remnant snow slanted down on all flanks. From the snow emerged streams of loose rock, flowing east through reefs of stunted conifer: no apparent place to camp.

The air was cold, but the sun touched my face with a quick heat. I stomped out a path through the drift to where the muddy trail emerged, once, twice, three times. I could smell the snow, a dusty, moist scent, and the air of the uninhabited canyon below. Pookie followed me dutifully, then stopped to roll in the snow and snap at the morning air.

The horses watched. On the pass there wasn't much to eat, but they nosed at patches of tough grass and jerked a few stems out. I noticed a faint trail along the ridge, leading north to the ramp of Prater Mountain. A fringe of pines seemed to hold it in place. To the south, the ridge curved up into a pine-shagged height that broke off into rubbly cliffs.

Leaving the drift, I walked back, four long steps to the western rim. The herd was struggling up. As they saw me, the lead ewes stopped and blatted over their shoulders. I had to get off the pass or the herd might turn back.

I mounted and drew a long breath. The packhorses balked at the snowdrift, and the rope snapped taut. Fat Tubby danced. I could feel her front feet breaking through the crust and her back feet sliding into the holes. I yanked Red's lead, and he jumped into the drift, dragging the others off balance. They collided and Red almost went down. Tubby floundered out of the snowdrift and slipped in the mud below—followed by all that struggling bulk—then clawed her way to dry ground. I yelled and pounded her ribs with my heels, and we dragged the others out of the snow and across the slick mud, to the security of the trail.

But the trail wasn't secure. In the angled plunge of rock and mud and ball-bearing pebbles into the bowl, it was barely present, a foot-wide scrape. I had a precise vision of how we would look, falling, a tangle of packs and rope and thrashing hooves, an avalanche of live things. Time was suspended in a great, fearful ball, spinning above the head of the cirque. "Don't get off once you start," Mitch had warned. "You'll knock your horse off balance. Don't look back, just go."

The first switchback was so abrupt that Tubby had to lift both front feet and wheel, grunting with the shock as her hooves struck down. Her back feet slid, and I yelped, but we made it. I passed the lead behind my back, looking at Elhon's big hooves level with my head, almost in reach. Tubby coughed and the bit rattled against her teeth. *Go.* One by one the packhorses lunged and recovered.

The second switchback looked worse, a shingly about-face on the spine above a tusky pinnacle. "If your horse slips," Mitch had said, "toss the rope down the hill and jump up. Then dig in, or you'll slide under the hooves."

I looked down the ridge. It was like looking down the bar of a chainsaw. The old mare hesitated. I shut my eyes for an instant as she spun and opened them looking south at the cliffs. Her back feet skated, and then she had them under her and I could feel her ribs heave as her breath puffed out in a big *whoosh*. I had to blink as each packhorse repeated the dance-step. But the horses handled themselves with care. At the tail of the string, Elhon lunged too far and her back hooves skidded off the trail, but she dug in and held.

Dizzy—I realized I'd been holding my breath. The next switchback was easier: Tubby didn't even grunt, and the rest of the string stepped through. Below, the trail was carved into the slope instead of sketched across it. I lined the horses out and then stopped. "Whoa up. Let's rest. Whoa up." My voice shook.

On the slope above, at eye level, there were tiny flowers bedded in the gravel, forcing their way up between rocks. In the morning light I recognized buttercups, yellow as tiny suns, and spring beauties, white with flashes of pink, seven-pointed stars rising from the earth. The air was alive and sweet. The sky, framed in the rocky cirque, was blue as an upside-down ocean.

At the first fringe of grass I dismounted and untied their lead ropes. They dropped their heads to graze, nodding, their colors brilliant: oiled rust, coffee, and ripe wheat.

On the pass I saw two wobbling white heads, then six, then a jostling mob. It took an hour to get them all down the slope. Mitch and Roger rode down the switchbacks, letting the dogs push the sheep. It seemed at any moment that the whole mass would come unstuck and tumble, as one, down the shingly slope, but only one lamb slipped. It rolled twice before gaining its feet, but that was all.

As the herd spread out in the basin, and Roger and Mitch rode through, I caught the packhorses and tied them together. Roger looked sideways at me. "Not too bad. The drift was smaller than last year."

"We made it," I said, and looked at him. "But it's bad. We ought to dig the trail out."

Mitch laughed. "We like it that way. Keeps the *turistas* out."

"Pretty early up here. We should get them down to some feed," Roger said. "I guess a guy could set up camp. Just follow this on down. There's a trail coming across. Make a right, up around the corner of the mountain. On top's a level spot under some pines, with stakes and stove rocks. That's camp. We'll get a scatter on the sheep. Then I have to ride out."

I was glad to go. I was still uneasy with Roger, and the high bowl wasn't a welcoming place, under its unsteady cliffs, blue-gray and ghost gray, streaked with mustard and white. The trail wound through heaps of stone, neither following the bony crests nor falling into the dips where snow held late. Between was a band of soil hedged by low, shaggy conifers, and the trail followed it down the pitch of the basin, curving with the contours, east.

Riding, I tracked the water's course, saw the snowmelt singing in rivulets then carving gulleys above which scraggly firs tipped. Dead fir trunks, none larger than a wrist, were jackstrawed in the chill cascades. Leaving the water we passed through fir thickets, twenty hooves muffled by dirt, then knocking on rock.

The trail dropped off the end of a moraine and out of the high basin. We sidehilled from one knuckled glen to the next, through lush pockets and big trees. From the lip of the bowl, the canyon's west face opened in softer curves and then dropped off again. Two headlands thrust out, draped with green and crowned with pines. Separating them was a narrow tributary hidden by its angle of descent. I could hear the roar of water, but the stream was out of sight.

The opposite wall of the canyon seemed too close. The snow on it had melted, and it was gray, not green, mostly talus or cliff. Conifers formed narrow ranks along each folded ridge, acutely angled from right to left, separated by landslips and gulleys. I looked for a trail but there was none. It was all ragged, all steep.

I wanted to be someplace where I couldn't fall off the edge. The bear's death, followed by the crossing of the pass, had left me with a hollow foreboding. And there was something else uncertain, unexpected, something I had missed. It was visible, not a scent or an emotion, something I had seen but not grasped. The thought was uneasy, so I tried to let it go.

After dipping low to a junction, the trail climbed south through pockets of green, loomed over by old firs, huge after the stunted growth of the cirque. There were berms of papery-scaled fir cones across the trail, dry enough that they crackled when the horses stepped on them. Knotted limber pines claimed the ridgetops and rock ledges as the trail roved south, up through eroding draws and cupped meadows, and then reached a narrow divide. I looked off: a headwater creek thundered down in a loose flume, then disappeared between cliffs. I waited until the horses stopped puffing and began to graze, and then rode along the ridge to the east.

It wasn't hard to find the camp: it was the only level spot. Tubby jigged her head and nickered, as if to say *This is the place.* We pulled up by a bleached stack of poles, and stove rocks like squat monuments. I untied the lash ropes, heaved the heavy packs down, and dragged them into the shade. Elhon had broken her britchen strap, and one end hung loose. The leather was rotten. Two more strings had broken in her front cinch. I'd have to ask Mitch how to fix it. I turned the horses out to graze, and they found a wallow of loose dirt and took turns rolling, then ambled off, tails flashing in the sun.

I got the camp up, and Mitch rode in and we ate. He opened the kitchen box and examined what was left of the food. "That damn *Rogelio* eats better up here than at home."

"Is he coming back soon?"

"Probably not. This part's steep, but the herding's not hard to figure out."

I built a fire and we made coffee and toasted bread on the stovetop, smearing it with peanut butter and raspberry jam. We sat outside and ate, scanning the country. Above the gorge, the head of Murphy Creek formed an amphitheater, curved walls without a floor. It was all either up or down; wild, crumbling slants, and creeks brawling white through boulders and deadfall.

"We'll work the *borregas* up and around the head of Murphy," Mitch said. "Wild and lonesome. I like this camp."

To keep meat in a mountain camp, you hang it in the night air, where it cools and acquires a dry surface film. At sunrise you roll it up in canvas and put it in the shade. If nights are cold, it keeps for days, even weeks: that seemed like primitive magic.

At midmorning I dug a pit with our sawed-off shovel and built a fire in it, under the wide, bright sky, then gathered more wood, carrying it up armful by armful. I unrolled a front quarter of mutton and cut chunks for stew. Then I rolled the quarter back up and stowed it in the shade. It struck me that there were varieties of knowledge that went with certain places and situations. Someone had found this way of keeping meat fresh, just as someone had thought up the sawbuck pack-saddles, and the trick of making rope.

I cut onions, potatoes, and carrots, the knife making a solid *chunk*. I set the dutch oven on the fire. When it was hot, I browned the meat, then tumbled in the vegetables: rudimentary and grand. I added salt and pepper and chili. The lid fit on with a satisfying *clink* and I felt gifted, suddenly, with this practical heritage, with these things that were simple and worked so well.

Beyond this work, there was space and light for me here. And I liked being unobserved. I made a gargoyle face at a limber pine. Hah! Nothing I could say would make the tree mad. That was a positive sensation.

I scooped hot coals out of the pit, set the oven in, and shoveled the coals on top. Then I buried it with ashes and dirt. Wonderful. I could leave and it would still cook.

At midday, Mitch was napping in the tent. I went to check the horses and found them in a green swale. A low burst of thunder crossed the stainless blue, followed by echoes traveling the ground like invisible trains. Then the first cloud exploded over the ridge, lifting to reveal a gray belly filled with turbulent darkness. As I hastened toward camp, cloud after cloud rose up, diminishing the light. The whole landscape shifted from the colors of hawk to the colors of dove.

A shadow raced down the talus, over me and into the firs, falling into the gorge and then climbing faster than any animal, up the east wall and over the Star Peaks. And the cloud trailed a sudden coolness, prickling the hair on my arms.

Then came more thunder, closer and higher in pitch: I could hear it burst in one part of the sky and then cross to another. As I reached the camp a bolt tickled the rimrock, burning a blue hole in my sight. Then a hard gust flattened the pocket meadow, and the leaves of the sunflowers flashed their silver undersides up to the racing sky.

I hear wind purring in the conifers, nudging dry cones into a stumble, and then I see the leading edge of the rain, the border of blurred silver, see the raw contrasts soften, hear the wind's brush and snare, see flowers dip and bow, and then: the air is rain, your skin is rain, your clothes, your breath, your heart, all rain.

I lowered my arms. Mitch watched me from the tent, nodding to himself: *Not enough sense to come in out of the rain.* He was starting a fire in the box stove. I stepped in and looked out through the door flap. The canyon was lidded. Clouds lapped over the high ridge to the east. I went out and brought wood in. The ground was wet, but there was a dry circle where I'd buried the dutch oven. "What about the stew?" I asked.

"The heat'll keep the rain out. It'll cook," he said. He started a pot of coffee. I dug out my classics text and opened to the chapter on the Chinese. "Do nothing and all things will be done," said Lao-Tzu. Check. I'd try that on Mitchell, next time he asked where the horses were. After scouting Lao-Tzu, I read an excerpt from the *Analects* by Confucius:

> Humility is near to moral discipline (*li*); simplicity of character is near to true manhood; and loyalty is near to sincerity of heart. . . . For with humility, a man seldom commits errors; with sincerity of heart, he is reliable; and with simple character, he is generous.

The rain ceased. I studied the sky. The clouds opened but then closed softly over us again, and rained again, gently. Mitch poured some coffee, and steam curled under the brim of his hat.

I asked him about the bullet hole in the ceiling above the big table in the Preston ranch house. "That was Ray," he said, and shook his head. "He's one wild bastard." A tale was about to commence. "Married a thirteen-year-old girl." I looked up.

"But this isn't about that," he said. "Anyhow, during lambing season, Prestons hired Ray to feed. Roger and I were doing shifts: I had the days and *Rogelio* took nights."

Another livestock memoir; I sighed.

"Anyhow, I was checking the ewes in the pasture north of the house and Ray was feeding from that little bobsled I showed you: the one-horse job."

"About the size of a VW bug."

"Right. Well, Ray'd been out on an expedition the night before. After leaving Dad's Bar, they got his six-cylinder Olds Ninety-eight upside down in an irrigation ditch during a little snow flurry. Took most of the night to get it out."

"It's a lie!" I burst out. "A *six-cylinder* Olds Ninety-eight?"

"*Potentially* it was a V-eight, but at that point it was, practically speaking, a V-six, or maybe even a V-five. Your average Star Valley native is tough on machinery."

"First threats," I said, "then the ball-peen hammer, with new spark plugs as a last resort. So, had he been partaking of spiritous liquors? Ol' *Ramón.*"

"Mmmmmm, not *Ramón* . . . he's Ray. These Star Valley guys don't like to be called by Mexican names, especially if they hire out as ranch hands. Good way to get your nuts kicked off."

I looked over my shoulder and hissed, "He's hiding behind that pine."

"Do you wanna jerk my cinch or hear the story?"

"Story. *Por favor.*"

"So Ray does everything really fast. He drinks a pot of coffee before he even gets his boots on and another with breakfast. And he eats so fast that it looks like somebody is vacuuming the food up—I don't think he chews. And when he goes to work it's like one of those old movies where it looks speeded up and jerky."

"So that's why he makes love to thirteen-year-olds?"

He ignored it. "So anyway, we're lambing and for April there's a lot of snow. Ray's feeding the ewes with the little bobsled, and he's whipping the horse up and making these wild strafing runs. You can see daylight under the runners. The horse is snorting and steaming, and Ray's face is red, like a balloon. And he's cussing a blue streak and flailing with the pitchfork, scattering a bale, maybe a bale and a half each time across the pasture. So the hay is spread pretty thin. The ewes aren't getting much to eat in any one place, so they're charging after the sled, trying to find a pile of hay bigger than a . . . a . . . ."

"Hamster."

"No. A . . . ."

"Dictionary."

"More than two or three damn bites! So anyhow Ray is flying low, and the hungry ewes are charging after him, and there's this other bunch of sheep in a pen by the shed . . . ."

"What pen?"

"We stuck some steel fenceposts into the snow and ran sheep wire around, to hold the ewes we wanted to take into the shed. About ten or so. So Ray goes cussing and tearing between the shed and the pen, a hundred and fifty miles per hour, and almost runs into the shed, and reins the horse hard right, and the right front runner catches the sheep wire, and *bing!*"

"Bing?"

"The wire. The pen goes right along with the sled, and the posts pop out of the snow: *bing, bing, bing.*" He takes a deep breath. "And those poor ewes are bagged up like fish in a net. By the time he gets the horse stopped he's dragged 'em halfway across the pasture, and they're squalling and kicking their pointy feet out through the holes in the wire, hell on earth!"

I laugh. "Yeah?"

"So he looks at the sheep all tangled up. His mouth's so wide open he can't even cuss. I'm standing by the shed and I start to laugh. I can't stop. And he looks at me, and at the sheep, and back at me, and I see little Zippo-lighter sparks in his eyeballs, and then he grabs that pitchfork and chucks it like a . . . a . . . ."

"Spear. Harpoon. Lightning bolt."

"Like a damn bolt of lightning. And it comes whooshing through the air right at my face and I can feel the cold breeze on my cheek and *SPANG!*"

"He kills you," I said.

"No, dammit. It sticks in the shed, right into the planks, and the handle is right next to my head, *k-doing, k-doing, k-doing,* just like a great big . . . tuning fork."

I nod, impressed.

"And Ray says, real slow: 'Laugh at me again, you're dead.' Like that."

Mitch's eyes are wide. "And it takes both me and Roger to pull the damn pitchfork out."

I wait a bit, to show my appreciation. But I'm still wondering about the bullet holes and the thirteen-year-old bride. "Sooo, did they have a Mormon wedding?"

"Mmmmmm. Rain quit. We'd better go out and herd sheep."

They were scattered in the bowls between the lip of the cirque basin and the camp, feeding contentedly. "Not much herding to do," Mitch said, taking out his pipe. "We'd better enjoy it while it lasts." He leaned back against a boulder.

I felt like exploring. I headed west and climbed into the huge bowl below the pass, over the piles and humps of loose rock. The more stable heaps of rock were capped by jungles of stunted fir and separated by scarce and verdant little pockets, with buttercups and spring beauties and nameless little purple devils starting up from the mud between the rocks.

Farther up, the north-facing slope was striped by slide paths and herringboned with dead fir trunks. The surviving firs were spiky with broken limbs, and their bark was peeled and scoured on the uphill side where they were ridden down each winter by the snow. These beat-up trees, I realized, lived more of their lives under snow than in the open air.

Above the trees, old avalanche tongues overlapped, like dinosaurs buried in the run-out. I sat on a big boulder around which the snow current split, thinking of how snow moves after reaching the ground:

either a creep or an avalanche, slower than water or faster. There were veins of dust on the snow, and dead flies and leaves embedded.

Pikas buzzed over the hollow expanse, and a raven circled high under a cloud. Walking on hard snow in the center of the bowl, I found the corpse of a weasel in full winter white, curled on its side in a melted-out cup. Its fur was soaked and transparent, and the brown skin showed through. The quick black eye was sunken and shut. The elongated form of the skull showed through the wet fur, a searcher's head. It was killed, I thought, in an avalanche, buried by more, and harder, snow than it could dig out through.

Why live in such a place? The conifers grew in little huddled villages, and the snow flowed in great cold waves around them or over them, crushing and breaking, as random and predictable as war. It seemed like a place where live things would always suffer. Yet the trees lived because it was their nature, as much as it was the snow's to layer and fracture and fall. And the weasel's to run, with black sparks for eyes, and to seek. There was no logic in it, only rhythm.

A shadow enveloped the bowl and clouds deepened. I hiked down again through krummholz and mats of snow-pressed willows, just melted out. A few large spruces grew on the south-facing slope, but what I noticed was the ragged skyline, the raw scarp faces, cracked and jointed cliffs, great spills of frost-split stone, and debris heaped in sizes from bricks to pea gravel.

Everywhere I looked there was breakage. Exposed to the weather, the bedrock separated along its layers: thin layers formed plates and shingles, while thicker ones split into angular blocks, sharp on every edge. Broken pines lay strewn on the avalanche run-outs, gray twigs tangled and moldered, and brown needles were matted and sodden underfoot. I walked through the wreckage, following the milky stream that appeared from under the snow. The water was turbulent, flowing over spalled rock, fractured wood, and cosmic trash. Joined by rivulets, it braided and twined, and took on a faint roar.

I hiked out of the basin and down toward the joining of the trails. I didn't know what it was I'd missed the first time, but I felt it again—an absence, or a strange withholding. I looked around at the clouds, the cliffs, the rock, the stunted fir, the stream.

But there was no stream. That was it: I'd started down with the stream on my right. Leaving the basin, I'd turned right and then climbed, without ever crossing it. That contradicted the laws of the landscape, as I knew them. What I felt was the stream's disappearance.

I hiked back and found the stream above and followed it through the stunted, springy fir jungles. At the basin's lip it roared into a bowl floored with coarse rocks, then sank out of sight, gone into the dark, its green and liquid line broken off like the fir twigs under my feet.

AUGUST 1

We shared the light of one candle, set in a jar lid on the kitchen box. Waiting for the coffee I read more of Li Po:

Journeying is hard.
There are many turnings—
Which am I to follow? . . .
I will mount a long wind someday and break the heavy waves
And set my cloudy sail straight and bridge the deep, deep sea.

I read it again, aloud. Mitch was listening. "That's good," he said. "Who?"

"Li Po. Wild old drunken Chinese sheepherder-saint. Here's another one:

"*Addressed Humorously to Tu Fu*

"Here! Is this you, on the top of Fan-ko Mountain,
Wearing a huge hat in the noonday sun?
How thin, how wretchedly thin you've grown!
You must have been suffering from poetry again."

"Hah! Suffering is right. I'll stick to Joe Back." Mitch had adopted my packer's bible and was studying it. In my classics book, Tu Fu was next. "Certainly he is finest in the classical tradition," I read, "though foreign readers and the commoners of China have preferred Li Po, his close friend." I was prepared to hate Tu Fu. But my cup was empty and it was time to go.

The plan was to move the herd slowly around the head of Murphy Creek. The sheep would naturally go to the best forage, so we had two tasks. The first was to keep them moving slowly around the headwater slopes. The second was to keep small bands from straying over the top.

Morning light showed the bony contour of the place. West was a steep climb to a hanging valley, backed by the spine of the Salt River Range, impassable except on foot. South was a complex set of curves where the creek began in small, snowy basins that gave into steep gulleys. Due south, a divide ridge was sparsely furnished with limber pine and fir. On the other side was Cedar Creek. If the sheep went down there, we'd have a hard time getting them back.

Mitch rode the red gelding back to the pass to hunt strays. Feeling both foreign and common, I clambered over the rocks and down steep dirt, herding as the day warmed.

The sheep moved slowly, nibbling and calling. I led Pronto, the young mare, and she jerked at the reins to gather clumps of grass. I could hear the wet crunch of it between her teeth. The colt played among the sheep, then charged Pookie. The dog dropped her tail and ran to me, and I laughed as the colt whirled away.

I liked it here. I felt free. And I felt a kind of peace, but when I looked hard at the place, I wondered why: there was no permanence, nothing static. In the steepest country, things move fast. Streams have the power of their high angle, and every loose slope speaks of movement. The peaks and ridges crest like slow waves. Limber pines come flexing and spiraling up from cracks in limestone, to cast cones and die and fall, to be caught in the gray torrent of scree, lost in the gravitational rain of all things.

I dozed off with Pookie at my side. From above, sitting on a cloud, the herd must have looked like a white amoeba, extending pseudopods between outcrops and pines. Loose herding—the idea of it—was to let wooly pseudopods extend and circulate without allowing them to break off and squirm away. When an amoeba grows too large, it yearns to divide, to become two, four, eight, or ten. And constantly, small bands of sheep struck out, each with its stubborn matriarch.

A fly bit me and I woke up. I stood up. The sheep had scattered all over the place. I spent a hot and itchy hour finding surly ewes and rogue lambs, dogging them out of the fir jungles, and chasing them toward the main bunch. Naturally, it occurred to me that I was harassing the poor, stupid animals because they wanted precisely what I did: to distance themselves from that critical mass of idiocy, the herd. But so what?

Mitch said I would learn to like sheep, but I hadn't. I hoped to discover at least a tolerant interest in them, but my hopes were confounded by the sheep themselves. They had a pissy, bad-cheese stink that clung to leaves and soaked into the soil. Their swarming numbers, the multiplicity of dumb looks, and the swath of broken stems and harrowed earth they left behind all aroused not simply dislike but a hot and active loathing. Sometimes the ewes would set their back feet and piss great yellow gouts, looking back, eyes witless and jaws quivering as they bawled sheepish curses. I had to restrain myself from picking up rocks and taking aim at their wobbly heads, as I longed for a machine gun.

Mitch said it wasn't their fault: they were bred to be stupid, wooly, and fat. The fact that generations of men had carefully debased generations of sheep to their present loathsomeness aroused in me, if anything, only a deeper loathing. And anyhow, who loves the whole of creation? A fool with a sandwich. Junkies, after a fix. Lobotomized nuns. So I hated sheep. It was okay.

The process of herding, quoth Mitch, required skill and patience, which I lacked. I tried to make up for it with verbal mayhem, wild downhill slides and uphill scrambles, and a wealth of extravagant gesture. But my bravura technique would excite the dogs to the point that they would chase strays away from the herd rather than back to it. Then my curses on the sheep were interspersed with death threats hurled at the dogs, who seemed to relish the barbarism and disorder. Yipping like coyotes, they acted proportionally worse.

I wasn't a good herder and would never be one. I simply hated sheep too much.

But I liked the swearing. My father had a gorgeous fluency when a tire sank in the mud or a horse stepped on the toe of his boot. I thought of it as a rich folk tradition, one to be cultivated. But if you spend hours yelling at sheep you become rather hoarse. Thus I found that Spanish, rolling off the lips and tongue, was better for cursing sheep than English. So I called them *borregas*—woolies—and also *putas, moscas, cresas, cabroncitos,* and *chingaderos,* none of which mattered in the least: animals care only about your tone of voice. Pookie, for example, would waltz up, tail a-flag, at being called a brainless, stinking, hairy sack of porcupine guts, as long as it was sweetly spoken. To dogs, and also *borregas, cabroncitos,* and *moscas,* Form equals Content.

With these weighty issues in mind, I bedded the sheep. (So as not to inflame the suspicions of the nonherding audience, I hasten to say *bedded* means that I stopped plaguing them until they dozed off.) Then I whispered a few parting threats and rode back to cook.

In the midst of my culinary operations, Mitch returned. "Beautiful morning. No strays," he said. The beans boiled merrily on the stove, still hard as stream pebbles. He tested them. "High altitude," he said. "Low boiling point." I'd been wondering why they wouldn't cook.

"We'll eat the beans tomorrow," he said. "Let me show you how to make tortillas."

There were two classes: flour and corn. Flour tortillas were quicker, so we'd start with the corn. Since the Mormon-owned market didn't stock *masa,* the ground hominy that went into real corn tortillas, we would use Christian Maid Bright Yellow Corn Meal, the best the Prestons could offer. It was somewhat coarse, so we would boil it to render it pliable. So said Mitch.

"Mush! I can do that," I replied. I set a pot of water next to the stovepipe. "Now," said Mitch, "we're gonna make beautiful flour tortillas." He took a bowl and mixed flour, water, salt, and a glop of lard. "Knead it like bread, but not as long." He pinched off a walnut-sized lump of dough, and sprinkled flour on the little kitchen-box counter. "Observe."

He groped in the box until he found a seven-inch piece of broomstick, glossy with frequent use. "The magic tortilla wand." He squashed the dough, dropped it into the flour, flipped it, sprinkled more flour on the top, and then began to roll it out. He worked on the dough like a painter on canvas, with pursed lips and intent gaze, as it rounded and thinned and assumed tortillahood. I was impressed.

"That's how Pancho says you pick a wife: wide hips and thin tortillas. Last year, he never let up until my tortillas were thin." He folded it deftly, lifted it, and then opened it onto the top of the stove. "No frying pan to wash."

"Right on the stove. Brilliant."

"Hah! You should see the Campos sisters make tortillas. They pat the dough out between their tender hands." He took a lump of dough and demonstrated, patting and flipping, but the tortilla fell apart. "That Aurelia Campos . . . prettiest girl I ever saw. She makes tortillas you could read the Bible through. And her mama watches her like a hawk."

On the stovetop, the first one steamed and bubbled and began to look like a real tortilla. He flipped it with fingertips, and it repeated the marvelous process.

"*Numero uno.*" He tore it in half and we shared it. It was a wonder of opposites: soft and crisp, thin and substantial, delicate and tough.

"Amazing," I said. It was something Li Po would have enjoyed.

"Now you try it." After a couple false starts, it worked. Then the corn meal was ready, so he showed me how to mix a little flour into it and then roll it out. I elbowed him away from the dough in my rush to create. He decided to take a nap in the shade, under a big limber pine poised over the stunning drop to the creek. Another small magic in hand, I made tortillas, joyfully alternating corn and flour, until I had a stack of each.

Time for a ramble. I stoked the stove and damped it down, for the beans. Then I dug out my clandestine bag of ganja—two tablespoons to last the season—and twisted a smoke, which I intended to appreciate along with the verses of Tu Fu, naked and dead center in the most perfect of all possible flowery bowls.

I scrambled up a rockstrewn gully into the hanging valley, and threaded broken blocks and fir jungles to reach the border of remnant snow. The valley was a sink, and the melt percolated out of sight, emerging in the little stream where we got water for the camp. Patches of the snow were red with algae. Mitch had told me it was poisonous, which I doubted: he had a way of testing me with fibs. So I ate a small handful and it had no flavor, apart from ice and dust.

There wasn't much reason for any living thing to be here, other than the opening in space. But it wasn't an easy opening, or a secure one. There's something depressing about shattered limestone, a kind of despair in its naked, unstable, razor-edged disarray. The only law here was gravity: rocks fell until they stopped, usually on a gray stack of rocks that had fallen just before. When a pile grew too high, it collapsed. Eventually the shards would be soil, but that would take huge gulps of time. But it was good to be on ground the sheep would never cross: too hard and worthless, and in August, still partly under snow.

A strange little fugue played in my head: *Jesus wants me for a sunbeam, to shine for him each day.* I couldn't get rid of it, and I could hear, one by one, squeaky voices adding themselves, as the kids in my Sunday school class found their places in the songbook, or were nudged by their teachers. The image I had was of buttery sunbeams squishing down onto tidy flowerbeds and row crops, and over the shingled roofs of identical candy houses. In perfectly square pastures grazed herds of cartoon sheep, pink bows around their necks. *Ugh.*

There were definitely plenty of sunbeams up here, where nothing could graze except imagination. I didn't know if Jesus owned them, and I didn't care. But if I had to be one, I thought, I'd rather light up this rich and meaningless disorder.

Broken limestone, or dolomite—I didn't know how to tell them apart—clinked and grated under my feet as I hiked south under a cracked wall, through a confusion of sinks and moraines, and into jungles of stunted fir. I saw a faint trail and followed it, quickly realizing that it was made by feet much smaller and sharper than my own. My foot slipped and I went to all fours, but it wasn't solid enough to crawl. My boot soles, white crepe rubber, were too soft to edge, and if I fell it would mean an ugly slide that wouldn't kill me but would remove most of my skin, embarrassing as injuries go.

There's not really a word for how I got across. Above, the slope eased and I breathed more easily climbing to the dip in the ridge, and the canyon's south divide. The ridge was chalky, softer than the gray stuff of which the peaks were made, and Cedar Creek was a fanged hole with no descending trail. In my little day pack, the classics poked at my spine and ribs. I sat in the breeze and read a poem by Tu Fu, written to his friend Li Po:

> . . . You sing wild songs,
> Your days pass in emptiness.
> Your nature is a spreading fire,
> It is swift and strenuous.
> But what does all this bravery amount to?

I delivered a gentle shrug toward the east and traded the classics for my book of flowers: here liveth paintbrush, arnica, lousewort, gooseberry currant, buttercup, bearberry, and mats of wind-flattened juniper. Then I got stuck—short-style bluebells or alpine forget-me-nots? I stared at the drawings and couldn't decide. *Your days pass in emptiness.*

Why not? There was a tiny yellow flower that might have been lomatium and a small white anemone-type blossom with a yellow-green center and a delicate, hairy stem: *Pubescence,* the book said, enough to distract me into longing, for the warm slip of belly skin and the curly shock of unseen fur and the soft clutch centered on heat, and then the moist bloom. Cassandra.

Life is a spreading fire. What does it amount to, the body's loneliness? Flowers amount to seed, and black winter sleep, and then the damp seeds spring up and amount to flowers, and the sum is nothing. Days pass in flowers.

I stowed the book and looked around. To my right, at the center of the dip in the ridge, was a giant limber pine, a tree that flowed, rough and brown, like a river into the sky. The trunk had a heavy grace, like the forearms of working men. Opening my arms—just over six feet from fingertip to tip—I measured the ancient body of the pine, the bark scratching at my cheek, four times, and stopped with my left elbow touching the knot that was my starting point: twenty-one feet. *Endure,* it said.

Far below, I saw light flaring on the tails of the horses as they grazed. I could see Mitchell stretched out under a pine, hat over his face. The camp was clean, tortillas cool and wrapped.

Run, said the pine. So I flew across the slope, reckless in my bliss, and leapt narrow snow gullies to land running in the mud.

I came to a sloping meadow, centered on a huge gray block upon which a lordly marmot sunned. The marmot reared, examined me—*a foreigner, and a commoner*—and relaxed into a noble slouch. The meadow was a vale of impossible greens starred with pink, yellow, purple, white, and heartbreak blue.

Above, I saw a cow elk, sleek and gorgeous. She looked back at me. Her coat gleamed as she dashed away, and I could feel a stirring in my blood. Tracking her, I traversed, up, down, over, and through the arteries of snowmelt, across the swoops of drainage east to the snow. I clambered up onto the melting surface, kicking and gliding, punching white holes in the dusty mantle, swift and strenuous, my boots soaked through.

The elk was gone. I came on a rounded puzzle-mound of mud, like a giant mallow chocolate, cracked at the top. I scratched its flank and found ice beneath. The world was inside out. I heard falling water on the breeze. A waterfall threaded over the rimrock and came down a steeply tilted trough of polished stone. Drunk with movement I scrambled and splashed up, and climbed the wall by the tiny falls, topping out, coming into another meadow, crowned with snow.

Go, it said. So I climbed the cornice, kicking steps, slicing my hands in for holds, up and up and over the melting lip. The snow leveled on the absolute top, and I stepped onto rocky soil, banding a line of krummholz fir. I burst through it and stopped. At my feet was a wild drop, cliff band to talus to meadow to forest around a tiny lake, and far, far down the long dark ridges was a river, Greys River, like a silver sword, sharp in its rocky cleft.

AUGUST 2

"Light the damn stove," Mitch said.

"Do nothing," I replied, "and all things will be done."

"Bullcrap. Says who?"

"Says Lao-Tzu."

"Son-of-a-bitch never herded sheep." He laughed.

I thought about that. "Maybe he just herded 'em really loose," I said.

But I lit the stove, started coffee, and set the beans near the pipe. Then I stepped out and stood until I heard a horse bell, not far off. Then Mitch told me that with the benefit of my ancient wisdom he could probably herd alone.

I was sated with exploration, so I cut up meat and started a cauldron of chili, red as a satyr's heart. And my cook's progress reached a milestone: a deep-dish pumpkin pie, baked in the dutch oven. The pumpkin was canned, but I made the crust from scratch.

I could smell perfection. And when the lid came off, it was perfect. I sat and looked at the buckskin-colored crust, the glazed moon of pumpkin, the entire, steaming wonder of it. Mitch came back early and was properly awestruck. Then we ate hugely, gluttonously, sinfully, and absolved one another with groans.

Mitch took a canvas pack cover and a lash rope, and showed me how to make a boondocks hammock. "Cowboy heaven," he said. "There it is." We stretched it between big firs in the breeze and then contended savagely for it.

"It was my idea," he snapped.

True. He'd shown me how to pouch the canvas over a pebble and loop it with rope. "I did most of the work," I said, "and I'm heavier—test flight."

"You might rip it," he said, and straddled the canvas, daring me to throw him out. "Tie up another one." We had plenty of canvas and plenty of rope, but it wouldn't be the same. So I stomped off and sat in the dirt and let my book fall open to the *Analects* of Confucius, hoping for moral armament, which I found: "The inferior man loves only his property."

I considered yelling that, but Mitch was already asleep, hat over his eyes: he loved his naps. Feeling lonesome, I wandered down to the horses. Red came and nuzzled me as I scratched his withers, and sniffed me, as I sniffed him. I had the stronger smell. The flies that accompanied him showed a sudden interest in me. My jeans were caked with flour, the thighs dark with spills and soot. My T-shirt felt sticky.

Digging through my duffle, I couldn't find anything clean except a wool shirt, which it was too hot to wear, and a pair of poplin slacks, which I hated. So I filled the dishpan with water and set it on to heat. That wiped out the water supply. I caught Red, and got a pad and packsaddle, and draped two panniers to hold the canvas water bags.

It was an itchy trip. The sheep had crossed the creek, and there were pellets of dung floating in the pools, so I climbed to where the water rose from the slope and found that it didn't rise far enough. I had to dip it, a cup at a time. There wasn't a tree or even a bush to tie Red, and he kept dragging his lead rope. So I tied it around my ankle. He tugged, and I quickly reconsidered. I untied the loop in what I hoped was a soothing manner while he sniffed the part in my hair, and tethered him to the full water bag, which would at least slow him down.

When I got back Mitch was swaying and singing a minor-key hymn:

> All day over the prairies I ride,
> Not even a dog to run by my side,
> My fire I kindle from chips gathered 'round,
> And boil my coffee without being ground.
>
> My ceiling the sky, my carpet the grass,
> My music the lowing of herds as they pass.
> My books are the brooks, my sermons the stones,
> And my parson's a wolf on a pulpit of bones.
>
> My books teach me constancy ever to prize,
> My sermons that small things I must not despise,
> And my parson remarks from his pulpit of bone
> That the Lord favors them who look out for their own.

The tune was elusive, and then unforgettable. I let the song end before I led the horse into camp. He looked aslant as I unloaded the water, then covered his eyes again. The water on the stove was hot. We didn't have laundry soap, but dish detergent would do. Should I wash myself before the clothes? Or wash clothes and bathe while they dried? The latter. Humming the tune I'd heard, I poured half of the water into a cooking pot and heaped my dirty clothes into the dishpan.

"Goddammit! You better boil that when you get done!" Mitch glared from the hammock.

"Boil yourself, grandma."

"Hah! Maybe you could wash up a few things for me." He laughed and settled back.

"Dream on. I wouldn't touch your socks with a welding torch."

I hung my wet clothes on the tent ropes and branches. As I started to bathe, Mitch objected again: "You can't use the dishpan for that."

"What? Wait until I get back to the ranch?"

"Go down to the creek and jump in. That's what I do."

"Right in our drinking water."

"My germs are all the way to the Snake River by now."

"Too cold. Can't get clean."

"As long as the horses don't stampede when you lift your arms, it'll do."

He told me about Pancho's morning ritual, which was darkly medieval. Pancho had only a few pairs of socks and didn't trouble laundering them. "He'd wake up and pull them out of his boots and then break them."

"*Break?*"

"Roll them around between his hands, to soften them up," he said.

I shuddered. "How did you stand the guy?"

"Got used to it. Horses don't smell good at first, or sheep."

"Sheep never do."

He shrugged and went back to his nap as I dried in the sun.

While my clean socks flittered in the breeze, I tried walking barefoot. I had the idea that toughening my feet was good practice, but up here the bedrock was cracked into shapes that were dangerous to bare feet: cubes, pyramids, and polygons. Besides, there were rock prongs sticking through the thin layer of soil. That I needed my boots to get around this place made me feel claustrophobic, but it was obvious I did.

Each place had its own laws. These mountains had hard layers and soft ones. Where it was hard, it was jagged, but there were handholds and footholds. Where it was soft, everything slid. Your boots shoved the slope downhill as you tried to go up. When you came down, the earth accompanied you.

That night, I heard coyotes. One howled, a questioning note. Another answered. Then another joined in and formed a wavering chord. As more coyotes sang, the night resounded as if darkness itself had found a voice. Mitch woke. "Damn critters," he said. The howls rose in crescendo and then fell into barks and yips. "Trouble," he said. "Bet they're in the herd."

He fumbled his way to the flaps. I heard a click and then the roar of a shot, stunning inside the tent. "Damn. *Sorry,*" he said, and stepped outside, jacking another shell into the chamber. "But maybe I can scare 'em off."

He fired two quick shots, the flashes inking his outline. The howls diminished. After the fourth shot, the coyotes stopped.

AUGUST 3

The shots repeated themselves in my dreams, and I saw the bear, dead and flayed. I woke up and lay with open eyes until it was time to start the stove. We did our tasks and didn't say much, but the silence grew easier. The sheep were near camp, and we split up and walked around them as it grew light.

Back at camp, Mitch sat on a rock and charmed the sun up with his lonesome harmonica. I caught the horses and brushed each in turn, with crazy momentum, until they shone. When I turned them loose they bucked and stampeded, glowing like jewels against the green, sunlit slope.

That afternoon the sky was a drum that played itself. Thunder boomed peak-to-peak, and the canyons opened under the sound, hollow and hard. Blue softness filtered over the ridge, and a rainstorm broke, chill and silver, a pelting beauty that sent the horses snorting and ducking under pines, as leaves dipped and turned under the sky's weight, and made the tent belly and stream at the eave, the canvas soaked through in spots, passing circles and streaks of light.

I started a fire in the stove. Mitch came in, hefted his saddle into the tent, and tipped it up to dry. I draped a canvas over a low limb and edged it with rocks, a makeshift tent for the wet dogs, and shooed them under it. But Tikki-Lo snuck into the tent behind the stove, and shook. A dog-scented steam rose.

"Git outa here, you varmint!" Mitch sprawled on his bedroll, settling into the smell of the wet wool and pine smoke. The coffeepot ticked as the storm wall passed over, leaving everything soft, quiet, porcelain-clean. *Your days pass in emptiness.* Or in flowers. Cassandra.

"What?" Mitch asked. I'd spoken her name aloud.

"Nothing," I said. Around us, the forest paused between breaths.

In his saddlebag, Mitch had a roll of tortillas and a can filled with beans, closed with foil and a string. His steel canteen cup held a little bag of coffee and two sourdough biscuits, for breakfast. Rolled on the back of his saddle, his bedroll made a big hump, and I had his shelter half rolled over mine. Because the east ridge had good forage, he wanted to take the herd up to the rim where I'd gazed off. But it took long enough to get there from camp, and was risky enough in the dark, that he wanted to tepee out: his phrase. He'd camp on the ridge. If the herd strayed back toward the main camp, Pookie and I would catch them. If they tried to go east into the Greys River Canyon, he'd be there with a horse and two dogs.

He picked a spot in the lee of old pines, overlooking miles of air. He unrolled the shelter half, army surplus—two of them snap together to make an A-frame tent—as I sharpened deadfall sticks with my knife. Then we staked it out. He'd sewn a strip of light canvas along the ridge to shelter the open side, and he stretched it with parachute cord.

He poured out some grain on a flat rock for Tony. "He'll probably raise hell all night, but I won't get much sleep—have to night-herd. Come up early and spell me off." I envied his bivouac on top of the world: it had a lonesome nobility.

In camp I luxuriated, in sole possession of a tent that seemed suddenly huge. I built a roaring fire in the stove for heat and tied the flaps back for the view. A few tiny drops hung from the firs as the last light washed from the air. Pookie whined outside, so I called her into the tent. She nudged me with her head before lying down at the back of the stove and licking her paws.

"Don't tell," I said.

AUGUST 4

A bolt of lightning tore the lid off the dark. I could see maps in my eyelids. I looked out. A gust slapped the tent and the tops of pines boiled, but there were only a few spatters of rain as the storm moved across. Watching bolts hit the Star Peaks, I thought about Mitch up there. I didn't envy him. The sheep would be on the move all night, trying to dash over the top and shelter on the lee side in the thick timber, exactly where we didn't want them to go. He'd be up, I knew, and trying to hold them.

I should help, I thought, but crossing the head of the canyon was dangerous even by day. I couldn't make it at night on a lightning-spooked horse, and I was too exhausted to go on foot.

But I couldn't sleep. I imagined a white bolt groping down to finger the stovepipe, which would go incandescent as the tent erupted in flames. I tried counting sheep, but instead of leaping one by one, they thronged over the ridge and into impassable wooded breaks. Bursts of lightning woke me, and between them I fell into torpor, finally dragging out of my bag at 4:45. Mitch had left his little clock: the sheep will wake me up, he'd said.

I moved in a daze, head buzzing with contingencies. If Mitch got struck by lightning, then I'd ride out for help. How. Over Prater Pass. No. Load him on a horse and lead it down to the guard cabin at Deer

Creek. How did a person struck by lightning look? What if the horse got struck? What if the dogs were eating the dead horse? My head spun with terrible sights.

I lurched out to pee and tripped over my bootlaces. I wanted to perform a courageous act, to equal Mitch's night out on the ridge, and in my disconnected state, I decided to ride Elhon. He'd been talking about making an honest horse of her. We'd saddled her a few times without too much trouble, and he'd circled her around a meadow. She was only a horse.

By first light, I got the saddle on. The trails were slick, and the big horse almost fell, so I got off and led her across the stream gully before I mounted again. The trail was barely visible in the rain-darkened soil. Ahead, it dipped under a brushy peninsula from which an old pine thrust roots into the air. The stream fell away faster than the trail climbed, and the next safe ground lay above a long drop. Elhon was reluctant, and I urged her gently, scared of her as much as the slope. Go, girl. Almost there. Then, from the forest edge, a weasel flicked out, quick as a lizard toward the stream.

I could feel her muscles bunch, and I grabbed for the horn as the weasel doubled and came back up the bank, right under her feet. She made two big jumps, straight back, and we landed on the narrow trail, but then she twisted and bucked out into space. The first buck took us twenty feet downslope. My feet popped out of the stirrups as I felt the dirt break loose under her hind feet. She bucked again. Thirty feet. Her front legs collapsed as her hindquarters whipped down the slope. I went flat out on her back, hands on the horn and boots in the air, as we surfed another thirty feet in a clatter of loose rock before coming to rest.

"W-whoa," I said.

I had the horn with both hands, and one rein. The cantle poked into my gut. My left boot touched the slope, and my right leg was stretched above the horse's tail. Her back feet were dug out of sight in a heap of debris. I could feel her shiver, so I cooed and quickly ran out of breath.

I rolled my weight up onto my left foot, careful not to push against the horse. She shivered again. If she lunged, I'd go under her hooves. I stroked her neck at the edge of the blanket. "Easy. Easy. Whooooooo." I managed a step up, keeping the rein lightly in my palm. Another step. Another. She heaved up and straightened her legs, and the slope shifted and gravel clattered into the creek, so I dropped the rein and clambered on all fours up to the first tree I could grab, showering her with dirt.

"Sorry, Elhon," I whispered. "C'mon. Up." The big horse stayed where she was, breathing hard, immobilized. I looked at the situation. Her two leaps had angled us away from the worst drop, to a set of ragged pinnacles where the creek plunged almost straight down. When her feet slipped, she'd swapped ends and was faced back the way we'd come, toward safety. That, at least, was good. She might slide or tip off the slope, but she'd roll into the stream just before it plummeted. If she didn't break a leg, I could lead her up the streambed to the trail crossing.

Pookie scrambled down and almost knocked me loose from my tree. I launched a slap and she cringed, anticipating the blow, but I stopped just short of her head. Then I stroked her. "Shhhhh. Good dog. Stay." I crept up into the brush, about where the weasel had emerged, and traversed the mats of juniper until I could step onto the trail.

"Elhon," I whispered. "C'mon. You can make it." She looked at me but wouldn't move. "Come on, big honey. Holy Christ. Please."

How could I lead her up? The reins were draped under her front quarters. I'd have to be almost on top of her to reach them. If she lunged, I'd go right underneath. But I couldn't leave her there. I took a tentative step, and Pookie shoved between my feet. "Damn dog. Get away. No stay. Sit. Stay." She retreated, whimpering. "Dogs. Horses. *Shit.*"

There was a flurry behind me. The gold horse tensed, lunged, slid back, and then dug in, gaining her balance as dirt and rock rained into the creek. She got her front hooves on the trail and then her hind ones and then she ran blind, right for me. I scrambled straight up and grabbed a hank of stems as she thundered beneath. Then she stopped abruptly, and swung her head, disoriented. My hand stung. Shit! I'd grabbed a wild raspberry bush.

Pookie was fleeing toward camp. Elhon stood wild-eyed but on solid ground. I inched toward her, soothing her with my voice, and caught one rein, then the other. I stepped closer and rubbed her withers until the shaking stopped. "Poor baby girl. Okay."

I decided she wouldn't let me on her back, as if I wanted a second chance. So I led her back to camp, stripped my saddle, and turned her loose. I thought she'd tear off, but she stood stiff-legged, watching every move I made. I took the food sack and canteen out of my saddlebags and put them into my day pack. "Screw this rodeo crap," I told Pook. "I'll walk, and live."

As I left the camp, the big horse followed me. I tried to shoo her away, but she thought I'd saved her life, or something like that, and she wasn't about to let me leave. I had to lead her all the way back to the other horses before she'd let me go. By then, the sun was over the ridge. I felt half dead, and I still had to relieve Mitch.

"Pretty damn slow," he snapped. He had the shelter half rolled and his bedroll ready to go. "How come you didn't ride up?"

I lied. "The storm had 'em all riled up."

"I sure didn't sleep a wink. The lightning was close. I felt a couple jolts through the ground, so each time it started, I got in my bedroll for insulation. When it quit, I'd run out and chase the sheep off the ridge. The meadow's a damn mess." I looked at what had been a field of sunflowers and bluebells: brown muck. Not a plant was standing.

"Well, at least you got here. Walk this ridge with the dogs. The *borregas* are hungry after running all night. Should be a piece of cake." He tied the bedroll behind the cantle, and rolled the tent up tight and lashed it in front of the horn. "Guess that'll ride okay. I'll be back after I get some sleep." He swung his boot high to clear the bedroll, settled himself, and rode off.

I was barely able to stay on my feet, but the sheep fed calmly below and then bedded down. I dozed, my back against a rock with my coat folded for a pad as the sheepdogs flopped on their backs in the sun. Pookie was the only mobile soul among us, and the pikas—little rabbity things—had a fine time teasing her. Ma Pika would pop up with a *tzcherrrrrrk:* half buzz, half squeak. Pook would pick her way over the boulders to chomp off her cute little round-eared head, and—*gone!* Then Sis would rear up a hundred feet away and—*tzcherrrrrrrk.* And the game would play out again: the dog laboring over the rocks, jaws agape, the pika diving, and then—*tzcherrrrrrrk.* Damnfool's tag with a permanent canine It.

At some point Mitch returned and told me he'd herd until sundown. I walked back to camp. I'd strained some muscles, unnoticed in the frenzy, but now I had to make an effort to keep my feet under me: to walk I had to stop thinking and to think I had to stop walking. I stopped at the spot where Elhon had almost killed us both. There were horse tracks and scuffed places, but you wouldn't notice unless they were pointed out. I climbed the loose slope back to camp and stood facing the tent, trying to summon the energy to get something to eat.

While I stood, a huge, brilliant cloud lifted from the rocky horizon until the sun was centered behind it, materializing soft and immense up toward the zenith, all glowing circulation, like a stirred bowl of pearls. It filled the sky with a tremendous presence, like God in a painting, but undeniably real.

Maybe it *was* God. I was too tired to judge, but I kept still under its gaze. At sunrise, the tall gold horse had almost killed us both. But I was alive to see this. It was beautiful. Sunlight through a cloud. Maybe that was enough. Maybe that was all. I looked up, hat in hand, my arms heavy, until it passed into the east and left the sky empty again.

4 ～

Murphy Creek

No day of rest. Given the mess the sheep had made during the storms, Mitch decided we should drive them out of the headwater bowls and move camp. We made coffee on an open fire so that we wouldn't have to wait for the stove to cool to pack up.

Catching horses, I saw clouds passing along the black ridges like a veiled procession. As I finished packing the camp, Mitch rode into the rising sun to start the herd. I got the horses packed and tied together in a line, but as we started there was a commotion and Tom's lead rope was jerked from my hand. Tony was bucking, his pack slipped to one side. With each jump it slipped farther and his eyes showed more white. I dismounted and circled around. The rope had burned my palm.

Tony stood spread-legged, rolling his eyes, but he didn't move as I cut the loop of baling twine that held Elhon's lead to the back of his saddle. Quickly I tied Elhon to a tree, and then cut Tony's lead rope loose from Tubby's saddle, which he'd jerked back: I'd have to unpack both of them. The cinches were loose; it was my fault. I got Tony calmed down to the point where I could loosen the lash cinch. I fought the saddle *cinchas* loose and then dragged the tangle from under his belly. I separated the tangled parts—panniers, saddle manty, lash rope, pads—and saw that the breast strap had broken. The rivets were in another pack, so I got a hank of parachute cord and cobbled it together to get us down the hill. When I finished Tony's pack I undid Tubby's, set the panniers on the ground, and reset her saddle.

I got baling twine out of my saddlebag and replaced the pigtails I'd cut, loops that were meant to break under sudden strain. As I joined the horses together, Elhon spooked and tried to uproot the fir to which she was tied, ending up on her hindquarters with her headstall twisted around her nose. Her breath whistled. It took more effort to get her calmed down. I decided to put her in front, where I could keep an eye on her. She balked and tossed her head, jerking my arm hard.

"I hate stinking horses," I said, "and rotten old gear." Pookie whined. "Dogs, too."

Below, a level mist filled the canyon, making ragged peninsulas of the ridges and forested islets of the hilltops. A half hour on, we passed the junction leading up to the pass. Turreted cliffs, the gates of the cirque, loomed above, and from the rocky moraines, new flowers had sprung: wild flax, a silky, heaven-petaled blue, and scarlet gilia, each flower distinct as a gunshot. Below the junction, the trail slanted down a deep headcut, where a spring dashed out of the ground: the hidden water from the cirque, I thought. It frothed white into a steep gully of bare dirt and shingle, edged with dwarf willows and patched with green: bluebell, coneflower, sweet anise, pink geranium, columbine, patches of currant, and grass. Each spot revealed a new combination of rock and earth, leaf and bloom. The mountains were like a huge, roughly patterned rug, draped over a heap of bones. Creation was a wreck, but it was a lovely one.

Where the steepness eased, I got off to check the packs. On the south, a split-topped limber pine stood out against the sky. There were outcrops of white limestone with black lichens like spatters of soot, held together by the sage green tufts of rockmat. I noticed something shiny on a rock. It was a shed insect shell, cicada or something like it, a tiny monster shape, translucent tan except for the eyes, which were like the gun-bubbles on an old bomber, and round and perfectly clear, with emptiness looking out.

As I mounted, my boot crushed a pennyroyal and its strong, solvent odor made me pause. I was balanced on a tall red horse on a narrow ridge composed of lithic trash. It bothered me to think of a hoof resting on such uncertain stuff, and of my horse depending on it, and of me depending on the horse. The water below was suddenly loud.

The springwater cut a deep gash, which turned from north to east. The trail followed its curve along a crumbling white rampart. The gash became a gorge and the water tumbled from sight, passing between two cliffs that seemed to touch above it. The trail clawed its way along the loose sidehill and disappeared between two ragged pines.

I prayed for good switchbacks, trenched into the slope. Instead, there were two bad zags. The horses skidded around yet didn't seem unnerved, except Elhon, who snorted and blew. After the second, I stopped and looked down. The gorge gave into the greater opening of the main canyon, and the trail followed a white spine out into space. *Go.*

Between Red's ears, the trail rose slightly before it reached a high outcrop and then slid off to the left. Above the trail two limber pines grew from the rock face, riding the arch of the layers like swimmers in a wave.

Off the spine to the north, the trail switched back twice in dry, rocky stuff and then entered a slanting forest of spruce floored with yellow arnica and brown duff, silent under the horses' feet. Cut into the bark were old blazes filled with pitch which had oxidized to opaque red and bronze. Going west, we crossed a dry gulley and turned south onto a broad slope with thick stands of spruce and fir relieved by flowery openings.

There were familiar flowers like wild carrots and pink geraniums, joined by various sunflowers, and a profusion of sweet anise and cone-flower. And there were new plants: a pungent mint, a tall larkspur, and several grasses. To the right was a solitary knoll that overlooked the creek. The horses buried their heads in the green, so I walked over to see it.

The knoll was pleasant, with nicely spaced spruces and low walls of rock: a good camp. Gentle above, it fell off sheer below and yielded a postcard view: the roaring creek walled by forest, sloped meadows to the west, and unscalable cliffs to the east. I was tempted to lead the horses over and set up camp, but I didn't see any stove rocks.

Stupid, I thought, walking back to the horses, not to camp there. From below, the knoll showed an overhanging wall, the limestone stained copper and blue by seeps. From its foot, dense shrubs rolled down to the creek: cow parsnip, twinberry, elderberry, and mountain ash.

I led the horses across spruce-walled meadows of goldeneye, butterweed, daisy, and aster. Grasses flourished among the flowers, and the horses lowered their heads to snatch bites, making our progress a halting one. A pair of hummingbirds circled and flashed away. Mitch rode out of the trees. "Thought you'd be to camp by now," he said.

"Tony's pack went under his belly. Busted strap. The leather's worthless."

"Sounds like maybe a loose hitch, too. No casualties, I guess."

Embarrassed, I looked down at my boots and saw green burrs stuck in the laces. I noticed a brown scuffler in the grass—chipmunk? The movement led my eye to a picket stake driven next to the trail. "Was there a camp here? On that rocky knob?"

Mitch gave me one of his measuring looks. "There was. Once."

"Good place. Maybe we should try it out."

"Hah!" he smirked. "Maybe not." He urged Pronto to a trot and I followed, fuming at the dismissal. Elhon balked, snapping the rope tight and almost jerking my shoulder out of the socket. Stupid horse. I looped the lead rope twice around the saddle horn and thumped my heels on Red's ribs, dragging the big mare along. "Hey! Don't do that," Mitch yelled.

"What?" I yelled back.

"Double-dally that rope. If Elhon throws back it'll lock up around that crummy saddle horn. Mine's the same way. We should wrap slick leather around the shank to build it up some."

Grudgingly, I let go the dallies and started out. Elhon threw back again, twisting my arm. "Ouch. You son of a bitch." I glared at the horse, then ahead at Mitch.

Rocks rattled as we crossed the dry streambed. The woods beyond were cool. I noticed sawn stumps, big ones, and the trail broadened into a logging road, partly overgrown. To the east hung rocky glens above cliffs, and above them a higher rank of cliffs. We rode through a clearcut, headstoned with great, bleached stumps of spruce and fir, tangled in raspberry and fireweed that sprung from the ruts and runnels.

The road curved through thick woods, joined by old skid trails choked with deadfall and shrubs. We crossed the creekbed, and it was filled with gray rubble, no water flowing. To the east was a meadow of pure grass, fairly flat, a rarity in both respects. But we turned to the west, and I could see good camping spots in the groves below.

AUGUST 6

The water rose again just across from the camp, negotiating a bed of worn stones and fallen trees. Along the east bank were springs trickling from crevices in the slope. The creek was thirty-six steps from the tent. Compared to the high camp, this spot would be easier to inhabit. What it lacked was grandeur. "We should have set up on the knob," I said, pouring coffee.

Mitch picked up his mug. "It's a sucker camp," he said. "Ray camped there. Once. After Warren had a stroke, the Prestons hired Ray and got this kid from California to tend camp: he had a long robe and meditated. They didn't hit it off that well. Anyhow, Ray looked at the knob, same as you, and decided to camp. But there was a problem. Maybe you noticed."

"What?"

"Rocky—can't get a stake in the ground, not one. But Ray said, 'What the hell, let's just pile up rocks to hold the tent.' So they did."

"Amen to that," I said.

"So-o-o, the second night they were camped there, the stars went out and the canyon turned black as the inside of a miner's boot. The wind starts to howl, and Ray and the kid can hear the tent flapping over their heads. Then the wind gives a big blast and *whoops.*" Mitch lifted his biscuit above his head. Then he lowered it and took a bite.

"Whoops?" I waited.

"They were looking up at raindrops. The gust picked up the tent and the stovepipe, and parachuted the whole damn kaboodle right off the cliff."

"Screeching Jesus! What'd they do?"

"Ray cussed. And they found some thick trees. The next day the kid rolled his gear and walked out. And Ray moved the camp down here. We better saddle up and go."

The moral, I decided, was that traditions were sometimes based on real events. Camps were in certain places because those places had worked out. Others didn't. If your tent blew over a cliff, that knowledge should be preserved.

Passing Ray's Knob, I pictured the tent whirling over the brink. Mitch was going to the top of the canyon to hunt strays, and soon rode out of sight, but I liked being on foot. I climbed through the woods and scuffed along the white spine, feeling better on my own two feet. It was loose and scary. The outcrops were like poorly stacked alphabet blocks. I plucked out a one-inch cube, then dismantled it: it split cleanly along each of five seams.

Limber pines and Douglas firs grew tall on the ridge, as it crumbled out from under them to the north and south. Underfoot grew common juniper, serviceberry, a smooth-barked currant, bearberry, and Oregon grape. There was arrowleaf balsamroot, a name I liked, and Indian paintbrush. Along the gully below the spring, there was a plant Mitch said was edible. Round leaves with pinked edges. I tried it. Peppery, not bad.

Mitch had told me to hike above the herd and then down the west slope to the creek, to bump them down. I saw the first bunches of sheep in the sinks above the trail junction, and walked close enough that they scattered downhill. Pookie woofed and made short charges, unnecessary but fun. I kept going until I thought we were around them and started down a loose gully, skiing more than hiking. Pookie barreled down the slope and slid into the back of my legs; we took off on a tumble that covered us both with dust and me with scratches. I glowered. "Dog Stew. Dog Steaks. Spiced Doggie Loaf." She stayed out of reach.

Farther down, water sprang out of the rubble and sparkled into thick willows and bluebells, which looked nice but proved to be terrible going. The thick leaves hid loose rocks and broken limbs. The other choice was a shaky traverse down the slope of the V. A third choice was to walk in the water: steep, loose, slick, wet, and stupid. So I took number two, and skated along the slope in a haze of dust.

The gully reached the main stream just below the joining of two forks, and I didn't see any sheep. To cross a succession of gullies seemed foolish, so I headed down along the stream. The water had cut fast and deeply, and both slopes spilled fragments to be carried off by the bounding flow, or just rearranged. In the streambed were rocks piled on logs stacked on more rocks, with just enough greenery to deceive the eye, and cold water blasting through the resulting mess.

It wasn't a stream you could stroll: to follow it meant hopping, straddling, teetering, and making desperate leaps. Pook fishtailed across loose banks, slithered between rocks, bellied over logs, and flipped upside down once with a yelp into a pool. Finally, we reached a tributary that dashed out of a slot in whitish cliffs, which had to be water from the big spring.

Damn. No sheep at all. The bastards were above us, feasting in the pockets. I didn't feel like digging my way back up the near-vertical slopes and clawing through brush just to see a sheep. Mitch said I was supposed to circle them, and strictly speaking, I had. That is, I knew where they were because I'd discovered where they were not. He never said I had to watch them like a goddamn hawk or anything.

In fact, there was a certain elegance to my method: to herd sheep while not troubling them, and vice versa, with an actual presence. They'd enjoy superior digestion and I'd stay serene. So I kept on following the stream until I saw Ray's Knob. I scrambled up and came out just above it, just as Mitchell rode out of the trees.

"Wow. What happened to you, sport?"

"I was, uh, circling the herd."

"It looks like you went underneath 'em." I did look somewhat the worse for my strenuous route. My arms were covered with deep scratches, my boots were sodden, and my clothes were caked with dust. Pookie, wet and slathered, looked like a giant chocolate-covered rat.

"I went up to the west of the sheep and bumped 'em, then crossed and came down the stream. There weren't any sheep above where I crossed, and I didn't see any below."

"If you waded the creek it'd be pretty unlikely that a sheep could get *below* you."

He rode back to camp, and I trudged ungraciously along in the horse tracks, kicking dirt in frustration. When I got back to camp, Mitch had bacon sizzling over an open fire. We fried potatoes and eggs, and then settled back.

"Up top," Mitch said, "I got charged by an elk. I tied Red up where I tepeed out that night. A spike bull came out of the timber, and we stared each other down. He bugled me," he said. "So I whistled back and stomped." He demonstrated. "That elk looked like it'd seen a ghost. It jumped up and tore down the mountain. Good thing I wasn't asleep. I might've been bred."

The horses wandered down, glonging their bells, and happily drooled water and nuzzled each other before they went back for more grass. Mitch lay on his bedroll for a siesta. I was too dirty for that, so I dug out clean clothes and trooped off to lie down in the creek.

By the water were low willows, mosses, and the bright pink of elephant's head, each tiny bloom eared and trunked, exactly like its name. Where they were wet, the mosses were vivid green. As the water level dropped, going into August, the drying mosses turned acid green, then yellow-green, then rust or orange, and then brown. I saw monkey-flowers, little snapdragons, yellow with rusty spots, around the springs under the east slope. More springs rose in the spongy meadow below the camp, willowed and mossed, sedged and rushed, each adding its flow to the stream. Two hundred yards down, the creek was roaring again, and I found a log-dammed pool with a waterfall that beckoned.

I stripped and waded in, then lay flat, head under the waterfall.

There was a white burst behind my eyes: so cold it hurt. I stood up and scrubbed with my hands, then flopped back for as long as I could stand it—three seconds—and then padded across the gravel and onto the grass to dry in the sun.

Pookie came over to investigate, and I caught her by the collar and dragged her into the creek. Dirt soaked out of her in tan streamers. Thrashing, she escaped and scooted into the meadow where she shook, becoming a silver porcupine in the sun. Then she fled toward the camp. Covered with mud and dog hair, I repeated my stirring dip, then wandered around naked, slapping at the bugs that dared my dripping form.

On a gravel bar among the sedges was a flower I had never seen, a marriage of water and night. I crouched until my face was level and my breath moved it; the color was richer up close, iridescent blue and violet, and it clutched at my heart. O Cassandra. All I'd ever wanted to say to her was in that color.

What was its name? The meadow was a cushion, the first place I could walk barefoot without flinching. I heard Mitch shooing Pookie out of the tent, in a sleepy voice. I went in. Mitch looked up and then quickly shut his eyes.

"Just getting my plant book," I said, realizing I was still naked.

"Of course," he replied, keeping his eyes shut.

I identified my way back. There was a large-blossomed butterweed, which dominated the sward with vivid yellow, and another that bloomed more discreetly. On the edge of the woods was northern bedstraw, with tiny white blooms, and mountain bluebell. On drier spots, old stream terraces, grew a tall white daisy and a purple aster, both with lance-shaped leaves, and harebells, delicate little magenta things. There were wild geraniums both pink and white, fleabane daisies, mountain dandelions, wild carrots, and a figwort with coarse, ferny leaves and pale yellow flowers. Brightest of all was scarlet paintbrush, which looked like lava, dabbed on the air. Fringing the meadow were shrubby cinquefoil and the ubiquitous coneflower, which didn't have much floweriness: it was a brown, upside-down acorn-shaped thing about three inches long on a tall stalk, all center and no petals. I found some yarrow and crushed it and held it under my nose for its rich, nearly sexual smell. I stood up and squinted and saw only colors: blue-greens, haze greens, fresh greens, and moist browns.

At last I came again to the flower on the bar: it was fringed gentian. That night I dreamed that it spoke in a woman's voice.

AUGUST 7

Above the white spine, in thick forest at dawn, in a net of deadfall, I waited for Mitch to arrive. I pulled the book from my pack and contended with the *Bhagavad-Gita*. Before a great battle, Arjuna stands in his chariot and says:

> O my Lord. When I see all these, my own people, thirsting for battle,
> My limbs fail me and my throat is parched, my body trembles and my
> hair stands on end. . . .
> Should we not, whose eyes are open . . . turn away from so great a
> crime?

Krishna, both a god and for some reason Arjuna's charioteer, replies:

> . . . cold and heat, pain and happiness, they come and go;
> they are not permanent. Endure them bravely, O Prince. . . .
> For death is sure for that which is born, as birth for that which is
> dead. So, grieve not. . . .
> Look at thy duty. Nothing is more welcome to a soldier than a
> righteous war. . . .
> So, surrendering your actions unto Me, thinking only of the Absolute,
> free from selfishness,
> with no anticipation of reward, devoid of excitement, begin thou to
> fight.

So Krishna whips up the horses, and the fray begins. I quit reading: when Arjuna raised his question, my question, Krishna told him to chop off heads with a clear conscience because: (a) the world's an illusion, (b) we'll all die anyhow, and (c) doing what's expected is the highest good.

But the world of life and death is less of an illusion than Lord Krishna and his sly arguments. Besides, if I was ever free of selfishness, devoid of passion, anticipated no reward, and thought only of the Absolute, why would I begin to fight? Lord Krishna worked both sides of the street.

Krishna's argument boiled down to this: don't give a damn and you'll be free. And I remembered Frank, telling me the only way to survive in Vietnam was not to give a fuck. But that hadn't freed him: he survived, but suffered for what he had been told, as much as for what he had done. So I dropped the book in the dirt. It was the color of dried horse shit.

It was true that appearances were misleading: a lush meadow that looked as if you could roll in it naked held sharp rocks and broken limbs under the soft green cover. In this broken country it was hard to stand straight, hard to walk straight, hard to find a soft place to lie down. And it was true that when you found a place to rest, death rested there too, in rusty needles, silver branches, and white bones.

The fallen trunks around me were marked by death: by beetle tracks where the bark had peeled and fallen, by the long splits of windthrow that slanted across the grain, forming scallops at each successive break. But even dead, the straight-grained spruce was still silvery and delicately checked. And the grain of a dead pine moved in a slow spin, like rising smoke, around old wounds—tines of elk, claws of bear, lightning scars—and the wounds formed burls that shone like watered silk. Something of each living form endured, and was transformed, and beautiful.

Death belonged. It swept things clean. I could fear pain and dying without being afraid of death itself. I put my hand on a dead spruce trunk. Why be loyal to spruce instead of pine?

Then I heard hoofbeats, and picked the book up and dusted it off. I slipped it into my pack and climbed out of the deadfall. I could see the edge of the herd across the gully to the south. Pookie greeted the sheepdogs with her usual snarls and shoulder-blocks as Mitch reined his horse.

"I started 'em down. Let's get out of their way. The fresh feed is toward the camp. Easy herding . . . for a while."

AUGUST 7

We were short on food: no bacon or eggs or cheese or peanut butter, no pancake syrup, no apples or oranges. Since we'd moved camp, there'd been no fresh meat. I'd been content with bread, tortillas, and beans, and Mitch seemed to be, too.

Most sheep ranchers, he told me, sent wethers up for camp meat. Wethers were castrated buck lambs that had been wintered over instead of being sold in the fall. *Buck* was the word the Prestons used instead of *ram*. The herd bucks, which fathered all the lambs, were purebreds. They wouldn't be put in with the ewes until after the range season. All the male offspring were castrated in June, and their tails were docked. After summer on the range, the castrated lambs were fat, and the Prestons tended to sell them all.

I was going to ride down to pick up supplies. I folded the list we'd worried over that morning; Mitch had vetoed some of my choices like a gallon of red wine and a canned ham because Royal wouldn't buy them anyway, and our asking would put him in a bad mood, in which case we wouldn't even get apples and oranges, just more ranch rhubarb. Fresh from reading the introduction to the *Iliad*, I argued that the wine would provide us a social safety valve and liberate us from conventional decorum.

Mitch laughed. "If we had wine we'd get liberated as hell: that's what Royal's scared of. After the kid left Ray, the conventional decorum wore him plumb out. So he rode all the way down Greys River to the Flying Saddle and got so liberated that he didn't feel like coming back. Finally he started charging drinks to the Preston Ranch, and they called Royal. Royal had to drive to Alpine to shut off Ray's safety valve, and then truck him and the horse back up here. The sheep were scattered from hell to Thursday."

Mitch let me take Tony, and I put packsaddles on Red and Elhon. That way I'd have three fast horses and not have to deal with the colt, which had been wandering off. Mitch described the landmarks: down past the big opening of Bear Canyon to the west, cross the tributary and around some beaver ponds, then down a narrow stretch to the ford. "Stay on the road," he said, "you'll meet Roger sooner or later. He'll park at the ford."

After the steep and sketchy trails, the road was easy. The stream fell from the low point of the meadow into thick woods. Dead trunks lodged in its way; some it slipped under, and others it swirled around or shoved aside. But where a trunk was level, buttressed by rootwads and trussed with branches, the stream filled underneath it with cobbles and gravel, then with silt and leaves, and made of the log a natural dam over which it spilled like a lace curtain draped across someone's arm. From its pool, whirling with bubbles, it hurried on, riffling and braiding, deep green in the shade and silver in the sun.

Besides seeing new country, I thought I might encounter someone. Since Roger left, we'd seen no one at all in the canyon. After plodding through the *Bhagavad-Gita*, I'd worked my way through the *Tale of Savitri* and the *Shakuntala*, and I fantasized about meeting one of the dark-eyed nymphs or hermit-girls who flitted through my dreams.

In more practical terms, I hoped to run across a cowgirl packing salt, or a couple of motel maids on a fishing trip. I realized that I simply missed women: their talk and their ways and their thoughts. I wasn't myself unless there were women being themselves around me. Cassandra, the dark flower of my life, had promised to come up, but she hadn't said when. And I would be up here until it snowed.

Despite all the jokes about sex with sheep, I couldn't understand how anyone could summon the necessary urge. I didn't want to touch them, period. Their wool was clogged with dirt, and the oil in their fleece got into your hands and wouldn't wash off. Besides the shit-balls dangling from the wool on their hindquarters, there was something about them I found inherently revolting. I shuddered so extravagantly that Tony stopped in his tracks and cocked his ears back.

The road switched down in forested arcs above the creek. There was thick Engelmann spruce (the big, common species) and Douglas fir, interspersed with subalpine fir, blue spruce, and an occasional lodgepole pine: a polyglot wood. Near the creek, the air was close and damp. Even in summer, these woods lay in the shadow of high ridges. The subalpine firs died young here and were covered by mossy beards of opaque pale green. Moss also hung from the dead limbs of larger trees. Did moss kill the trees, or did it live on wood already dead? Another question, of thousands that I was accumulating.

The road led into the creek and came out on the other side: it was easy to see where the bridge had been. I waded the horses through the ford and tied them to trees. I heard an engine and the sigh of gears, and a pickup ground into sight. But it was Royal who slid from the seat.

"Where's Roger?"

"He had a good run at the hay, so he decided to stay with it."

"I'll bet he decided," I said.

Royal laughed at that. Dust streamed from the hinge as I let the tailgate down. "The boxes got dusty," he said. "The river road's a hell of a mess." There were two cartons of groceries, a big sack of dog food, and six sacks of stock salt. I started to pack the food into the panniers: cheap staples, mostly. Some fresh celery and carrots and canned peas. There was one grudging bag of oranges and one of apples, small and bruised. And mail: a letter from my brother and one from Cassandra.

"Any trouble with the coyotes?"

"We heard some, but I don't think we lost any lambs."

"Get a count?"

"When Roger was up. Not since then."

Royal reached into the cab and brought out a bulging plastic sack of rhubarb. "It's near as good as fruit." I must have looked skeptical, as he brought out a box from his shirt pocket: cinnamon dots, the candy I most loathed. "Put these in—makes a hell of good pie. Louise won a ribbon at the county fair."

"Thanks. Looks like plenty of stock salt. I didn't see a can of coffee."

"Oh my hell! Must've forgot. I'll send some up when the ranger drives up from Bedford."

"We'll run out. We have some tea, I guess."

"If you run out of the tea bags, there's raspberry leaves and all up there . . . makes good tea."

"I hear the Flying Saddle has great coffee," I said.

The sheep are eating stars. It is cold, almost dawn, and my eyes are half closed, and this is what I see. They cross high heaven in waves, devouring the lonely fires, one by one.

On a long slant of meadow above me, the sheep are eating flowers: helianthus, goldenweed, and golden-eye. In the near-light, which deepens the leaves to blue and black, the yellow of each bloom glows with weird intensity, the color ghosting in the air between the flower and my eye.

The sheep in the front line touch nothing but blooms. Their necks stretch, their teeth nip, and one by one the stars wink out. The sheep pass and the sky's field goes dark, still green but somehow bare and blind.

The sheep are ugly.

The sheep are stupid.

The sheep are hungry.

The sheep are too many.

The sheep are owned.

I hate them most for being owned, somehow. Up close a single ewe and lamb seem like real animals, but as a herd they become property with legs, walking globs of wool and fat, bred to move in a noisy crowd and to exist without souls.

The flowers were gone, and it was too cold to sit and think, so I started my circuit.

We'd let them drift downcanyon and then spread out to the west. The east side was notched with gullies and rockslides, too rough to herd, and my task was to keep them from crossing the creek and going up it. After crossing the steep slopes and abrupt gullies, my ankles felt as if the small bones were disconnected and grinding like stones in a sack. Rather than fight across the ribs and gullies, I decided to walk along the bed of the creek.

It was dry where I reached it, the rocks stained brown where the water had flowed. From a flowery pocket, a spring tumbled into the creekbed and sang through the stones, but in twenty steps it disappeared.

Following the bends, I came into a dry meander lined with blue-bells, and an old ewe stared me down. There were other ewes and lambs behind her. They looked at me and bawled. The old ewe turned east, so I waved my arms and she stopped. Pookie started a run, but I held her back. The old ewe tried to make a rush around me. *Bitch.* I let the dog loose, but the old ewe stood braced even as the others fled. Pookie stopped and then ran past the defiant ewe to chase the others west, her tail whirling as she plunged into the brush.

The old ewe made another dash and almost knocked me down, and I caught her by the wool. She retreated, leaving a greasy tuft in my hand, and then circled. I grabbed a stream cobble and flung it without aim. It hit her between the eyes. I heard it strike bone.

"Ouch. God."

She fell to her knees, eyes shut. She tried to rise and shook her head, eyes unfocused. I heard gravel spilling behind me and turned to see a lamb coming fast down the east slope toward the ewe. It dodged around me and butted the ewe in the flank, almost knocking her down, and started to nurse even as she stood dazed, still shaking her head.

She wouldn't leave without her lamb.

"Sorry," I said, knowing it did no good. "I didn't understand."

She recovered and led her lamb out of the creekbed to the west. Feeling guilty, I walked down the dry streambed, rocks crunching under my boots. Pookie came back and I scratched her head. The slopes fell back, and I could see downstream: no sheep. So I found a pocket under big spruces level enough to sit and watch, and opened my book to the *Iliad.* I had read the start, but I read it again: "Anger be now your song," it began.

But my anger at the sheep wasn't a noble or a righteous one. And I could kill, as quickly and irretrievably as I'd thrown that rock at the old ewe. I would never be innocent, but that didn't mean I would be the willing instrument of murder. I flipped forward to my mark and read of the death of Patróklos, Achilles' best friend, who was first struck by the god Apollo, who knocked his helmet off, then speared by Euphorbos from behind, and then gutted by Hektor: a gang killing.

Trip mines, punji pits, belly wounds—I thought of Frank, who came back, and of Lawson, who didn't, and I read on:

> Sorrow fell on Achilles like a cloud.
> he swept up dust with both hands
> and poured it over his head. . . .

> His mother found him groaning. . . .
> "My child, why do you weep?"

> . . . I could not help my friend in his extremity.
> Far from his home he died; he needed me
> to shield him or to parry the death stroke.
> For me there's no return to my own country.

I felt a sorrow that was more than my own distance, then. That distance wasn't only the number of steps I had taken into the mountains, or the number of nights spent under open sky. For their awful games, the old men had presumed too much. What they demanded was not loyalty but blind obedience, and that was a death that took place in the heart, before dying. I wouldn't give that up, and it set me apart. But my friend had gone to the war and been killed. *I could not help.* And there was no return.

The lines blurred and I closed the book. It took an effort to rise. The sun was hot, and flies were circling, then touching down to bite. The sheep were all out of sight, and I started down. The rocks in the streambed grated and clacked with my weight. They looked so lonely, those rocks, split off and thrown down, tumbled into heaps and assorted by water. Each rock had been part of the earth's body until it saw the light, felt the air and weather. Split off, it would never fly back to the parent cliff to sleep in darkness and safety. Instead, it would be broken again and again, losing its sharpness and mass, gathering distance until it was no more.

I came to the gorge where water from the big spring rushed down and filled the streambed again. There was hope in water. I knelt and washed the salt tracks from my cheeks, and drank the cold water until my jaw ached, and dried my face on my sleeve. The stream cascaded through cliffs that overlapped, and there was a chockstone wedged in the narrow gap, water spraying around it. The gorge seemed like a refuge. I had to see what was there.

I reached the chockstone and chimneyed up between it and the wall, then jumped down into the creek above. Pookie scrabbled at the walls and then squeezed under the boulder to come up soaked and wheezing. She shook, wetting the rock walls higher than I could reach.

Above, it was lovely, wild, and rough. The cliffs rose in fractured columns, stacked yellow and white. Thick spruce and fir overhung, roots netted against the sky. At my feet the water had scoured to bedrock and turned the limestone a wavering light gold.

Huge deadfalls lined the narrow reach, some bridging the flow and others aligned with it. Looking up, I saw that avalanches had snapped trees and gouged out boulders. All the force of winter had funneled into this slim opening. But through the confusion of rock and wood, brooded over by columbines, the creek came sweetly down, catching, swirling, and springing free.

I passed a side gully and saw a pine trunk lodged across it, sanded smooth: if the water broke some things, it polished others. Big spruce trunks had rolled and wedged in the gorge, and I walked on their backs, careful with my balance, hopping from roots to broken crowns as the water spiraled underfoot.

I saw a strange rock in the creek and started to jump to it, then stopped. It wasn't a rock. It was a sheep. Dead. I could smell it. Pookie wound through currant bushes and sniffed eagerly. "No," I said.

It was starting to bloat. The water in my stomach, swallowed a hundred yards below, seemed to writhe inside me. Old, dead thing. The damn dog nosed it. "Jesus, Pook. NO!"

I stepped around the carcass and started upslope, feet digging and sliding, but I stopped. The dead thing lay in our water.

I had to get it out.

Impossible. Too heavy to lift. If I dragged it downstream, I'd have to raise it above my head to roll it over the chockstone. I imagined the sodden wool dripping onto me . . . no. But the south slope was too steep. So I'd have to drag it up the loose north side of the stream cut. I stepped close and grabbed a front leg and pulled.

The leg came off. I dropped it and windmilled up, dirt and stones flying, and reached the top, where I heaved, belly water burning out of my mouth and nose.

I lay there until the spasms ceased. Which solved nothing. We'd been drinking straight out of the creek. I could leave the sheep and not say anything to Mitch, but how could I trust the water? If I told him, he'd ask: "Did you get it out?"

How could I touch that rotten thing?

How? I needed rubber gloves up to my shoulders, a gas mask, gallons of rubbing alcohol, and stainless steel hooks. Lying there, I looked a flower in the eye: heartleaf arnica, pretty but no help. I sat up and rubbed my hands in the duff. Beyond the arnica was a patch of yarrow, and I buried my face in the feathery leaves.

They made the air clean. So I crushed them and packed my nostrils. Breathing their scent, I swung over the edge and skied down the bank to look at the dead sheep again. From the way it was lying it had probably broken its neck, pushed over the south rim by the others. Gingerly, I gripped a hind leg and dragged the waterlogged carcass out of the creek. It was far too heavy to drag upslope. I groped for my knife.

Left hand for the grip, right for the knife. Quartering the big, bloated ewe was worse than bad. With my jaw clamped hard, I breathed through the yarrow and had to blink just to break up the sight of it. As it came apart, I retched so hard and so often that it seemed like my way of breathing.

I laid the four legs out on the slope. The body was heaviest; I'd drag it up first. But what do you grab, on a sheep with no legs? The ears. The tail. The neck. I leaned into the slope and hauled, one and two and three, hearing it slosh. Then I stepped up the slope and hauled again. It was a hundred feet and it took a hundred years. At last I dragged it over the rim and into the woods and lifted it over a dead log where it couldn't roll back, *done.*

I scrubbed my hand with pine duff and changed old yarrow for fresh, jamming my nostrils until they hurt, breathing the pungent, green scent as if it were the only real air. The legs would be easier, but there were four of them.

Pookie wanted to roll in the dead thing or gnaw it; she keened and pawed as I cursed her and made her stay. I slid down the loose gravel, grabbed a leg, climbed up. Again. When I tossed the last leg into a mat of juniper, it lodged with its black, heart-shaped hoof pointed up to the sky. This was a living beast, I thought, *alive.* But I fell on my side and shut my eyes and retched again.

Who cares?

AUGUST 10

Anger be now your song, immortal one . . .

Trying to read the *Iliad,* I kept going back to the first line. I was thirsty, waiting for a pot of water to boil, but the fire was almost out. I fed it some sticks, the last of the pile. We were out of wood. I picked up the axe and noticed that the edge was dull. Where was the file?

I looked in the box panniers, then in the kitchen boxes, accumulating anger as a snowman gathers snow. Where had Mitch put the damned file? I looked in the sack of leather-working tools. It wasn't there. Son-of-a-bitch.

At first, nostalgia, tradition, the frontier myth—whatever it was—had spread its golden haze around each object and circumstance. Being in the tent felt good because it *was* a tent. Cooking was less onerous because it was done on a box stove or over an open fire. Even washing dishes had shed its misery because of the smoke-blackened dishpan and the way the dishes steamed in the cold air. But chores were far more laborious in camp than they'd been at home.

I looked in the roll of horseshoeing tools and found the file. I started to sharpen the axe. The fire was out and the water was cooling. If the material of our lives was simple, life itself was not. To eat anything but our jealously rationed cookies or cheese or apples, I had to spend hours cooking. I'd tried eating raw flour at one point and had sampled the other staples, but they weren't very good. Raw rhubarb was amazing on the tongue but not really edible. Ketchup was nice, direct from the bottle, and so was the evaporated milk Mitch used in coffee, but such furtive pleasures made me feel low and mean.

So I had to cook, which involved long hours of being near food and thinking about food without being able to consume it. It took about nine hours of boiling to get beans soft enough to eat. And to cook anything, even cornmeal mush, I had to go out and find dry wood and carry it to camp and build a fire. To gather wood, I had to have my boots laced and my hat on. And just then I'd notice that we were out of water. And so on. Deprivation didn't make me feel saintly, or even soulfully detached. It just made me mad.

As I stacked wood on my arm I blamed the ills of a suffering world on the Prestons. Of course Royal couldn't think of bringing us a beer or two. Beer was really expensive stuff, like *thirty-five cents* a can, and besides it brought the devil out in innocent men, *that quick*. Even Roger—who drank like a champion at college—had ignored my pointed hints. Our present lowly station—sheepherder, worker, servant, serf, slave—outweighed all past acquaintance.

As I built up the fire, I speculated about the bullet hole in the ceiling at the ranch. Left by Ray in a rage, no doubt, at being designedly starved. After a long, hard day minding all that fresh meat on the hoof, he got another penny-pinching Preston repast of microscopic pork shreds in white-flour gravy with mealy potatoes, and boiled rhubarb for dessert: a thrift victim.

I spoke Royal's part: "Oh the hell! Guess we're out of butter. Don't know how I forgot that. It's just so damn expensive these days. Plenty of salt, though. Mmmmm. Have some more salt on your rhubarb, Ray. But go easy on that sugar, it's gone way up."

La violencia. Ka-bam!

I was a hedonistic brat, and with each inconvenience, each petty struggle, each dull, recurrent stress, the specific causes merged into one great cause. Mitch didn't have much tolerance for my fits of temper. He worshipped tight-lipped western gods with names like Verle and Rex, whose salient characteristic was fox-under-the-cloak stoicism. That was my heritage—that weatherbeaten, expressionless squint—

more than his, but I wasn't sure if I wanted to retreat into it, or escape to a higher plane of self-indulgence.

Okay. At last the water was boiling. If there were dead-sheep germs in it they were now likewise dead. Ugh. I decided to filter it through cloth, but the towels were disgusting. And my bandannas were all dirty again. The only clean piece of cloth in camp turned out to be my hated poplin slacks, and I stretched them over the bucket and poured water through the seat.

My tongue felt like a dusty leather strap, but the water was still too hot to drink. So I got two mugs and poured steaming water from one to the other, to cool it down.

At first, each day had been full of novelty: even frightening, ugly, or bloody, it was new. But the newness had turned grim. It was hard to live on the mountain's terms.

AUGUST 11

There was only enough coffee left for a half pot, and that was thin. And I dazedly poured my coffee into my bowl of mush instead of my cup, and then stared at it, hissing, as Mitch giggled. I tipped the bowl and drank it off anyway, nasty with bits of cornmeal. He said I'd better stay in camp, but could he leave Tikki-Lo tied up and take Pookie? Fine.

When he tied Tony to a tree to saddle up, the horse bit him on the thigh. Rattled, Mitch forgot to tighten the cinch, and when he stood up in the stirrup to mount, his saddle rolled. As Tony was a fairly short horse, Mitch was able to do a nice high-speed hop on his right foot and jerk his left boot out of the stirrup before Tony reached high gear.

Naturally, all the other horses joined the stampede away from camp, so we had to go wrangle them back. The saddle had slipped horn down and Tony was wild-eyed, so Mitch pulled it off and saddled Red, who was only slightly less spooked. He mounted up and the horse promptly stepped on Pookie's foot. Red snorted and pranced in place as the dog ran to me, anguished wails echoing. Her foot was bruised but not broken.

"Lord. What next?" Mitch said, as Red sidestepped and a spruce limb took his hat.

"Don't ask," I said, and picked his hat off the ground and handed it up. He finally set off, looking warily first to one side and then the other, on a stiff-walking Red with Ansel on the flank and Pookie limping at a cautious interval behind.

As soon as he was out of sight, I felt a hungry resentfulness steal over me. Breakfast? Cornmeal mush with lousy coffee in it. Ugh. I had a sudden desire to eat the whole three-pound can of peanut butter. After holding myself to one loaded forefinger, I felt my gaze pulled to the cans of evaporated milk. I hefted one and wondered if Mitch had counted. Probably. I felt like biting a hole in the top. It was hard to put it back, but I did, and shut the kitchen boxes.

To be near food was torture. I slipped a stalk of rhubarb out, bit the end off it, and chewed. Arrrggghhh. My tastebuds shrank and my tongue tried to crawl back down my throat. I spat it into the bushes and still had the urge to take another bite.

Is that obsession, or is it compulsion? Or both? I had to get out of camp for a while.

The best remedy for my mania was to walk. Walking felt good, and there was always some distraction not far off: a bizarre orange mushroom (I wondered how it would taste—probably poisonous, though) or a historic maple syrup can (Could I drink a gallon of syrup? It seemed like something to try). Since the previous herders had tossed their empty cans into the brush, I decided I had to get farther from camp to relax.

For distraction's sake, I'd developed some odd sports. Walking blind had proven to be strangely absorbing. The flat, grassy meadow above camp was one of the few spots in the canyon where you could walk more than a few steps with your eyes closed, so I went there. I learned to judge the angles of the sun and the unseen ground, and the drift of the air, and to recognize where the grass became low shrubs, which meant I was at the fringe and likely to run into a tree.

The puzzled horses gathered to watch me, so I made them part of the game, trying to sense where they were, and to decide which horse I was approaching, and to touch it without scaring it away. Once I touched the horse, I could tell which one it was. The only ones I failed to tag were Elhon and the colt.

Keeping my eyes shut was a test of will that I liked better than resisting food. Another trial was to scuff a mark in the meadow and see if I could walk a circle blind and return, guided only by instinct. My first attempts were laughable, so I made small circuits—four steps, eight steps, then twelve—until it began to come. I also found that circling to the left worked better, maybe because my left-footed steps were more cautious.

I'd also begun to concoct songs, shamelessly borrowing a tune and bellowing out whatever lyrics popped into my head. So after voluntary blindness palled, I did that:

Some demented evening,
in a frenzy utter,
I'll smear peanut butter
on yooouuuu . . .

Obsession? Or compulsion? Whatever it was, I noticed that the words *peanut* and *butter* made me salivate. So I got out my journal and started a poem about Ray:

Upon a lonesome hump of rock, Ray Wolfely pitched his camp.
He was squint of eye and bowed of leg, an alcoholic scamp,
And he herded sheep to earn his keep, up high on Murphy's Creek,
Where the rocks are rough and the flies are tough,
and each day lasts a week.

As I scribbled away in my journal, I forgot about the peanut butter. I'd never met Ray, but suddenly I could picture him up here, glowering and craving. The poem was a cheap imitation of a fairly inexpensive poet, but it made me feel better than I'd felt all week.

AUGUST 12

I could hear the sheep from camp. Mitch worked them down and then let them drift back up as they fed. He didn't need much help, or want it. The sheep blundered and wormed through the profuse green, making passages and leaving the rich growth broken-stemmed and yellowing. At night they gathered in the openings, preferring them to the deep woods.

But I went out to see more country, and wandered back to camp in loops and curves. The mid-elevation woods were thickly grown in with cow parsnip, currants, Utah honeysuckle, mountain ash, serviceberry, Rocky Mountain maple, buffaloberry, birchleaf spiraea, fireweed, grasses, geranium, raspberry, thimbleberry, and blueberry elder. Much of this growth, Mitch said, was good bear food, and these were good bear woods. He claimed to have seen fresh tracks and sign. The notion that I might run into one added spice to my explorations.

"The bears are good, too," I said.

"Not if you're a sheep," he said.

After arguing, we agreed on a Bear Contingency Plan. If the bear was near the herd, we would watch it first, to identify it, and then try to scare it off. I refused to pack the rifle, not even wanting to touch it, so I'd yell and throw rocks. Mitch said that he wouldn't shoot to kill unless a bear had actually downed a sheep and then ignored a warning shot, which seemed fair.

"Anyhow," Mitch said, "you always lose more sheep to accidents, sickness, and poison plants than to predators. Bears and coyotes will feed on sheep that die of other things, so it can look like a kill. But most ranchers just blame all their losses on coyotes, to get a government trapper or poison baits."

"Bunch of damn liars," I spat.

"It's traditional. They've done it for so long they can't back off. And it'd be hell to be the first one to break ranks."

So this was my proud heritage: boots and saddles and lies. I stomped off, smoldering on behalf of all the coyotes and bears that were poisoned and shot and trapped, and Pookie followed me with a whim-

Despite all, the ranchers would carry on their private war and justify it by counting up as coyote kills every sheep that died of bad genes, ill-treatment, clumsiness, crowding, lupine, bloat, or old age. They just wanted to kill coyotes, period: they couldn't live without an enemy. And like the generals, if they didn't have a real enemy, they'd create one.

Why were cowboy-and-sheepherder books such deadly crap? Because you couldn't tell the truth, except about the design of your saddle and what kind of rope you hung from it and how many conchas glinted on your batwing chaps. We stumbled along, one boot sunk in sentiment and the other in obsessive detail, because the interior was too dangerous, too dark with lies.

Lying was a sign of defeat, of psychic domestication, that had worked so deeply into our fiber that it passed as a form of truth. With only three or four generations in the West, we had learned to lie determinedly, almost religiously about what happened on the land. We didn't know this country we had tried to possess. And we didn't own the sheep: the sheep owned us.

It made me so mad that I spun like a top and howled. Pookie beat a retreat to the woods as I threw rocks at a big gray boulder that looked—momentarily—like Richard M. Nixon, President and Father of Lies. I caught up fist-sized rocks and fired them—*spack, spack, spack*—filling the air with razors and dust, and the senseless rhythm made me feel better so I kept on until my wrist and shoulder ached.

None of this was Mitch's fault, or that of the sheep, or mine. Which of us asks to be born? Even the ranchers saw themselves as victims, trapped between the idiot government and the ravenous coyotes. There was a nasty, encompassing humor to it. I flipped the last rock straight up and dodged it as it came back to earth. *Spack.*

Then I sat in the dirt. Pook rejoined me, hesitant, and I scratched her ears. *Go.* In search of punishment, I contoured through the rankest brush and crossed a rattly avalanche chute northwest of the camp to see if there were aspens there. There weren't. There weren't many aspens in this canyon, and I missed them. Likely, the sheep ate them up.

I dropped straight down and came to a clearcut. The loggers cut what was too big for the sheep: a sensible division of labor. If we ever bred a beast that could eat rock, then we could finish the whole place off. I bounced a rock off a stump and it made a satisfying *bonk*.

The bare ground in the clearcut was netted with wild strawberry, its thin red runners trying to bind the world back into one. There were white blooms, so I got down on my knees and searched but couldn't find a single berry to eat. As I looked, Pookie stropped herself on me and licked my ear. I realized that I'd stopped acting crazy.

We followed a skid trail down and started walking back up to camp on the old logging road. Where there were people, there would be lies. It was a simple equation. My own mother lied to me, at fourteen, when she said my hair, greased like a wheel bearing, looked nice, or that I looked handsome in my skintight iridescent slacks. I lied to myself when I affirmed these propositions, knowing they were false to the core. So maybe it was the scope of the lie that mattered, and the result. Lies pivoted on desire, and large desires gave birth to tremendous lies. When a president lied, and called out the bombers, it was disastrous.

I was distracted by a huge porcupine that was waddling with insular dignity down the logging road. After a few button-eyed glances of alarm it chose the left rut and stubbornly kept its course, so I walked in the right. Pookie trailed us and had the grace not to attack, and the whole thing made me happy somehow. I hadn't been this close to many wild animals, even unglamorous ones, and some animals, like bald eagles and bull elk, were so impressive that you didn't learn much from them because you were too busy being awed.

I stretched out my hand. The shadow of it crossed the porcupine's face and it stopped and switched its tail, warning me. I drew my hand back and it set off again, determinedly. The porcupine seemed magnificently sane, insisting on its right to walk down this particular logging road without being turned aside, or touched. While I was musing, the porcupine reached its home trail and turned off, and I bowed deeply to the barbed and lumbering shape.

I got back to camp, fed the dog and ate, then lolled in the hammock with the *Iliad*. It was such good poetry that it even took my mind off the flies for a while, but for all its grandeur it was basically a hacking match, with gods slamming onto the scene like runaway locomotives, mashing good and bad alike. One thing that struck me—the Greek warriors were all sheepmen at heart. Maybe too much contact with sheep could ruin a person's character, I thought, and turn a gentle herder into one of these flesh-hewing, bronze-plated maniacs. They were self-righteous, possessive, and paranoid: traits I associated with my own ranching heritage (though we thought of ourselves as proud, enterprising, and independent). But the *Iliad* was clearly written from a shepherd's point of view: attacks were likened to the charge of a wolf on a grazing flock, and defenses to the frenzied efforts of the herder to drive the shaggy, sheep-gnawing beast away.

Thinking of the *Iliad* as a sheepherder epic made me uneasy, since the idea of sheep as the basis of Western civilization was depressing, but I also felt closer to it in an odd way. As the horseflies swarmed with the heat, I swatted and made up a new verse:

As a wild, black pack of wolves will race down, with moon-glinting
     fangs,
Upon a hill-bound flock, so drove the horseflies upon the Campjack's
     nape.
Vainly he slapped, as they chomped the vital cord that bound his body
     to his brain,
And then with a thud he fell, breathing dust, as darkness veiled his
     eyes.

Ouch. I dropped the pencil. Damn flies. It was impossible to sit still, so I got up and checked on the horses. They were in the shade at the edge of the grassy meadow, tail-swishing and tossing their heads. Mitch had rolled tortillas in a plastic bag and filled an empty can with beans for lunch, closed with waxed paper and rubber bands. He'd be making a little twig fire, to heat the beans and brew a canteen cup of tea. I was restless but couldn't think of anything that needed fixing. Then I remembered the joint I'd rolled and forgotten the week before. I decided to smoke it and go on a hike, up a reach of the streambed I hadn't seen yet.

I set out, feeling as if my boots didn't quite reach the ground, and

Pookie followed. Where the stream crossed to the west side of the canyon, the bed was deeply incised and the flow was a thread, bounded by watermarks on rocks and logs. It turned into a gorge, with deadfalls crossed and jammed, and I climbed over and through, testing each foot before committing my weight. At the top of high, eroding banks the spruces loomed and passed the light, complicating the linear puzzle with bars of shade. Passing between shadow and sun, I had to pause to let my eyes adjust. The boundaries between glare and shadow were diffracted, like slim rainbows draped along the ground and over fallen trunks.

"Somewhat ripped," I told the dog.

A cloud swallowed the sun and my skin felt cold. The spruces seemed to touch above. I wondered how often they fell. Maybe nature hated us. How was I to know? There was something else going on here, some thing else.

"Way ripped," I said.

There was a remnant pool ahead, with its own cloud of gnats. I walked up to the log that dammed it and put my hands on the bleached wood and looked down at concentric rings of color that expanded around a reflection of the clouds and overhanging trees. There was an oily glimmer in the mud along the edge, and wet soil crumbling, and water filling a set of little rounded holes and scores that resolved into a fresh bear track.

Big track. Big bear. Still-filling-in-with-water fresh. I held my breath and looked up the loose bank and saw a trail freshly scuffed. I looked at my hand on the log, and the bear track was bigger. I tensed my fingers into claws and my lips into a snarl, and felt like a bear, interrupted at my drink, water dripping from my half-open jaws, my nose full of man and dog. The dog clambered over the logs and sniffed the track, too loud. "Sh-h-h-h."

I scanned the banks above, such a confusion of rocks, brush, live trees, dead trees, and the shadows of clouds that poured into the gorge and were sucked as quickly out again. The gravel in the streambed squeaked under my weight as I turned to go, and as I fled, the cobbles made a nasty clatter. When I reached the first opening, I ran. Pookie thought it was a game and nipped at my ankles, and I aimed a kick at her and fell. I listened for the bear's charge and its huffing breath, but nothing came except the dog. She nosed my neck. I sat up. There was a long gouge, showing white, under my forearm. I watched as blood seeped in. Oh God! The bear would smell the blood. I sprang up and started a jerky sprint, trying to outdistance my dread.

The horses stood exactly as before: they hadn't smelled the bear. They tipped their long faces up, acknowledging me, allies and familiars, and went back to switching flies. The tent was just exactly where it had been. Of course it was. The tent wouldn't change places because I'd seen a bear. And I hadn't really *seen* a bear.

Too ripped. It took an effort to hold my shape, to keep the words in place, to pretend that they meant anything. The blood on my forearm was scabbed. It itched. There was nothing that could be kept safe. Because the impetus, the hurtling, headlong rush was the only rule.

In self-defense, I started a fire in the pit and filled a pot with water. Rice. A pot of rice. If Mitch came back I'd be cooking a pot of rice. I scooped a cup of rice into the pot. How much water? A cup at least. Then I scooped another half cup and dumped it after the first. Was that right? The rice was cooking. Now I was cooking rice. Check. I crawled into the tent and lay on my side on my sleeping bag. I stared at the canvas as the light defined the weave, threads and crossings, buff and brown and gold and amber. The breeze moved the fabric close, then away.

"Lazy bugger," the voice said. I woke up fast.

"Rice," I said. I stood up and walked over to the firepit. I lifted the lid. The rice was done, but it was cold. I held it out.

Mitch nodded. "It's definitely rice," he said.

"I saw bear tracks," I said.

"How big?"

I held my right hand up and spread my fingers. "Big."

"How far?"

"The streambed above the ford. Fresh. Still filling up with water."

"Pretty close to the camp. We better hang the meat up higher." I noticed two hindquarters, tied together at the hock and slung over a limb.

"I didn't hear a shot," I said.

"A ewe prolapsed—the uterus gets turned inside out. Usually happens during lambing. Sometimes you can wash it off and put it back, but hers was hanging almost to the ground. She was pretty weak and the flies are so bad, I cut her throat. It saves killing a lamb for camp meat. We can try it. If it's no good, we can feed it to the dogs."

As Mitch sliced the mutton, I built a fire and got the frypan out. I felt shaky but whole again. The thought that I was about to eat the hind leg of a sheep didn't bother me at all. My world centered on the fire, and the deepening blue of night seemed friendlier than the day.

"Cut up some onion and toss the rice in," Mitch said. "I'd better drive a bigger picket stake, in case that bear comes around. Then it'd be good-bye horses." He took the axe, walked over to his saddle, and touched the rifle in its scabbard. "If you hear me sing out, grab the saddle gun."

"I won't shoot any bears."

"If it's chewing on my leg, you better. Or stick your foot in his mouth and toss the rifle to me. Hah!" Laughing, he faded into the dark.

AUGUST 13

"Is it Monday?" I asked.

"How should I know?"

"You have the herding notebook." I crawled out of my bag and lit the stove.

"You have your journal. I'm staying right here until the coffee's up," he said.

"No coffee, remember?" I heard his frustrated grunt. "I'm supposed to ride down and get it from the forest ranger on Monday. That's why I asked. And my brother might be up soon. He's hitching from Cache Valley. If he goes by the ranch, he might bring the coffee."

"I'm sick of that dime-store tea. Let's have cocoa."

"What's up with the *borregas*?"

"They're trying to go over the ridge to Bear Canyon already."

"Why can't we let the sheep drift over the top?"

"We'd kill ourselves. We still have to get a week's feed down here and move the camp."

"Where to?"

"Beaver ponds, where the creek from Bear Canyon goes under the old log bridge. We'll hold 'em low to catch the south slope—it's lush in there—and then turn the corner and let 'em go up the east side of Bear Canyon."

By midmorning I had a rhubarb pie cooling, perfect except for the color: a red so violent that it looked like melted lipstick. Mitch rode in, stripped his saddle from Tony, and turned him loose. I followed him out and caught Pronto, the dark mare. She and Red were my favorite mounts, but the colt was a nuisance when you had to cover ground.

Mitch surveyed the pie. "Looks like a brake light," he said. He lifted the coffeepot from the coals and poured a cup of hot water, then draped a tea bag in. "Cut a hunk?"

"Be my guest. Primary colors are a vital element of Mormon cuisine. We need green punch and yellow Jell-O: a stunning display, charged with beet sugar. Mormon opium."

He ignored my tirade and tasted it. "Not bad. Maybe use half as much candy. But now we can tell Royal it was great and he'll tell Louise, and everybody's happy."

"And he'll bring up rhubarb instead of canned cherries."

Mitch sighed. "I think rhubarb season's finally over," he said.

"Thank heaven." I saddled Pronto, and her colt tried to nip the bandanna out of my back pocket. I whirled and kicked at the colt as the colt whirled and kicked at me. Its pointy hoof nailed me in the ankle-bone, and I sat down hard and watched the colt dance away through the flashbulbs as Pronto sniffed daintily at my hat.

Mitch laughed. "Hah! The colt wins," he said, and cut another piece of pie. "Red Wing boots have pretty soft soles. No match for a hoof."

I pulled my pantleg up and rolled my sock down; two white Vs were indented in a fiery blush. Mitch grinned. His teeth were shocking pink. Clearly, it was time to go.

To ride off down the road was a holiday: new country to see, a forest ranger to meet, and the chance of a stray cowgirl. Pronto had a sporty walk and a stylish, rolling trot. I was beginning to like riding, now that I trusted the horses. More or less, anyway.

Pookie and the colt followed, swapping spots behind the mare. We swung down the steep curves and came to a big opening with a stream entering from the west. The tributary canyon forked not far up, and the left fork turned south around a peak that looked like the pyramid on a dollar bill: that was Bear Canyon. The right fork rose straight up. I could see hanging bowls up there, and long bare skylines, trailing skirts of broken stone. That must be the Double Heart.

The road looped around the beaver ponds, and I noticed plenty of camping spots at the edge of the woods. Above the ford I noticed a trail and kept to the left bank instead of crossing; we went along the terrace near the creek through groves of lodgepole, and came out in a pleasant flat, another nice camp. Behind it the ridge was edged with a green I recognized: aspen.

I found a shallow riffle and we splashed across in a line, Pronto, colt, and dog. I rode through stately, open woods as the canyon broadened, and then onto the road. Down a turnoff I saw a lake among the trees, small and almost round, under thick pine woods.

Below the lake the road made easy curves around a pair of ponds, one with a beaver lodge. On the left, another canyon opened up: North Murphy Creek. The creeks joined in a boggy flat, willows quilted into rush and sedge. There were more signs of travel, a new bridge, and a beaten campsite under lodgepoles with two-by-fours nailed between. The road skirted a boggy flat and climbed a hill on which the forest was mostly lodgepole pine.

Ahead I saw a larger opening, where Murphy Creek swirled into Greys River. The river was fifty rippling feet across and stoutly bridged with log stringers set on concrete piers: a government bridge, for hauling logs. Screw that, I thought, and aimed Pronto into the river.

There were two channels where the river came up to her belly. I lifted my boots up like a jockey as Pronto strode across like a movie horse and emerged dripping on the east bank. I looked back. The colt, no fool, was crossing the bridge, mincing at the sound of its own steps. Pookie looked desperate-eyed at me, then at the colt on the bridge. I tried to wave her onto it, but dog ethics demanded that she go where I had gone, so she gave a disconsolate wail and hurled herself into Greys River, and was swept under the bridge and washed downstream. Paddling frantically, she reached the east bank two hundred yards down and clawed up into a mat of willows. I got off the horse and called her, and praised her as she licked my hand, whimpering. "Brave dog, good dog," I cooed, stroking her draggled fur. "Rin-Tin-Tin was a girl, y'know."

Royal was right about the Greys River Road: it was a mess of sharp rocks awash in limy dust. The horses' wet hooves turned grayish white, and the dog looked as if she'd crossed a freshly poured sidewalk. But not far along I saw a loading chute and pole corrals. Then there was a log fence and a road leading to a neat brown cabin on a gentle slope.

Wanting to arrive in style, I rode to the porch and stepped from the stirrup onto the bottom step. No one applauded, so I dropped the reins and knocked: no response. I looked in the window at a painted tongue-in-groove floor of old fir, army surplus bunks, and sunlight falling across a green Formica table. Nobody home.

I sat on the porch and scratched the drying dog as Pronto grazed the lawn and the colt nursed. I walked to the drive and looked: no recent track. It was Monday, so the ranger must be on the way. So I loosened the cinch and sacked out on the grass, hat over my eyes, listening to the horsey chomp and the suckling of the colt, smelling bruised grass and the mare's milk. Pookie rested her muzzle on my arm, and sighed. I heard a diesel out on the road, but it went by fast—logs, bound for the mill.

An hour passed, two. Lodgepole shadows striped the mare and colt. I stood up, stiff and disappointed. I tried the door, but it was locked. If the ranger had coffee inside, I could borrow some and leave a note: use what you brought up for us, and thanks. The back was locked, too. I decided to leave a note and thought about tearing a page out of my journal, but then I saw a garbage can, and found some discarded forms: Report of Timber Sale Inspection. Good enough.

Dear Ranger Sir:

I work for the Preston Ranch and Royal said he would send a can of coffee up here with you, but there's no you yet. Alas! Will try again tomorrow, thanks.

C. Rawlins, Chief of Culinary Arts
Upper Murphy Creek (no phone)

No coffee. I was so bitterly cast down that I even used the bridge. The breeze moved upcanyon at the same speed as my horse, so the ride back was dusty, morose, and plagued by flies. I cursed the bugs, and my footsore dog, and the mare for balking and trying to turn back. At the ford I turned to curse the colt, but the colt wasn't there. That's why Pronto was acting up.

Pronto jigged and fretted until we set off down the road again. Pookie followed with a sad, tipping gait, blurred by our dust. We reached the cutoff road to the lake and Pronto gave a gusty cry as the colt bounced up, squealing: Mama, where *you* been?

It wasn't a hundred miles back to camp, but almost. The mare was cranky. The dog was half dead. Mitch was disappointed and sulked. And I was too tired to cook, so I ate a fluorescent slice of humble pie and went to bed.

AUGUST 14

The mountains keep their own time, in the water and the rock, under gravity's slow, inescapable pull. Time is also a kind of distance, between the ridge and the streambed, or a palpable difference, between the rainstorm and the tent. And when we sit perfectly still and watch, under the slow-rolling sun, the land's time seems to open like a sunflower, radiating in all directions as it blooms, sets seed, and cures under the August sun.

In the broken country, our eyes travel farther and faster than our bodies, so we're learning to use them well: to see not only the ridgetops but the sky's light breaking across them, and not only the pines and the firs but their moving shadows. This wasn't a gift I sought, or even understood at first, since it came from dull hours spent scanning the landscape for stray sheep. But then you begin, in the half of creation you face, to watch all things at once without stopping on any single thing. When you can touch the whole fabric, world and light, with one gaze, then it may be yours, even though you don't possess it. It is not something to be taken but something to be felt, a quick certainty of what *is*.

And given that other sense, for it feels like a sense quite beyond the sight we have from birth, you notice what moves, or is out of place, or interrupts the weave. And in watching and knowing the world as a fabric of light, you discover a different, unbounded time. There's a quality in this kind of sight I can't name, but I imagine it as the strange light in the eye of a wolf or a hawk, that deadly state of heed.

It's easy to be foolish about such things: words tempt us with their shapeliness. But time is everywhere, and always real, and yet time here is not as I knew it. We inhabit the canyon like a world.

Mitch stirs. Time to light the stove. Time to light a candle on the box. The tent is a reservoir of light. And then the tent is darker than the sky. Morning. Each day full of going: the sun's; the going of the horses and the herd; and ours, afoot or on horseback. Strain in the thighs, the creak of leather, wind. Midday heat settling between the gusts. A cloudscape building high. In the grassy meadow, I try to outrun the shadows.

Camp. Smoke and the smell of frying meat, and our little theater on the range:

> LORD MITCHELL: I say, dear chap, was this lamb *hung*?
> PADDY: Couldn't say, bejasus. The poor bugger was docked before we met.
> LORD M.: I say! I mean, was it *aged*?
> PADDY: Aged? It wouldn't be fughing lamb, then, would it?

We fried our mutton and potatoes and ate under a mountainous sky, clouds sailing over at tremendous speed. Then we decided to flip, to see who'd ride down to Deer Creek and fetch the coffee. Since we didn't have a coin and couldn't find one, we flipped the baking powder lid. Mitch quickly claimed the upper side, with raised letters, as *heads,* and won. And chose to stay.

Tying Pookie up in the shade, I set out on Red. The canyon looked different under broken, cloudy light, but not different enough to compensate for sore thighs, and I rode fast: the curves, the beaver ponds, the narrows and the ford, and North Murphy all came into sight and passed. I saw a shadow crossing shadows on the road, a figure under the pines. I rode closer, and the figure was familiar: "Chris!"

My brother stopped and waved. I thumped Red's ribs and he sprang to a gallop. I could see Chris's face now, and his long blond ponytail draped along his shoulder. I reined up hard in the proverbial cloud of dust. Red reared: it was *perfect.*

I stood in the stirrups and whooped. Chris hollered back, shaking his fist in the air.

"Nice scalp!" I cried. "You're buzzard bait, White Boy."

He doubled over laughing, under his brown frame-pack with feathers hanging from the top bar. I slid from the horse and we hugged.

"Don't take my scalp," he said. "I've got trade goods: look—brown gold." He opened the pack and produced a big blue can: Maxwell House.

"Whoa, Red!" He was dancing; I stroked his neck. "This is Red. And the camp's about three miles up."

"I caught a ride with the ranger. He's real nice. He said just walk up this road and you'll find those guys. And if you get lost, open the coffee and they'll find you."

I led the horse and we chattered. He'd been home and had hitched up to Star Valley from there. "Dad's still pretty hot," he said, "but cooling. He blamed my long hair on you." My brother had my father's looks, a clean-jawed handsomeness, like the Arrow Shirt man with straight, shoulder-length hair. I have my mother's blood, and my hair is wavy and thick, full of reddish glints.

We rode double across the ford, and then he walked. As we went he stopped to look at things: Murphy Lake. A deer skull. A beaver in a pond. I babbled stories at him, family questions, and nonsense. "I guess you don't talk much up here," he said.

"Yeah, we do, but Mitch is turning into Livestock Man. I'm glad you're here."

We got to camp and I turned Red loose, and Chris took the coffee can out of his pack and put it on the ground and we did a war dance around it. Mitch stumbled from the tent, rubbing his eyes. "Long ol' day," he said. "Hey, Chris. Welcome to Never-never Land." Then he saw the coffee and swept it up in his arms like a child.

We cut mutton from the bone and fried it. Chris ate his share and more, with big slabs of dutch oven bread, and then we cooked another pan of meat and he ate nearly all of it, and finished off the bread. The sky cleared, the climbing shadows reached the Star Peaks, and the smoke from the fire made blue eddies along the creek.

"You want some pie?" I asked.

"Sure!" he said, and finished that, too. "I'll sleep outside," he said.

"Good thing," said Mitch. "With that bellyful, you'll fart like a grizzly bear."

"Speaking of bears," I said, "there's one around. Big. If you hear the horses charging through the woods, or the dogs go nuts, come inside the tent."

"Okay," he said, with a silly grin. Bear bait, for sure.

5 ～

Beaver Ponds

That morning we woke to the first, light frost, white on the blades of the grass and the margins of leaves. I stoked the stove and Chris wandered in, scratching and yawning widely. "Cold out there," he said. "Let's eat."

I tipped a lid of coffee grounds into the pot. Mitch sat up.

"Smell that," he murmured. "God's alive. And magic's afoot."

Mitch took Chris up to the herd, along with all the dogs. I packed up the camp alone, feeling cheated at losing the chance to swamp my brother with lore: *pannier, sawbuck, lash cinch, manty.* But just yesterday I got to ride up shrieking in a cloud of dust, and my horse reared at the perfect instant—that had to count.

But they came down in time to hoist panniers and throw hitches, so I got to swamp my brother after all: *box hitch, diamond, off-side, jerk-end, pigtail.* Mitch and I set out with the pack string down the road, riding slowly as Chris hiked. Where we rode, the main canyon was narrowed by landslides and heavily wooded. We crossed the creek that flowed from Bear Canyon and reached the beaver ponds at noon. Mitch pointed out the stove rocks in a little glade. "Too close to the road," I said, looking at a spot farther east and nearer the creek.

"No big deal," he replied. "No one drives past the ford. You could dance buck naked in the middle of that road at noon all week." And that was true.

The camp was on a dry terrace north of the tributary creek, which braided clear and cold through willows on a gravelly fan deposited by floods. The woods in back of the camp looked disheveled, marked by rough little mounds and overflow channels that now were dry. Crowded east by the wash of rock and silt, Murphy Creek cut deeply into the bases of three conical hills that walled off the sky. North, above the beaver ponds and willows, a dry ridge rose, steep and patched with conifers and brush. Bear Canyon yawned to the west, our only long view, and beyond it rose the mystery of the Double Heart.

We loosed the horses and raised the tent. The stove rocks were light gray limestone filled with swirls and twists and tiny, collapsed arches that suggested fossils, although there was no shape that I could name. As we set up camp, the clouds massed and flowed into the canyon, dulling the sharp points of the peaks, then muffling the barbed tips of the firs. As we hurried to get our gear under cover I could feel the moistening of the air, feel my pores open, and smell the pitch of the conifers and the sharp tang of the willows. Then the rain broke free, dousing the road and the rocks, darkening the tan-and-gray soil to burnt brown and slate, burnishing dark surfaces to silver: leather, willow leaves, ponds.

Rain divided the world: inside the tent, or out. I had only enough wood to start the stove. Then I shrugged into my slicker and went out to fill a bucket from the creek. I returned dripping to put the coffeepot on. Mitch and Chris were swaying by the stove, soaking up heat. So I kept my slicker on and went out again to find dry wood.

The rain hadn't yet penetrated the forest canopy to the ground, but by tomorrow morning everything would be soaked. I scrounged the skirts of spruce and fir until I had a bundle of dry limbs, then packed it in. The coffee was done. Mitch and Chris both held blue mugs, and Mitch was weaving his hands in the air, telling about Ray and the

Knob, and how that tent blew off in a storm "just like this." I squeaked the stove door open and fed the flame. Three loads would be enough, I thought, and went back out into the heavy, dripping green.

This was my sacrifice, stooping and fetching with the rain sneaking chilly down my neck, so my friend and my brother could bask in the heat, and drink the hot brown brew, and tell tales. I brought in the last armful of wood and stoked the stove again, and here we were, protected, warm, complete. I loved the ease I'd created, and had the urge to point it out. But then it wouldn't be ease: to claim my credit was to lessen it that rainy afternoon.

Mitch slickered up and rode off to check the sheep. "They scatter in the rain, but they're too smart to go over the ridge in a storm like this, I hope. Back at dark."

Chris lay down to read a book he'd brought and fell asleep. I checked the horses and gathered more wood, keeping the stack replenished.

Mitch returned early, looking out of sorts. "I had a gold crown put on by a dentist in Salt Lake City. A fast-buck artist," he said. "It just fell out."

"Did you find it?"

"It didn't fall out of my mouth. Just out of the tooth." He pulled a knotted bandanna out of his shirt pocket and showed me the wrinkled piece of gold. "Aches like crazy." He shook a couple of aspirin out of our first-aid box and swallowed them. "I'd better ride down and see if the ranger can radio out, to get me a dentist appointment."

"Want me to go?"

"I will. It'll take my mind off this tooth. I'll take Tony and be back at dark." He switched his saddle and took to the road in a trot, splashing through the puddles, and disappeared. Chris slept through it all.

Living wild is fine, I thought, until you get a toothache. Then you want a nice, balding, boring dentist. I thought about what Mitch could eat with a hole in his tooth. Soup, I decided, or stew with the meat cut up small. I opened the kitchen boxes. Chris woke up and stood looking over my shoulder. When I got up to cut meat from the mutton leg hanging out back, he was eyeing the can of peanut butter. When I came back in with the meat he wore a dreamy smile and was clutching our largest spoon, with about a quarter pound on it.

"Go easy on that: it's three or four days 'til we get supplies. Put it on some bread and fill up that way. I can make more bread." He ignored me and stepped outside to finish his snack in peace. Once the stew was bubbling, I mixed sourdough and flour into a sponge, keeping a significant eye on the peanut butter as Chris wandered in and out.

There was wild food in this country, but I lacked the knowledge to use it. Given our canned and dried staples, we were always hungry for greens, but we usually ate them as we found them, and seldom gathered them to use in camp. I liked the plant that Mitch called miner's lettuce, though it didn't look quite like the miner's lettuce in my book, and since it grew by the creek I'd pick a handful whenever I fetched water. It had a mild, fresh taste. At the melting edge of snowbanks there'd been glacier lilies with juicy, peppery leaves, and spring beauties with crisp, peanut-sized corms, but their season had passed.

Mitch introduced me to waterleaf, which looked unlikely—the leaves were fuzzy—but it was pleasing raw and a delicacy cooked. It grew under aspens, though, and was scarce here. I'd gathered a handsome plant called false Solomon's seal and cooked it up. Mitch tasted it and begged off, so I ate what I could: bitter. It turned out to be a pretty efficient laxative, too. That night I had to dash to the woods in such haste I forgot the roll of toilet paper.

But I was tantalized by the idea that the woods were full of food. If bears ate cow parsnip, maybe we could, I thought. But boiled, they smelled like old saddle blankets: full of vitamins no doubt, but then saddle blankets might be, too. Leave cow parsnip to cows, or the bears, I thought, and tossed it out.

To know this country we had to have names for things. I'd gotten that far, but you can't eat names. So I wanted to know what could be of use. My plant book mentioned uses casually, with few specifics. For instance, it said that stoneseed was used by the Indians for birth control, but didn't say exactly how—not that we needed it, but I was intrigued by the possibilities. I'd tried yarrow tea for sunburn, and it worked. I remembered hearing about arnica salve but had no idea how to make salve—simmer the flowers in bacon grease?

Some names were obvious warnings: stinging nettle and death camas. And some plant names were a kind of code: *wort* meant that you boiled the plant and used the liquid. There were Saint-John's-wort, soapwort, liverwort, and figwort. But was liverwort good for your liver? What about figwort? Or lousewort? That must kill lice, or at least make them unhappy. And what about the various *banes*? I'd heard of dogbane and had the vague intention of trying it out on Pookie. My book said that the ancient Greeks mistakenly believed it was poisonous to dogs, which argued that in terms of naming things, old mistakes could persist right along with truth. How could I know whether they'd gotten it right? Did fleabane daisies really kill fleas, or was that another ancient goof?

And there were puzzles: speedwell, for example, could be either a tonic or God's own laxative. Or it could be neither. The code was confused. Not only were there mistakes and superstitions, but we had old names from the old country, which in these mountains didn't always hold true. Salsify, for instance, sounded not merely edible but absolutely delicious. Mitch said it was called oyster plant. Good enough. He heard you could use the roots in soup, but he'd never tried it. So I dug up a bundle of the roots, which didn't look oysterish. Instead, they were like mildewed ⅜-inch rope, and boiling didn't improve them. Maybe they grew fatter and softer in Massachusetts or England, where there was richer soil or a different species. You could put these tough bastards in soup, I told Mitch, but the results wouldn't be very salsifying. Hah!

There was a whole green world to learn, and trial-and-error just wouldn't suffice. Sampling at random you'd spend a lot of time with diarrhea, or worse. And it might be like jumping off a cliff to see if you could fly: plants like hemlock or death camas didn't give second chances, and dying, at least in an individual sense, isn't a good way to learn. In a movie, an old Shoshone would come strolling in with his medicine bag, eager to teach us rough white punks his lore. But so far only my brother had shown up, and while he was deeply interested in edibility, he didn't know much about plants.

The rain ceased. Chris was prowling nearer and nearer the kitchen box. Mitch had mentioned that fireweed was good tasting. It was a pretty plant, with long leaves that my book called *lanceolate*. I'd seen it all over but hadn't tried it yet. There was a big burn at the mouth of Bear Canyon where the fireweed should be thick. That was an idea: we'd go foraging. At least it would get Chris away from the peanut butter.

We crossed the road and struck west through thick willows toward the burn, crossing dry channels and levees of gravel. There was a lone rank of narrowleaf cottonwoods along the creek that rushed from Bear Canyon—unusual, with none above and, as far as I'd seen, none below in this canyon. Soon we reached the first bleached trunks and deadfalls. Some burnt trees, pines, spruces, and firs, were still standing, stripped of their bark by the weather, while others were jackstrawed on the ground. In places the ground was still black with ash and fireweed grew thickly, some of it in full magenta bloom. I pulled a leaf off a young plant and tried it: good. The older leaves were leathery. So, moving slowly, hunched like two bears, we picked a few rain-washed leaves from each young plant. Chris was absorbed, picking leaves and eating every sixth or tenth one with a dreamy satisfaction. When the plastic bag was a quarter full, I begged off to check on the stew and the rising dough.

I took a different way back and had to breast through thick willows. By the time I got to the road, my pants were soaked. So I stood on a rock and took them off to wring them out. I'd hang them by the stove when I got back to camp, so why put them back on? I thought. I'd given up on underwear, so I walked bare-arsed along the road with my jeans rolled up under my arm.

Why not? We had the whole canyon to ourselves. There weren't any trout in the creek, as far as I could tell, so except for the lake, which got stocked, the fishermen left it alone. It grew big, lovely trees, and the loggers had cut the easy stuff and gone. When hunting season began, deer and elk would be shot and hauled off. And here we were with our hungry sheep, taking the best of the forage. Nobody came to this canyon except when they wanted to take something out.

The Tetons weren't far off: you could see them from the ridgetops. Being a national park, they didn't get logged or hunted. And unlike this canyon, they were crowded, like a movie set where the brave deeds never lacked witnesses. There was a book of rules, and you signed in and out, like checking into a hotel. The park even had a domestic staff: scuttling rangers cleaned each camp, renewing its virginity for the next wave of pioneers. If you broke your leg a helicopter would sling you out in a matter of hours. This range was unspectacular and scarred, but it felt wilder than the Tetons somehow.

What was *wild*? I'd been thinking of wildness and order as opposites, but this canyon was heaped with the wrack of every form of natural violence except tidal wave and volcanic eruption. And it all fit. Or at least it felt that way. My feeling of disorder and wrong was aroused when I saw the clearcuts and the crudely bladed roads: they were the interruptions. The wild animals I saw, from elk to porcupines, came and went with dignity about their own lives, unlike our jostling, bawling, devouring horde of sheep. The sheep disturbed things, like drunks fighting at a concert.

So maybe *wild* was something I felt up here, because we were so alone. Or maybe my ideas of order were slipping. If order was keeping your pants on, I'd already slipped.

Chris came back smiling, with a bag of tender fireweed leaves, and I praised him. He didn't mention my lack of pants. Maybe he didn't even notice. "There's a bunch of raspberries over on the left side, in the rocks," he said. "Way ripe."

"Did you pick some?"

"Yeah." He beamed. "But I didn't have anything to carry them in except . . . me."

The bread rose and the stew stewed and my pants dried out, so I put them on. Mitch rode in and turned Tony loose. The ranger had radioed out, and the clerk would call the Prestons about a dentist. Counting on that, Mitch would ride down the next day about noon and catch a lift with the ranger going home for the weekend. "I'm not sure if they can get an appointment. I may have to wait until Monday. That's four days I'd be gone. Or more. Can you herd that long, if Chris helps out?"

"Without going nuts? Sure. If you aren't fixed up, Roger can bring us the grub and help us get things under control. No sweat. It'll work out."

The camp was wreathed in fog, and we sat by the candle and schemed: horse tactics. Mitch wanted to coach me on the herding. I wanted to ride Red, the picket horse, so I had to catch Pronto for Mitch. Coaching accomplished, he'd turn Pronto loose and ride old Tubby down to the ranger station. Tubby would be less likely to jump out of the fenced pasture.

"Tony or Red would fly over the rail the first night," he reasoned. "If I ride Pronto, the colt's likely to stray on the way down, plus she's broody enough that she'd get in a scrape with the ranger's horses. Elhon would kill me. And Tom's too damn slow."

Chris was scooping oatmeal out of the pot, and Mitch was nursing toast on one side of his mouth. I went out and picked a halter from a stub behind the tent, and shook some oats into a feedbag. It was dark and foggy: the woods were indistinct, a heavier darkness, and the willows looked like sleeping bears. I walked over to Red and checked the picket stake and rubbed his withers. He faced toward the willow jungle and neighed. An answering whinny came from the fog, so I knew where to look for horses, more or less. Feeling crafty, I set off. The leaves of the willows painted me with wetness as I threaded their leafy maze. Then the willows ended and I looked back, but the camp was lost. I came into rushes and the soil was spongy, burbling water up around my boots. I couldn't see the ponds, but they were close. Damned horses. Why couldn't they stay on solid ground?

I saw a tall, black blur and a smaller one: Pronto and the colt. I cooed and rattled the oats in the canvas bag, and the tall shape started, ears pricking the belly of the fog. I walked slowly toward the horses, and the fog made known forms look odd: the mare's head was distorted, bulbous at the nose, and the colt looked top-heavy. I rattled the oats, and the big shape backed off a step, then planted its hooves with a squelch. I held the lead rope out, preparing to drape it over the mare's neck. Then I realized that I was about to halter a big cow moose.

The moose's mane, stiff like the roached mane on a horse, flicked up, down, up. In the fog her neck seemed to swell and deflate. I could see the shine of her big black eye, fixed on me as her mane kept time like some infernal clock. I backed up slowly and stepped into a hole. Then my left boot sank into the mud and I almost fell. I wrenched it out with a *plop,* and the moose snorted. The calf moved close to her and she nosed it, then fixed her glinting eye on me again. I backstepped as comfortingly, as gently, as apologetically as I could.

She waggled her head and lowered it, and my breath caught, but her feet stayed put, braced in the muck, and her black bulk softened: forty feet, fifty, sixty. Rather than diminishing, she seemed to grow larger, to rise into the fog, to loom and then disperse.

Reaching the solid ground, I tripped on a sagebrush and then charged in belated panic toward the tent with the fog swirling at my back.

I stopped and listened for the drum of hooves, but all was quiet. I heard Chris laughing, his mouth full of oatmeal, and Mitch's quieter voice. Then I could see the candle, a circle of bright amber diffused by the canvas flap. "Holy shit," I said.

Mitch looked out. "Where's my horse?"

"I just tried to halter a *moose.*"

He thought it was a joke. "Hah! Anything you can catch, I can ride."

I was too shaken to join in. "No. In the willows. I saw these two shapes, a big one and a little one. I thought it was Pronto and the colt, but it was a moose and a calf."

Chris joined Mitch at the flap, eyes wide. "How close did you get?"

"Arm's length."

"You're lucky she didn't kick your damnfool head off," Mitch said. "Moose can strike straight out with a front hoof. Bang! Kill a horse just like that! Where'd she go—run off?"

"Stood her ground," I said. "If you want to track a pissed-off cow moose through the fog, be my guest. I'm gonna wait till it gets lighter to wrangle horses."

"I'll run her off." He caught up the dishpan and a big spoon, and stepped out of the tent. He banged on it and yelled into the fog: "Git! Git! Shoo!" I shuddered and Chris shook his head.

"Whoa! That really sucks," he said.

Under a coat of soot, the dishpan's bottom was already wavy with dents, since the colt had been stealing it out of the tent and kicking it around when we weren't there. I'd had to beat the bottom flat more than once, and it wasn't in good shape. The racket was awful.

"Hey! If you knock a hole in it, we'll be washing dishes in your hat."

He stopped. But Red, on picket near the camp, had begun to whinny at the noise, and the rest of the horses thundered over to see what kind of hell had broken loose. As they materialized like ships out of the fog, I rattled the bag of oats. Pronto came to me. As Mitch saddled her, I decided Red was too nerved up to ride, or maybe vice versa, so I turned him loose. I'd walk.

Mitch left Chris and me on the ridge. The sheep did sheep stuff, and we wandered around them until they fell asleep, then followed the horse tracks down the steep east-facing slope, where spruce and fir were thick. The forest was dank and enclosed, with dying trees bearded by moss, a vivid, pale green. Where light could get in, there was dense brush that exhaled a sticky humidity. Our feet seldom touched the ground, and we couldn't always see what they touched instead. Every step had to be tested, and we were both sweating when we struck an old logging road that carried a slight breeze uphill. We followed it down through swales and dips and came out on the main road not far above the camp.

We finished what remained of the stew, with slabs of sourdough bread. Then Chris sacked out in the tent while I lay heedless as a dog in the aromatic shade. I rested my head on Pookie, but she let out something between a yelp and a snarl, clearly offended, and stalked off to the next patch of shade.

So I got up and idled toward the stream. Good old boring nature, I thought, same old water wearing out the same old rocks. Then my eye was caught by an egg-sized pebble of a deep red. It was a kind of rock

that I hadn't noticed before, harder and heavier than limestone, o
grained welded sand. Okay, Mr. Hard-to-Please, I thought: Now find
another one *exactly* like it. Don't just think about it—try.

With the lovely red pebble in hand, I quartered the dry bed of an
overflow channel. At first glance the rocks all looked the same, but that
wasn't the case. Looking closely, I found a few pebbles the same color,
none of them quite like the one I held. The size or shape was off, or
there was a yellow stripe, or a crack.

And around me the forest seemed all one thing, but when I looked
closely there were no two trees alike. Meadows seemed to be filled
with identical plants, but each one was really a balance of likeness and
difference. Some plants grew together, but no two groupings were
identical. And no two places could ever be the same. That was hard to
think about, somehow. The idea of variation as the only constant made
me feel insecure. With my nose rubbed hard in the immensely complex, I wanted to believe it absolutely simple, a big yes-or-no. When I
got to the creek, I tossed the red rock in and felt like a nasty little
monkey, unworthy of grace.

Was this wisdom, or distraction? For some reason it was easier to
think when I was moving. I walked along the edge of the woods, passing from sun to shade, shade to sun, and ticked propositions on my
fingers. I mean, how dare I be bored?

1. Because I'm lazy and sinful.
2. Because I don't know enough about all this to make sense.
3. Because of the rhythm and repetition: how to pay attention to
   ten million raindrops?
4. Because the scale is too large: climatic cycles, geologic time,
   planetary time, continental drift. Or too small: molecules, en-
   zymes, genes.
5. Because my interest is usually reduced to us and what we
   brought: horses, sheep, peanut butter. If I don't need to know
   which plants taste good, I can ignore them, mostly.
6. Because I have the illusion of being exempt. Things that increase my comfort and security lend a deadness to the world.
   But, be honest: suffering will do the same.

7. Because—aha!—I need to be known. A rock warms up in your hand, sure, but it never says hello. Wild animals attack or flee, but mostly they keep their distance. They see me, but they don't recognize me. I'm just another thing.

Ouch! A fly bit me in the soft spot under the lobe of my ear. Gripped with insights, I'd stopped moving for too long. Deflated, I walked back to stand in the opening of the tent. My brother mumbled inside, and the flies continued to zoom and circulate. If each fly had trailed a silk thread, like a spider, I'd have been immobilized in a white cocoon.

The big flies were frank predators: they bit out a chunk of flesh, leaving an oozing red point of fire. Their eyes had three beautiful stripes—copper, leaf gold, or tinsel green, black-edged and floating in a nervous polychrome. Their bodies were flattened and clad in overlapping scales. The pressure of your hand against your skin wouldn't kill them. You had to stun them with a slap and then, as they twitched in the dust, grind them with a foot; otherwise they would rise again. Pookie simply snapped them out of the air and chewed them up. Uck.

The large jewel-bodied ones that bit were called horseflies. The medium-sized ones, gray with stripes, also bit and were called deerflies. There were regular houseflies in plenty—and a tiny breed that looked like baby houseflies and had no sense of danger. These smallest ones roamed boldly, entering nostrils and ears, stepping onto the wet, rolling globe of an eye, or trekking into sleeves. They were called nose flies, according to Mitch, and my body offered them both grand scenery and hot meals. There were also clouds of tiny blackflies that hatched in the dung of horses, and furry bee-flies, which had black spindle snouts and kept mostly to themselves. Not to mention the midges and gnats.

In the day's heat, when we large animals sought shade and rest, the flies reached a sizzling peak. Some tactics I learned: shimmy, twitch, flinch, flail, flap, and curse. Keep moving at all times between midmorning and sunset. Tuck in your shirt, button your cuffs, tie a bandanna around your neck, and drape a dishtowel over your head, à la

Bedouin. Rip up big wads of fresh pennyroyal and rub yourself green. Create new, explosive words like *phwabbbb* and *fnooop*. Lie down in a stream with only your lips exposed. Haunt a cliff edge with a breeze, and when it fails, resist the urge to jump off. Or jump. Either way, the flies will have you.

Chris emerged from the tent, flapping his hands. "If I get under a blanket, it's too hot. If I don't they chew my skin off."

"Let's wallow in the mud," I said.

"Mud," he said. "I'm hip."

I had a particular spot in mind, where beaver ponds flanked the creek. It offered great mud, and the clear, cold stream was nearby. We trotted over and stacked our clothes and smeared ourselves a bilious gray-green. I slathered his back and he slathered mine. The mud was cool on our skins. It soothed our bites. I noticed a cut bank with a streak of ochre, so I daubed mustard stripes on my legs and made two bold handprints on my chest, a flying bird. Chris got into the spirit with a yellow target, centered on his navel.

"Good thing Mitch is gone—he'd think this is pretty weird," he said.

"Cowboys keep things buttoned up," I said.

"Too bad," he said. "For all of us."

I ate some miterwort, or miner's lettuce, or whatever it was, and Chris ate some, too. His eyes and teeth shone through the olive drab of drying mud, as we shambled up and down the creek, trying the textures—rush, sedge, sand, and silt. I paddled my bare feet in the lovely ooze, *blap-blup-blap*, and hooted like an ape. Chris shrieked and jumped on a hummock.

"Bugoonzi," I yelled, my old kid-password.

"Potty-Buzumbo!" That was his. In an instant we had become our child-selves, inciting one another to our old madness, and we spun and capered, slinging mud and ripping up tufts of grass, and hollered and screeched until we got dizzy and had to lie on our backs. Then it was nice to let the sky spin over us, slowing to a calm and perfect blue.

Quieted, we washed off in the cold stream and started fresh, looking for different colors of mud. I painted his face and he painted mine. We noticed that the flies didn't follow us across the water. So, barber-poled with red and yellow clay, and dizzy with relief, we lounged in midstream on the mossy crest of a gravel bar. The mud was like a pair of tights, constricting gently in the sun.

"Nice old place you got here, bro." He waved a hand.

"Land of the Flies, Home of the Bees."

We washed off. Slipped into clothes. Went back to the tent. I opened the peanut butter can and plunged a spoon in, then slurped it clean. I handed Chris the spoon, and he dipped it and licked it silver. "Okay. Let's pay the rent," I said. And we hiked up to the sheep.

The heat had kept them bedded late and they were hungry, so they fed quietly and stayed together, and all we did was watch until the sun went down.

Hiking down, we followed the eastward strike of shadows into the canyon's depth. "Let's make a loop," I said. We waded through cow parsnips and blueberry elder, and climbed the modest summit of Ray's Knob. "So this is where the tent blew off," he said.

The sky was full of rosy light. I fetched out my journal and read him my poem:

The tent ballooned and cracked and flapped, like the sail of a pirate
    ship,
And it jerked at the ropes like a hungry horse as the rocks began to
    slip.
And the wind roared like a thousand lions, as it caught up the
    stovepipe and tent.
Up from the ground it whirled them around, and over the cliff they
    went.

He laughed, and reached for the book. "Just read the poem," I said. "Not the other stuff."

As we walked back down the main road, the moon bloomed over the spiky eastern ridge. The bare dirt lost its day color and took on the moon's blue and lavender, striped by the shadows of pines. Near camp, the horses spooked and ran at our approach, and then circled, trailing long-legged shadows across the expanse, their coats glistening in the pale light, their eyes soft as water. And Red came to nose my hand, and I rubbed his neck and breathed into his face.

AUGUST 17

Steam puffed from the black spout of the pot. I lifted the lid and ladled cold water in, to settle the grounds. I tied the flaps back and there was fog outside. First the nearby sage and willows took on form, and then the dark woods at my back, and the standing dead trunks in the burn, and then the lift of the ridges, as all things sharpened their edges on the morning light.

The tent was pitched in a small glade formed by outlying spruces, and shaded except at midday: when a woodstove is your means of cooking, shade is more desirable than sun. And when you're with the herd at sunup, early sun isn't vital, but afternoon shade makes the difference between a nap and a roll in your own sweat. Southwest of the tent, a tight group of spruces formed a rectangular cove, like a barn composed of living trees. There we stacked the saddles, tied horses, and hung bags of oats and quarters of mutton.

I stepped out and a Steller's jay flared down to grip a limb and squawk. Above my head a pair of mountain chickadees was picking seeds, eyeing first the jay and then me. The horses watched from the boggy meadow, alert for the prospect of oats. And Chris watched me from his sleeping bag under the pines.

We ate our cornmeal mush and fed the dogs. While Chris washed up, I laid the plans. We'd hike up the logging road we'd come down the day before and follow the ridge up to check for sheep. If all was steady with the herd, we could take a good, long hike.

There was a stately morning breeze, cool but not cold. We saw sheep from the main road and I counted four markers—a sign that they hadn't gone over the ridge. The old logging road branched off and climbed through swales of Douglas fir, then dipped into pockets of young lodgepoles and grass. I saw a scratch trail that led through a delicately grassed little bowl and cut off on it, stooping under the bottom limbs of the pines. From the edge, as the sun found us, we looked down into the big burn. It made a streak of livid green from the canyon floor to where I stood, and there were charred stumps along the rim and in the lodgepoles. The fire had crowned up the slope and burned like a furnace in this swale, which now held grass and young lodgepoles.

The road swung south and grew steeper, then ended in a big clearcut on the ridge. There were sheep in the shadow of a thin fringe of woods to the east, tugging leaves from the shrubs. The dogs whined, wanting to herd, but I held them back.

We walked the west side of the clearcut, where it rolled down into cups and bowls with sedges and willows. I could see a trail leading off to the west, toward Bear Canyon. In the clearcut the soil was patched with fireweed, thistle, strawberry, raspberry, geranium, and blueberry elder, all broadleaved plants that made it look solid green from a distance. But that was more impression than fact: at my feet the ground was exposed mineral soil, not the brown duff of the wood this had been, nor the matted thatch of a meadow. The cushion of organic litter had washed away, and it would take years to build it back again. Our feet came down hard as we found a scrabbly trail and went up the ridge. Most of the sheep were feeding on the sunny side below. Only a few were on top, and we pushed them down to the east as I counted three more black ewes.

We hiked up until there were no more sheep to see, but a great deal else. We stood between the crest of the range, which ran north to south, and Murphy Creek, which carved a deep parallel. East of the creek rose the rough and precipitous block, drained by waterfalls and cascades, that was crowned by the Star Peaks. But on our side, west of the creek, were great bowls and cirques in the crest, formed by the tributary creeks: the long one under the Pass, then the head of Bear Canyon, where morning sun gleamed on a theater of broken stone.

"That's where we take the *borregas* next," I said.

"Looks pretty rough. Are there places to camp?"

"I hope so. Mitch knows a spot. He says." West and north was the complex of cirques that Mitch called the Double Heart, and a long north ridge that led our eyes down to where the canyons joined, and our camp. Below the beaver ponds the main canyon turned east, out of sight.

We turned back and walked the sunny east side to push the sheep down, letting the dogs have their pleasures. They charged and growled and nipped, and it looked like fun. Chris tried a snarling run at a clot of sheep, which stared horror-stricken until he got close, then dashed off in panic. But his antics drove the dogs beyond themselves, and we finally had to catch them and calm them and tie a rope to Tiger's collar.

When we reached the clearcut, we turned west and headed down into Bear Canyon. Through brush and over deadfalls, we scrambled down into the canyon's mouth, crossing the creek where it issued just above the burn. You couldn't ride through it at all, I thought. The dead trunks were lapped and balanced, two deep, four deep, six layers deep in spots. It wasn't a half mile straight to camp, but it would probably take us an hour to cross the maze.

So we turned west again and followed a set of rocky channels up the other fork, toward the Double Heart. The canyon was floored with rubble so loosely heaped that the water flowed underneath. The dry, rubbly channels were likely full only a few days each year, and that's when whole highly inclined landscapes moved camp. I could imagine these gullies in flood, after spring rain on saturated snow, each one filled twice my height with a churning slurry.

It was gravity's wrecking yard. Where channels were blocked with broken trees, we sweated through scrubby thickets of willow, alder, aspen, shrub maple, and thorny currant. First Anselfrond disappeared. Disgusted, I thought. She'll head for camp. A minute later, Tiger peeled off and followed her. Pookie looked dubious but stuck with us.

The south side was a green wall, overhung with spruces and firs. The north side was barer, warped outcrops that rose between a succession of funnel-shaped ravines. From one gorge so much rock had spewed that it formed a dike, fifty feet above the rest of the slope. We climbed up it and edged between the buttresses to peer inside, and it was a goblin rookery.

The morning air was still and the flies were unrelenting. The big ones bit right through my T-shirt and left dime-sized spots of blood, browning in the heat. The canyon pinched down and then forked, steepening into walls. I couldn't see a good way up. "Go on? It's looking pretty rough."

Chris shaded his eyes. "Yeah. But the way back is obvious. And it looks neat up there." We waded into sweet anise and horsemint, an aromatic shag that concealed loose rock and broken limbs. As the watercourse choked down we climbed up to the right, choosing a fresh rockslide as the easiest route.

There were scrub aspens at its foot, and a few raspberries had grown up through the slide itself. We stopped to pick berries, one on the tongue for each fly bite. How far did the roots go down? And how would it feel, to rise up and bloom and set fruit, only to be shredded and buried again, how many times? Something about the raspberries in the rockslide caught me unawares and touched me at the heart.

"These berries are poems," I said.

"Make one up."

"Okay. Hmmm. Like poems on a thigh-high, thorny cane . . . sweet and blood-red . . . rooted . . . ten thousand years . . . through fallen rock . . . and pain."

"*Whoa!* It even rhymes. Write it down." Chris waited while I slipped my journal from my pack and scribbled, collecting two fly bites: one for History and and one for Art. Then we struggled on. A big hawk circled over us, plagued by a smaller, darker bird. Then the breeze struck up, and some sharp rocks clattered down into the gully: dislodged by the wind.

Neither fork looked passable: the right one was a steep vault of talus, and the left a scoured, overhanging gorge, all tilts and shatters. But we reached the fork and found a trail that climbed, steeply and improbably, onto the central rib. Twenty steps up, we had to stop and breathe. The elk must keep this open, I thought. You'd kill a horse before you got this far.

Farther up we heard water and saw a milky pool in the right fork. The trail switched back over the rib, and I heard water falling. Above, a rivulet threaded out of a hanging forest on the south in a long spiral and spattered on the sharp rocks far below.

Steep and scratchy. Hateful. Sweat. Hard to find a decent place to stand. Too blown to talk, we climbed in spasms. As I stopped, Chris staggered up and passed, stopping twenty steps beyond. Vile. Hot.

Pookie left claw marks in the baked dirt. There was a kink in the trail as it went up beside a jagged point, over the collapsing gorge. You could slide right off this stuff. I imagined us traversing a bad slope over toothy hollows. Why did we come up here?

A springy, drumming squeak. Hummingbird, close to my face. Buzzing Chris's red bandanna. Hovering to probe a scarlet gilia: the thin trumpet of the flower agrees with the slender beak. Which came first? Who cares: it's a perfect fit.

Watching the hummingbird gave me a fresh burst of resolve. I reached the airy saddle and looked down into a massive headcut. On the headland from which all else fell away, a single big spruce rose. The tree was doomed, the earth abandoning it in three directions, and its brace roots clutched only air. Chris made it up and we looked east. The rockslides looked like bolts of gray tweed, draped from a chair to the floor. Distance gave things beauty.

"No way in hell you'd ever get a horse up that trail," I said.

"Great way to suffer, though," Chris said. "Lots of good mortifications."

My fears weren't realized, since above the headcut the trail climbed more easily along the slope, and then we saw not agony but heaven itself. Heaven with pink geraniums.

"Sweet Jesus, take me home," Chris murmured.

Rising smoothly the trail led into a flowery groove. A breeze spilled down and ruffled the blooms. Pookie fell on her side and panted, as we sat and rested and marveled. I watched a white butterfly tip past. Two breaths later, a seed on a white parachute rose from the gorge and drifted at eye level, west. So calm. We ate flour tortillas, rolled around beans. Our apples were half brown, so we ate the parts that weren't and tossed the rest to the chipmunks. This place was strange and hard to predict. Where I'd imagined a horrible, scary defile we found instead a scoop of blossoms, easy as thought.

We hiked up it and entered a flowery, flat-bottomed sink, which seemed quiet and separate. The right-hand slope was dry and loose, forested above. On the left, yellow castles loomed far above the sink and had filled it with shattered rock. There was mud in the lowest part, but the wild, slurry-piling flows of the canyon didn't go this way. The lower end spilled a bit of snowmelt, but most of the drainage sank into the broken floor.

A pika buzzed in the talus. In the mud were many elk prints and a few left by deer. The far end of the little sink rose in a short, steep slope that looked like a man-made dike, though it couldn't have been: the spruce and fir that topped it were too old. We climbed it and then dropped into a lovely, open-floored grove with a cathedral feel.

The pleasant woods opened west. The canyon broadened above, centered on a dry streambed that turned to the north. We walked down that way, and a thread of water appeared and then fell off into a cavernous headcut, deeper than the one we'd passed. I peered over the edge—not a way to get down. But I was looking, I realized, into the right-hand fork, and we'd come up the left. As we hiked up the streambed, I looked back. Between the two forks was one of those odd, conical summits, and I filed the puzzle away.

The day was slipping out from under us, but we could see the crest so we drove ourselves, climbing the north slope past big limber pines, and up into long sweeps of grass and open sky. There were landings with islands of conifers, each with a fresh elk bed in its sheltered lee. This was where the elk had gone. The wind held the flies off and the grass was thick: good summering. We held high to the right and climbed until we could see over a dip in the crest into Star Valley. Northwest was a high summit on the ridge and above us northeast was what looked like a pass. With our last strength, we gained it and ducked under limber pines—*ka-whoop!*

It cracked off in a sheer drop. Between two reddish peaks there were big cliffs of untrustworthy gray-brown rock. We were looking down into North Murphy, I realized, and around at everything else on earth.

To the north rose the Teton massif, across the canyon of the Snake. Northeast was the Gros Ventre Range, and beyond it I could see the hazy wall of the Absarokas. Across Greys River, the Wyoming Range filled the east, and through a gap I could see a bigger range, still snow-capped in August—the Wind Rivers, Wyoming's highest mountain range. I recited the names I knew, and Chris repeated them in a reverent voice.

I didn't like these vertiginous rims, since it was clear they had broken away in massive chunks. The wall below us fell so steeply that we couldn't see the cirque below without leaning out, which neither of us was willing to do. My fear of falling was so present that even a tiny misstep called it up. The wind buffeted us, and I rested my hand on a pine to have a third, steady point. The stones of the rim were a deep, sunwashed red that was somehow familiar. And then I knew: this was where my red pebble had started from.

Coming down, we faced two hanging bowls that made heart shapes under a broken face. The upper one held remnant snow, and the other a circular lake, of a curiously opaque green. The roll of the slope was interrupted by gullies, and we avoided two or three, but then had to cross one with rotten snow in its maw. I started traversing south, with the lake in mind.

"Whoa up," Chris said.

"What about the lake? Eye of the goddess."

"Too tired. Let's head straight back."

He was right. I was tired, too, and Pookie was licking her paws. So we descended and found an elk trail. I heard water splashing and slid down for a drink while Chris bore on. I caught him in the grove, and we went through the flowery scoop, and then down the gravelly horror. I kicked a rock loose, and it rolled to the end of the switchback and off into space.

Soon we were picking our way across the rockslide and it was growing dark. In my fury to see new country I'd forgotten the sheep, but I had to check on them. The camp was about a half mile away through the burn, and Chris didn't want to climb up Bear Canyon.

"Can you get through the deadfall?" I asked. "What if you fall or get tangled up?"

"Crawl on my belly, if that's what it takes. It's not as bad on the north."

"Okay. I'll do the maggot-watch. Why don't you start a fire and get some food on?"

He hiked off and Pookie swiveled her head until I called her.

"Come on, ol' hound. Let's go herd the herd."

My thighs burned, climbing up to the clearcut. There wasn't a sheep in sight. I hiked for twenty minutes up the ridge and found sheep shit but no sheep. I was worried, then. Where were the stupid things? A couple thousand sheep couldn't just take flight. Pookie sniffed the air and whined, no help.

Then it was dark. I'd find them in the morning, I decided. What the hell. Ray had ridden off and gotten drunk for days, and the sheep survived. They were filling their bellies somewhere. They didn't need me. I came to the main road and shuffled toward the camp. The bottoms of my feet felt whipped. Pookie limped behind me and stopped to gnaw at her paws. We followed the swings of the road down toward the creek, as the moon came up. Then I heard a *baaa*.

Weird. They'd come down and crossed the creek on their own. I counted three markers in the moonlight, four, five, six. We'd talked about getting them to come down and cross the creek as a problem, and here they were. I couldn't explain, but I was glad.

And I couldn't rightly take credit, I thought. But I might.

AUGUST 18

"*¡Que barbaridad!*" My ankles wouldn't flex. I shuffled to the stove, stooped, and got a double charley horse. "Goddam biting sow," I screamed. I heard whimpering behind me in the tent and turned to shoo the dog outside, but it was Chris. Then I noticed another sound.

It was raining, hard.

I got the fire going and coffee on, and a pot of water for oatmeal. Then I remembered: no butter. We did have a can of shortening, but I didn't feel up to that. Chris had wiped out the peanut butter last night, on his return, before I got back. I opened the jam jar and there was mold on the few spoonfuls that remained. There was brown sugar and white sugar and maple extract. I could make sourdough cakes and use the boiling water to make syrup.

Unbuttered flapjacks? Spartan fare, for sure. I slid back into my sleeping bag. But the sheep might scatter in the rain, so I had to go herd. Oatmeal would be less work. No butter, though. What would Achilles do? Crack skulls? Beat on a slave? Sulk in the tent? How about Odysseus? He'd trick the Trojans into tossing butter over the walls, or swipe some from the table of a god. What about Li Po? He'd scratch his belly and make up a poem, to cheer himself up. Short and to the point, like:

> *Oatmeal*
>
> When there's no butter,
> eat it without.
>
> When there's no sugar,
> eat it without.
>
> When there's no salt,
> eat it without.
>
> When there's no oatmeal,
> *everything's perfect.*

I started to giggle in my sleeping bag.

"What?" Chris looked at me from his bag. "Did you crack up?"

"Made up a poem. This one's funny, though."

"Let's hear it." I repeated it and he hummed appreciatively. "I don't necessarily get it," he said, "but I think it's very deep."

We tried some shortening in our oatmeal, for the calories. It wasn't bad if you looked away as it melted, and it gave me the strength to lace my boots. Chris wasn't much inclined to herd. He wanted to stay in the tent and read Li Po. Pookie issued after me, sad-eyed and dutiful, into the rain, but the border collies didn't want to come. They gave me exasperated looks and shook, though they weren't wet, as we set off into the storm.

Low clouds touched the pines, and the peak at the mouth of Bear Canyon looked like a Mayan pyramid, overgrown. The willow stems were vivid red and orange, and the pebbles had taken on deeper colors underfoot.

Red came over, and I draped the rope across his neck. "You're it," I said, and fed him oats from my palm as he blew warm breath into the crook of my arm. Riding up the road, I spread my slicker out to keep the saddle dry and noticed that Red's heat rose up inside: nice. I rode past where I'd seen the sheep, then forded the creek. The dogs gave me tragic looks as they breasted the stream.

The sheep were spread for a half mile up a thickly wooded slope that I recognized as the toe of a landslide. We circled north, above them, and then came down a rocky rib along a stream. At the edge of the woods there was fireweed in bloom, rich magenta, and tall-stemmed wild hollyhock with flowers of pale pink, and banks of thimbleberry that held big, soft leaves and white flowers up to the rain. As I rode west, the stream fell faster, its voice distinct above the low drumming of Murphy Creek below, and clear through the surrounding whisper of the rain.

Smoke curled from the stovepipe, rising a few feet up, then losing itself in the willows. In the tent Chris was sprawled in his long johns, reading my book and absently brushing his hair. A can of pineapple slices was opened and empty with a spoon inside, and there were only two thin sticks of wood left to feed the stove.

As I tried to think of a crushing remark, I heard something else and stepped out: it was the ranch truck, and I could see the twin glints of Roger's glasses. He pulled up, and I could see a box of groceries in the passenger spot and a tarped mound in the bed. Mitch rode Tubby into camp. "Let's get this stuff unloaded and have some lunch," he said, as he slid off.

We'd done better this time, but having both Chris and Roger up here at once was a terrible risk to the food supply. Roger looked sunburnt and cheerful. "Old truck made the ford," he said. "I figured Mitch could pull me out with the horse, but it didn't even spin."

"Where are the *borregas*?" Mitch gave me a bossy look, which I ignored.

"They're fine. How's your tooth?"

"The dentist in Afton put the crown back on. Nice old guy. He said it may not hold, but it feels good. I'm ready to chew that old, tough mutton again." He shot a look at Roger.

The killing of the bear still echoed in my memory as a crime. But it couldn't be undone.

"Hey, Roger," I said. "Good-looking grub. No rhubarb. Thanks."

He grinned, and his glasses flashed light. "Sure. No sweat. Mitch and I did the shopping this time. I know how it is. Dad's big on rhubarb. It was always the first thing ready after winter, sometimes before you could get out with a wagon and a team. And they leaned on it pretty hard in the Depression, too. So the old-timers all swear by it. Hey—my ass is chewing on my undershorts. Let's eat."

I opened a fresh can of peanut butter and set out a round loaf of sourdough, along with oranges. As we ate, I stowed the rest of the food, tucking prizes—pie cherries! canned ham! cookies!—behind sacks of flour and meal. Mitch asked again about the herd and I told him where it was. "Good," he said. "I figured they'd run all over hell up there."

"Chris and I stayed above 'em." Strictly speaking, that was the truth. I looked at Chris, hoping he wouldn't mention yesterday's exploration, and he caught the glance.

"With the four of us here," Roger said, "we can count. Mitch and I can ride up and gather. You and Chris hold the front. There's a gap in the pines we can run 'em through."

It was raining lightly as the sheep spilled down into the meadow like a white landslide; the lambs butted heads and porpoised over logs, like clumsy deer. Roger and I stacked limbs to make a gate between the pines, and he and Mitch kept count as sheep squirted through, shifting pebbles from hand to hand at every twenty-five.

Last to go through was a clutch of bum lambs and a footsore ewe. "What'd you get?" asked Roger.

"You first," said Mitch.

"I got seventeen sixty-nine."

"Seventeen seventy-three."

"Split the difference, say, and we're out twenty. Any kills?"

"Broken necks and legs from falls, about eight or ten, and two prolapsed. One jumped over a log and got hung on a sharp stub." Mitch looked at me. "Any more?"

"The one I pulled out of the creek. Fell off the bank. Might be some that I missed."

"I didn't see any," Chris said, and stroked his chin, looking grave.

"I'll back-ride for strays," Mitch said. "But that seems pretty good for this rough country. Hell. There's probably a couple old ewes watching from some hidey-hole, each with a little band of bums. We'll round 'em up."

Roger led the way back and started digging in the kitchen boxes. "Where in hell are those cookies? A guy could use a little extra feed for the drive."

"I hid them." Roger and Chris both gave me bad looks.

Mitch snickered. "Wolves in the smokehouse: hang your bacon high."

Chris and Roger blushed, and I got the cookies out. Roger took ten or so, and an apple. "Oh, Mitch—don't forget," he said with his mouth full. "That ranger'll be up to inspect."

"Yeah. He and I set a date," Mitch said. Roger drove off.

Mitch waved at the truck. "We'd better ride down to the ford and brush the tire tracks away," he said. "Otherwise, every Boy Scout in northern Utah will be up here. There're some down at the lake."

"Why can't it be *Girl* Scouts?" I looked up at the sky.

"Order some up," Mitch said.

"It's not exactly something you'd pray to Jesus for," I said. But maybe the *Iliad* could do us some good. Pausing between lines, I declaimed:

> Noble Hera, highest Queen of earth's high beauty!
> Sweet-limbed Aphrodite, with your lover's mercy!
> As rain may soothe dry woods and comfort dusty ground,
> As clouds embrace these harsh and heartless peaks:

O Hera send us *Girl Scouts,* in green uniforms unbuttoned;
Girl Scouts, Aphrodite, full eighteen or older, frisky,
Dark-eyed, with bright hair unbraided,
Bearing wine in golden cups . . . and . . . and . . .

"Great big jugs . . . *of whiskey!*" Mitch finished it with a shout. Chris laughed.

"I'd settle for beer," I said. "That ol' Homer sure goes to your head."

Chris rolled his eyes and stroked the beard that was appearing on his chin. "Sounds like he got to you a little lower down," he said.

"Damn," Mitch sighed. "If that doesn't work, we'll just have to stay pure and lonesome."

"I'll settle for lonesome," I said.

AUGUST 19

The burnt forest had grown leaves of fog. We were late rising. The sheep were on good feed and close to camp, Mitch said, so we could sleep for a change. I liked the rain because it held the flies down. The day after rain brought hungry mosquitos, though. You couldn't get away from hunger, in one form or another.

The grass bowed down and shed droplets to the dark soil, and wet sage perfumed the air. I could hear the sheep from camp but didn't want to wade through wet brush, so I caught a horse. Mitch rode in his rain chaps, tubes of coated nylon that tied to his belt, and lacking those I tried to keep my horse from brushing my boots and jeans against the soaked shrubs.

We pushed the sheep across the creek, southwest, so they'd work over the ridge at last and up Bear Canyon. Then, Mitch said, we'd take the horses up and camp high, with a minimum of gear. Above the clouds, I thought.

We met the ranger riding up at a trot. His horse was a tall, sleek bay and Mitch admired it. He said it was his own, and that if he rode government stock he'd never get anywhere on time. They laughed and rode off to check where we'd grazed, as I rode back to camp. Chris told me he'd decided to explore the canyon's head. Robed in a surplus poncho, he vanished up the road.

I made a loaf of sourdough and two good, round stacks of tortillas. Cooking was comfortable now; its laws were familiar, and most things I tried turned out approximately well. Into the dutch oven still warm from baking bread, I put the beans I'd soaked all night with chunks of bacon and black pepper and a bay leaf, and heaped it with coals, then banked it with ashy dirt. Buried thus, it would cook for hours.

My legs and ankles were still stiff, but I decided to fill in a blank on my inner map: the big burn. I'd looked down into it, and gone around it, but hadn't gone through. That morning, the fog made it look mysterious and desirable.

And there was something odd about the north slope above the burn. The tent faced it, and I'd been watching it for days, morning and evening, in the rain and under clouds. It was grassy rather than bushy, and had horizontal brows of a shrub that Mitch called snowbush. Most of the vegetation grew in stripes up and down the slopes, not across, and I wanted to look at a snowbush. I took my day pack and journal with my slicker rolled around my waist and set off, with Pookie dancing figure eights, across the road and into the willow jungle.

On the north, a trickle had been dammed by beaver and backed up into sinuous pools and silty runs. There were fresh beaver tracks in the mud, and the dog sniffed them and searched the willows. I'd seen beavers in the ponds near camp but hadn't watched them quietly or for long. I liked them, but they slapped their tails and dove when I came close.

The floor of the side canyon was all flood-washed gravel, higher at the center than the edges. In the high spots, gophers and ground squirrels burrowed in the gravelly soil, churning and mixing, and bears and coyotes and badgers tried to dig them out, leaving pits. I saw coyote prints in a fresh spray of dirt, and I'd noticed bear digs under roots and in banks, with large stones prised out and roots broken. Grizzlies would leave amazing digs, I thought, but here they'd been shot and trapped and poisoned long ago. The wolves had been wiped out before the last big bears.

Wolves, it was said, had killed fifty or a hundred lambs a night in the early days. I'd heard tales of grizzlies slapping ten or twenty sheep to death, in sheer annoyance, to clear a path. The black bears and coyotes, smaller and more furtive, were holdouts against the ranchers' long campaign. Mitch had told me that Royal was hopping mad because last year President Nixon had signed an order to ban the poisoning of coyotes. Poison was easy and sneaky and cheap, and while banning it seemed out of character for Nixon, it was good news to me. There'd been tons of strychnine and 1080 spread out in Wyoming, at taxpayer expense. At times there'd been so much poison set out that you couldn't let a dog run loose.

And it was poison, more than trapping or shooting, that had killed all the wolves and grizzlies. I wondered how it would feel to share this canyon with a grizzly. While it appealed to my imagination, it would be scary, too, with mutton hanging just out back. I wouldn't sleep as well. But, given my sheep-ranching heritage, maybe I didn't deserve to.

The little creek had disappeared. I cut north and saw that it came from a spring upslope, its water threading stones and greenery: sapling aspen, monkeyflowers, balsamroot, lush grass, and sedges. I climbed up and drank, felt the soft, cool pulse on my lips. Fallen logs were locked in the rivulet and overgrown, exposed only where the water washed them bare.

The snowbush hedged both sides of the small cascade. Its leaves were cupped and leathery, with a waxy shine and three veins extending the length of each leaf. They had a fine aroma, tangy and spicy at once. *Ceanothus*, said the book; in May and June, its flowers looked like small drifts of snow. They smelled so good—spicy—that I picked some to try as a tea.

Then I sat and looked into the burn, as the sun emerged and dazzled me, glancing off the wet leaves and making the standing trunks gleam silver. I opened my journal:

> The burned forest
> is a field of swords, raised
> in a slant of sunlight
> under the blue-black wall
> of approaching storm.

Swords? That was the *Iliad* creeping in again, I thought, and started another, trying not to imitate, and trying not to reduce the whole world, in my mind, to a war:

> Between the trunks scorched bare,
> unbarked by years, grass covers
> black despair, and roots in the old, red dirt,
> spreading thick as green fur, under
> the blind back-curtain of the air.
> A burnt forest is so empty,
> white and razor-clean, so new,
> showing all past, all wounds, all pain:
> I never could explain myself
> so well, or stand so bright
> under storm.
>
> These tears, as if I, too,
> had burned.

I closed the book and looked east. The spring sent its water east, and beaver had captured it in ponds, softly couched above the main creek in varying stages of usefulness. Some were deep with fresh-cut willows in their dams and silty grooves across their beds. Between the active ponds stretched runs just deep enough to cover a beaver's back, kept open by the circulation of thick-furred bodies, by animal intent. Other ponds were partly filled with sediment and too shallow for a beaver to submerge, their dams overgrown with sedge and sapling willow. And others remained as wet depressions: beaver history. New ponds lapped over the traces of old ones. From above, I could see that the whole watery flat was sediment, trapped and held by beaver dams.

I left the spring and headed into the fire's country, toward the white trunks that leaned above a labyrinth of fallen ones. Besides grass among the fallen trees, there were flowers: fireweed, of course, and sulfur-flowered buckwheat, false Solomon's seal, cinquefoil, geranium: a few of almost every plant I'd seen. Some would multiply, and the others would give way.

It was hard to hold a course through the deadfall. The rain had left the maze of fallen trunks slick. I hopped and ropewalked, following each trunk like a compass bearing, changing direction with each step. One trunk pivoted under my weight and almost shed me, but I caught myself. The deadfall was six or seven trunks deep and offered strange geometries, like a stockyard designed by Braque. But it was a maze without gates, all tight compartments, and where the deadfall rose high the soil beneath was bare and ashy.

I was almost in the center of the burn, balancing ten feet off the ground. Pookie had a hard time getting through, making detours, taking leaps, and squeezing under logs. Maybe I'd have to turn back, I thought. I was looking back for her when my foot peeled the dead bark from a slick, wet bole, and I went down. I grabbed, missed, hit my elbow, and then the burnt forest exploded, the fallen timbers flying up into the blue.

Yellow. Tooth. *Cold.*

My head pulsed like a frog's throat, huge and wet, then tight and cold. Iron. Spit. Leg hurt. I made it onto an elbow, saw black waves, and tasted blood. Awwwww.

Pencil. *Randy! You fucker!* Lead poison. Pull it out. Crying. *What?*

Crying up there. I opened my eyes and the sky went black and confusion plummeted out of it, a wheel of hair hitting me in the chest, knocking my breath out with a sudden weight. *Wolf.* Claws raked my arm, and I sucked air, fighting, and slammed an elbow drawing back. It was real, the thrashing weight, it wrenched my trapped leg. Teeth. *Stink.*

I wrapped an arm around and slugged it. It struggled, cried, relaxed. No. *Dog.*

"Okay. Whoa up. Pookie. Good."

She licked my face, frantically. *Okay.* Where? Gray pipes. Ship. No.

I saw dots and sparkles, whether my eyes were open or closed. I focused on a stick, and it was painted at the tip with blood. I dabbed my hand on my shirt and left blood there. My left foot was caught between two trunks above my head and my ankle hurt. There was pain in the middle of my back. Broken? No. Feel toes. Wiggle. There. Breathe out.

"Good. Good dog."

She fell on top. Okay. She'd scratched my arm and it was bleeding. I couldn't get up. Maybe the dog could lead them. Lead them over the bridge. *Who?*

Down. Fires. Guns with wheels.

My head burned like phosphorus and I couldn't breathe right, tasted blood. My tongue was bitten, swelling, glued to my teeth. They'd never find me in this. Couldn't hear me yell above the sound of water, over the wind. Could the dog climb out?

Raining. *Cold.* I put the heels of my hands down and twisted my foot sideways, and it flopped onto the ground. Not broken. I was free. I managed to sit up. The back of my head felt pulpy. There was blood, but the skull felt solid. I stroked the dog and found a blunt stub with my hand and gripped. Up. I had a tilting flash, ship in a storm, and it was gone. Okay. Get out. I slotted a boot between two logs, stood straight. Okay. Hang on. Hooked a hand over the top. Pulled. Okay. Up.

The earth spun, then slowed, then stopped. Nothing broken, except the inside of my head. Things had an ugly warp and I saw bubbles when I moved. And below me the dog cried, whirling in the dark enclosure. The cribbed walls overhung the ashy trapezoid of earth.

"Pook. I can't get you out."

The trapped dog howled, then leapt and fell back in, rebounding, her breath punched out. Tears blobbed my eyes.

"O God! Pook. Hold on."

Testing each grip, I lowered myself back into the maze. She leaned on my leg and panted. I bent down and hugged her around the ribs and she kicked. As I straightened up, she flopped in my arms, pawing at the logs, and I felt her claws dig in. Then she ratcheted up out of my hold, hooked front paws over the top, tail spinning, and flipped out of sight.

I straddled a log and retched up acid gouts of air. *Cold.* I couldn't see the dog. No. There. She was waiting for me. She'd make it back. It was raining hard. I started to crawl, a busted monkey, along the wet logs. Wrong direction. There. Cottonwoods. Willows. There she is. Good dog. Stand up. Okay. Camp.

Raining. Where was my hat? The road. Camp. Tent. I threw the flap back and fell onto my sleeping bag, then squirmed inside, aching like a broken tooth.

AUGUST 20

"You all right?"

"What happened? You okay?"

"He said he was tired. 'Let me sleep,' he said."

The light filtered slowly into reach. Mitch hovered, his eyes dark and wide.

"I'm okay," I said. "I fell down in the burn."

Chris spoke. "We thought you were just being an asshole," he said. "You rolled over and cussed us out, and pulled the bag over your head. Mitch said you were just bummed out on cooking and the rain and stuff, so we left you alone."

"No. Hit my head. Up in the burn. I'm okay, I guess." My tongue was swollen, and it was hard to form the sounds. I struggled out of my bag, needing urgently to piss, and realized I still had all my clothes on, even my muddy boots. My sleeping bag was a mess. I peed next to the tent, the hot stream burning out. Pookie loped over. I saw the shapes of horses in the mist, and stroked the dog as she pressed her head against my thigh.

I looked around for my hat. "Lost my hat," I said. I had a vision of my hat, brim up in the deadfall, catching rain. That's how quickly you could lose your life. Then you were trapped in that bleak, confusing place, lying there alone as night came. Then, nothing. That image seemed more real than my being where I was.

It had been like the slap of a giant hand; I could understand how the Greeks thought a god had struck them down. I went back in to wash my face, and Chris took a wet cloth to my matted hair, and Mitch kept shining a flashlight in my eyes. It took them an hour to satisfy themselves that I was whole and sensible, more or less. Then Chris tied Pookie up to keep me company, and they went off to herd. I slept.

When she pulled the box stove over, I woke up fast. The stove was on its side, spilling ashes, and Pookie was looking at me with frightened eyes from the end of the rope, squatting to pee. The upper sections of stovepipe were dangling from the steel thimble, strewing soot. *What?*

Chris had tethered her to the flap, to one of the webbing ties. Dumb-ass trick. She'd gone around the stove and gotten three wraps on the lowest piece of pipe. I was glad the stove wasn't burning, but on second thought I wasn't glad at all. My head ached and I felt filthy. It wasn't enough to be stuck up here with the flies and the sheep, with horses running away, and dogs that chased the sheep instead of holding them, and no showers, and no women, and no beer, and now a god-damn busted head.

And my own miseries weren't all of it. I had to have a brother who did crazy shit like this, tying the dog to the tent flap. I made a noise that wasn't really a word. Pookie tried to flee, which gave the stove another flip, sending a cloud of ashes across the front of the tent.

"How long?" I yelled, but that made my head throb. I sat on the ground for a while and punched my leg a few times, but it hurt too much. I felt the hard scab on the back of my head, and the round one on my hand, and the clotted scores on my arm. I assessed the pains in my back and ankle, and the ringing emptiness in my skull. No help for it. Buck up.

So I calmed the poor dog down and turned her loose, and set the stove up, and plugged the stovepipe in, and shoveled the ashes into the firepit. Then I went to the creek and knelt, and scrubbed the ash from my hands and face. Cold water made the headache worse. I came back and the flap of the tent gaped open like a jaw. Morbid. I opened the first aid kit and took two aspirin, and then two more.

I'd better wash my sleeping bag. The sun was out, so it would dry. I didn't have to get it completely wet. Just scrub the lining, nasty with blood at the top and mud below. I got a brush and a bar of soap and carried the bag to the creek. Then I went back for a plastic basin, and dipped water and scrubbed. Most of the stuff came off. I tossed the dirty water into the willows and dipped some for a rinse. And got bitten on the hand.

I smacked the fly, and it fell to the mud and I stomped it, then danced on the spot, growling. The bite hurt worse than anything else. It was forming a whitish lump in a corona of bright red, and there was a stinger hole: not a fly but a yellowjacket. If I'd stirred up a nest, my day would really be complete.

I ran back toward camp, trailing the sleeping bag, ready to dive inside it. No swarm followed, so I crept back for the basin and the brush and soap. I dipped water to finish rinsing at the camp, and my right hand throbbed. The sting was right on the knuckle of my forefinger. I'd already taken four aspirin. I wanted to crawl into my sleeping bag, but it was wet.

I couldn't think of anything to *do.*

What? Chris burst in at a dead run, white-faced, startling me. I jumped, and my head flashed lights as he wheezed and sucked air. His hands flapped, but he couldn't talk. God!

"What now?" I asked, as he tried to get his breath.

"A bear. Big mama. On the skid road. Two cubs. They saw me. They climbed a stub. I always heard the mother. Bear was dangerous. I turned. Around. She stood up in. The brush and made a noise. Like *Whoof.*" He raised his arms, acting it out.

"Holy shit," I said. "Did she chase you? Where's the mama now?"

"Don't know. I took off. I never ran like that before. Up on the road. Or maybe she ran off. I swear to God. I didn't stop. Until I saw you here."

"Where's Mitch? If he jumps that bear, the horse'll buck him off."

"No way I'm going back up. *No way.*"

"Where's Mitch?"

"We pushed the sheep, but they wouldn't go to the top. So he rode up. I guess they smelled that bear." He shivered, head to foot. "She stood up out of the bushes. No way I'm going back up there."

"You probably spooked her as bad as she spooked you," I said. "Damn horses. Scared of the smell. Buck you off and stomp on your head. Shit! I'll go, then. I could get eaten by a bear and feel better.

Make a fire and start some dinner. I'll take Pookie. By the way, don't ever tie her to the tent flap again."

"How come?"

I resisted the urge to slug him. "It's bad luck."

I hiked the skid road one step at a time, watching the dog as she sniffed the air. We reached a saddle of old, fire-scarred Doug firs with a deep green hollow to the left, a bear's dream: punky stumps, berries, shade. Pookie made a funny circle and sniffed. The hair was standing up along her spine.

I didn't see anything except some long scuffs on the road. Chris's tracks? But I had to warn Mitch. If he got bucked off and hurt, we'd be in great shape. The road rose, then dipped through the pocket where Chris and I had gazed down off the rim, a swale of young lodgepoles and juicy grass: another lunch counter for bears. Pookie hugged my steps.

The road climbed into the big clearcut on the ridge. I didn't see the bear or Mitch. I didn't want to yell or to plunge into the jungles of Bear Canyon. *Bear* Canyon. No way!

Head up the ridge in the timber? Could bears run uphill? Probably.

I looked down and saw wild strawberries. I caught my breath, and bent and picked one, crushing it between my bruised tongue and palate. The sweetness calmed me down, so I picked a handful. The ones that looked dark and overripe had the best flavor.

Mitch rode out of the timber on a snorting, dancing horse, followed by the border collies. They barked and bristled, and Pookie snarled back at them as Mitch reined up.

"Pesky critters! I didn't think you were up and around. Where's Chris?"

"There's a mama bear," I said. "With two cubs. Chased Chris down the skid track."

"That's why the damned *borregas* wouldn't come up," he said. "I found a couple dead ewes up there. One was chewed up. And there's an old, lame ewe holed up with some bum lambs. She won't move, so I need to rope her and drag her down."

"Maybe we should just go back. With that sow and cubs around."

"Yeah." He dismounted. "I'd hate to get pitched headfirst into a stump."

"If we can move the herd up tomorrow, why not pick up the bums then instead of dragging 'em all the way down now."

"Makes sense," he said. "If we can find 'em. Show me where he saw the bear."

We dropped onto the skid trail and went around the hill. I gave his horse plenty of room, in case the bear showed up. We got to the lush pocket, and I said I thought that was the place and pointed out the footprints. Mitch got off and handed me the reins. He pointed out scrapes on a tall, rotting stub.

"The cubbies climbed up here." He walked a circle and found the big bear's tracks in the shrubs. "She took off near as fast as Chris. Look at this." There were little trenches in the duff, the marks of claws.

"She's big," I said. "Could it be a grizzly?"

"Not here. Pretty good-sized black bear, though." He walked over to the horse and pulled the saddle gun out. "Lead Tony down the road and hang on. I'll count two hundred. Then I'm gonna fire some shots. Try and run that old sow out of here."

A downdraft flicked the leaves, and Tony got a whiff of bear and seesawed as I held him by the reins. Mitch set the rifle down. "Use the lead rope. Damn reins are too short. Been stepped on so much they hardly reach the ground. Prestons need to get new ones, but they never do."

I untied the rope from the saddle string. It was already snapped to the halter, so I knotted the reins and draped them over the horn, then led the horse down the road. Mitch fired five shots. The fusillade made Tony buck, but I held on. Then Mitch came down the road and we went back to camp.

AUGUST 21

"All things are God," my brother said.

Too early in the morning for that: "So God stung me on the hand yesterday?"

"Nope," he said. "God stung *God* on the hand."

"Oh, *right*. Then God smacked God into the dirt and mashed himself flat."

"Sounds good to me."

"Inspiring. I'm really getting enlightened here."

"You could use it."

"Okay. How come you ran from the bear, if it was God?"

"God scares me." He laughed.

I stomped out of the tent. Mitch was tying Red and Pronto to trees.

"Hey, Rasputin: God's out here tying God and God up to Gods. Check it out."

"Amen," God said, with vast calm, from inside the tent.

"Don't be stupid. It's not a particularly useful way to talk about anything."

"You've been acting really weird. Since you hit your head, especially."

"Everything's *been* weird. First, I crack my skull, among other stuff. Then my own dog falls on top of me, knocks the wind out of me, and scratches the living shit out of my arm. Then I'm delirious and you guys think I'm just being Mr. Potty-Mouth. Then you tie the damn dog to the tent flap and she pulls the stove over. When I try to get cleaned up, a yellowjacket stings me on the knuckle. And now you tell me I'm God, and Everything is Everything? *Give me a fucking break.*"

"Hey. Life is suffering, asshole," Chris said.

I balled up my fists. "Check. The question is who and how much."

Mitch stifled a laugh. "Whoa up! No religion in the cook-tent. Nor dogs, neither."

"You haven't heard? They aren't *dogs.* They're gods."

"IF YOU WEREN'T SO DAMN PISSED OFF ALL THE TIME YOU'D BE A WHOLE LOT BETTER PERSON." Chris's bellow startled us both. There was a moment of silence.

"That's true," I said. "And it really pisses me off."

Mitch spread his palms. "Now, whoa up. Let's have breakfast. You two are as bad as Ray and that camptender from California."

Chris looked out from the tent. "The one that walked out after the tent blew off the cliff?"

"That's only part of it. Ray was pretty bent out of shape, and the kid told him that he should think fewer negative thoughts and things like that wouldn't happen."

"What'd Ray say to that?"

"He threatened to kill the kid. That's why he left."

After breakfast, Chris announced he was leaving. "I've got some rice and stuff. I think I'll just camp out by myself, and sit by the fire, and mellow out."

"Already? I didn't even threaten to kill you yet."

He laughed, but I could tell he didn't think it was funny.

"Help us get the sheep started," Mitch said. "We could definitely use your help." That made Chris feel better. And being a born diplomat, Mitch sent me south and Chris north, which kept us a quarter-mile apart. We got the herd up into the clearcut and over the top. And after a couple hours of screaming, cursing, and rock throwing, I felt almost human again.

Chris and I hiked back to camp, not saying much. He got his pack filled, and I gave him some fruit and cheese and two onions, and we hugged. "I'm sorry I yelled at you," I said.

"I knew that stuff about God would piss you off." He grinned. "It sure did."

We'd been doing this all our lives. I had a scar on my left eyebrow, where he'd nailed me with *Levallois to Marimba,* an inspired shot. He was my brother, after all.

I walked him to the road. We hugged again. He walked away, then stopped and waved, rounding the long curve east, a dust cloud trailing his ratty basketball shoes like a little dog.

6 ~

Bear Canyon

The scent of the bear lingered on the skid road, and the horses spooked
and hung back. But we cut across the slope, started the sheep, and
once they reached the big clearcut, rode through them. The sheep
traveled in parallel lines, like slow trains on adjacent tracks. One would
set out in hunger or thirst or restlessness, and others would fall in
behind, from a corresponding need or simply because they were sheep.
In the sun they looked like rows of dirty white houses, a city of hunger
forced off its foundations, trailing its dusty streets and mourning its way
across the earth.

That was how my thoughts tended. There were distinct pains in my
head, back, ankle, and hand, along with a general weary ache. I'd lost
my hat in the burn and hadn't gone back to find it. The last days
had demonstrated how chancy my life was in this place. I wanted to
hold still for a while, to let the aches leave me, to have some good
luck. But Mitch was unyielding: the herd must be fed. So I tried to
keep my disquiet unspoken as we set out to camp for three nights
up above.

We'd cached our heavy gear in the woods. When we packed the

camp, the horses were cranky: not ridden enough, Mitch said. I rode Pronto and led three horses: Tubby and Tom, old horses and steady, with Tony in front. Tom, the eldest, barely had a load at all, just our sleeping rolls and some oats. Mitch rode behind on Red, leading Elhon with the kitchen boxes, lashed tightly and padded with towels. They were carrying light loads with no top packs; as Mitch remembered it, the trail was rough. No one used it except Preston's herders and maybe a hunter or two. The axe was sheathed and strapped to my saddle, and the rifle to Mitch's, and our sawed-off shovel was lashed to Tony's pack, for quick trail work.

As we swung west into Bear Canyon the trail was choked with large deadfall, and we made detours into the brush and jumped our horses over down trunks. Twice I had to get off and chop fallen trees and heave them out of the way while Mitch held the jittery horses, talking to them and exhorting me to get a move on.

It wasn't as if there was more than one way up. At a narrows, the trail dropped into the jumble of the streambed, and we clattered over dry, sharp rocks until it climbed out onto the west slope, climbing under limestone fangs and talus, under a sky filling up with clouds as gray as the rock. What we followed wasn't a trail so much as an imaginary line between where we had been and where our intentions might lead us, and much of it was either washed out or covered by fresh slides.

Ahead, the canyon rose in an abrupt swoop, and water fell from a stained gray rim on the east side, spiraling off into gleaming strands, then breaking white on a heap of rock. I watched the falls as they undulated with each draft of air, as the trail switched under us, steepening to make the rim. Gaining the rim I saw that the falls came from a spring that issued from a hole in the mountain's flank, a low cave softened by moss and bracken fern. The upper bowls collected the snowmelt and rain and gave it up here, from the underworld to light, in a single, frothing burst.

The canyon was dry above, all tumbled rock like a staircase in a ruined cathedral. Farther on, Mitch had said, it was level enough to camp, but I saw no sign that such a place existed. Clouds were begin-

ning to cover the crest—this was not a place to meet a storm—and the
head of the canyon looked precipitous and entirely devoid of refuge.
The trail clung to the right side, a scrape, such as you could make by
dragging the point of a pencil across the flank of an anthill, and we
clung to the trail. Just ahead it had been cut away by a slide, and I
stopped.

"Too steep to get off," Mitch yelled. "Try to ride on through."

"I can't," I yelled back, "there's no trail and it's loose."

"I can't get around you. Elhon's plumb spooked. Do something
quick, or we'll wreck."

I chose a way and checked my preparations, such as they were: reins
in the left hand, lead rope in the right. If a packhorse slipped off, the
jerk would spin me toward the wall, not out into space. No loops in the
lead rope. Okay. I eased my boots back in the stirrups, in case I had to
bail off. *Okay.* I urged Pronto forward.

She balked, and then bolted. The lead rope snapped taut in my hand
as she hit the landslide a little higher than the trail, front feet digging
and back feet skidding down. No. *Jump,* I thought, and then she was
over, her hind feet kicking rocks off into the deep as she scrambled
onto the trail. I heard Mitch yell and reined her up, giving slack for
Tony, hoping he wouldn't crash into us if he jumped, which he did, and
as his shoulder hit Pronto his nose almost touched my back. She stumbled and then caught her balance, and I let out the breath I'd been
holding.

Tubby managed to pick her way over, giving Tom enough slack to do
the same: the old horses took a higher line across the slide and came
without skidding. My horses were all across, and still on the trail. The
colt skipped across easily, and Pookie followed, and I settled my weight
into the cantle and breathed in again.

But I saw that our passage had loosened the rock and dirt in the
scoop. Any semblance to a trail was gone.

"I don't know about this," Mitch called. He shifted his weight in the
saddle. Red stood firm, but Elhon was dancing at the limit of her rope,
eyes white and rolling. "A big bunch slid off. Can you tie up the horses
and shovel it out?"

"I'll give it a shot." I heeled Pronto on past a single fir that curved out under the trail and hung its needles over the drop. A hundred yards on, the slope eased into patchy firs. "Yeah," I yelled. "Got it. Back in two shakes." I slid off Pronto, careful not to upset her balance, and tied her up short to a tree above the trail. Then I scrambled above her and untied Tony's lead and tethered him. As I pulled the shovel from under the hitch, I could hear Mitch's "Whoa, whoa up, whoa."

Planting my boots in the steep, loose gravel, I started digging to the hard ground beneath. Rocks rattled down into the canyon, skipping in mad curves, tearing through brush and whacking the boulders. At the noise Elhon threw back, snapping the rope tight. Mitch cursed and jerked his boot out of the stirrup and then bailed off toward the slope. His left boot strummed the taut lead. At that, Elhon sat down in the trail, hauling Red's front hooves off the ground.

Still gripping the reins, Mitch tried to stand on the loose rock as the red horse struggled, whipping his head. The jerk of the reins pulled Mitch off his feet. With a startled yelp he slid down on his back under the horse. Red gave a desperate hop, hooves pounding the trail as Mitch in a cloud of dust rolled onto his knees and scrabbled up, limbs milling, to clutch at a bush.

Panicked, Red dashed straight toward me, jerking Elhon to her feet. I plunged the shovel in and paddled my way straight up as the red horse charged just below me, hauling the gold one. Red made it across, drawing himself onto the trail with a leap. But Elhon's hind feet went over the edge. As Red passed the lone fir, the lead rope sang tight and he flipped, his front hooves swimming. Both horses fell.

And stopped. I could see them falling, end over end, down onto the rocks. But my brain played me a trick. I blinked, and they were hung in space, thrashing at the ends of the lead rope as it sawed a green gouge in the bark of the fir.

I scrambled over, using the shovel like an ice axe. Mitch moved across more slowly, flinching each time a horse kicked or heaved. If either horse got back onto the trail, I realized, it could knock us off.

Two turns of the lead were locked around the saddle horn. Red hung there with space between his withers and the saddle. If the cinch broke, he would fall. Elhon was stretched hard on one flank, iron shoes flashing as she flailed, suspended by her head with the halter wringing the end of her nose. She couldn't breathe.

"Don't move," Mitch said, " 'til we get this worked out." He gripped Red's part of the rope and pulled, but horses are built to go forward or back, not straight up. The horse dug and got his back legs firm, but the rope sawed over the tree and Elhon slipped farther down, breath whistling. Her position was hopeless: strangle or fall.

"Shit! Get ready to run," Mitch said, and light flashed in his hand. I looked up from the horse as he cut the rope. He scrambled straight up from the trail. I was too horrified to move.

Elhon slid on her side, caught a hoof, and then flipped out into the air, thirty feet at a turn, flying in a cloud of gravel, slamming down, bouncing up, and then crashing on her back into the dry streambed. Red hooked his right front hoof on a rock, clung, and then lurched onto the trail, where he stood too dazed to move. Mitch slipped down and caught his reins, and laid a hand on the horse's neck as Red heaved, nostrils distended, blowing white droplets into the air.

Mitch looked down, then at me. Elhon lay on her side, bone-still. "Is she dead?"

"I can't tell," I said.

We stood for what seemed like an hour without words. Then she pawed the air, feebly, one front hoof describing a slow arc. She lifted her head and then let it fall. Again. Then she rolled onto her feet, and stood up in the stream of shattered rock. She trembled, end to end, but that was all. She didn't look up, or call out to the other horses.

"I'll get Red to safe ground," Mitch said. "Look at these damn reins—if they weren't busted off short, I could've held on to the horse and none of this would've happened." The cut lead rope still hung from the saddle horn. I stared at the dallies wrapped hard around the horn, and Mitch caught my look, but neither of us said a word. He led Red up the trail and tied him to a tree, then came back.

"I'd better go see about Elhon," he said.

"I'll go." I started down the trail.

"Want the rifle?"

"No. If it's bad, you can climb down. Do we have to come back this way to get out?"

"Yeah," he said. "Unless horses can fly."

"Dig a trail across this mess, then." I handed him the shovel.

"Wait—you'll need this." He opened his saddlebag and came up with a spare lead rope.

I had to walk back a few hundred yards before I could see a way down to the streambed that I could lead a horse back up. I walked up the streambed toward the big horse. She faced away, shaking at intervals but otherwise unresponsive. I didn't want to startle her and get run down, and there wasn't much room to dodge, so I spoke as I got close. Uphill in the narrow defile, the gold horse looked huge.

I scrambled around a boulder and came abreast as she shuddered again. "Hey big girl. Okay? Okay?" I stretched out my hand and caught the frayed end of rope. She cocked an eye at me and continued to shiver. I put a hand on her neck. It was chilled with sweat. As I stroked, the shivering stopped. There was blood on the rocks in the streambed, and blood was dripping from a score along her ribs, and her legs were badly scraped but they looked straight and true, and her weight was on all four. Good sign. I gazed up at the path of her fall, where newly exposed dirt showed dark at points of impact. She ought to be broken in half.

"Mitch—I think she's okay. She's in shock, but her legs are all right. I'll try to turn her around. Okay?"

"Good deal. I'll keep an eye out." I could see that he'd traded the shovel for the rifle, which put ice up my spine. He was prepared to shoot the horse if she looked about to run me down. "What about the load?" he yelled.

The britchen strap was dangling loose, but that could be fixed. I checked the kitchen boxes. "Packs are still snug. Can't believe it. The hitch is even tight." I rubbed her neck under her mane, and held my other hand where she could sniff it, and that seemed to calm her down. She could move, I thought, but she believed that she'd fall if she did. I'd have to lead her forward, so she'd trust her feet again. I stroked and cooed and put a hand down and pulled at her front leg, ready to jump away. She took a faltering step, breathed hard, then shivered. I gently pulled the lead, and she took another.

"See? It's solid, big honey. We're okay."

I turned her around slowly and we started down the streambed. We're all still alive, I thought. A few minutes ago, that didn't seem possible. Mitch yelled that he was moving the other horses up the trail, and disappeared. Pookie was picking her way down the slope. Dammit. I tried to shoo her off and she wouldn't go. But Elhon barely noticed the dog. With coaxing and resting, it took a half hour to get her up to the trail, and then I had to lead her down it to find a spot wide enough to turn her around.

Mitch had done a good job on the slide. You could ride a bike across it. I'd expected to fight with the big horse, but she went steadily across, as if in a trance, and then halted on the far side for a long spell of shivering. Mitch looked the big horse over and checked her load. "Have to treat those cuts. Might be some stuff broken in the boxes, but we can wait to find that out. I guess you just got your horse-packing diploma."

"I can think of better ways," I said. I knotted the britchen together with parachute cord, enough to get us up the trail. I rode Pronto and led Elhon while he took the other horses.

The storm was on us. Lightning burned a ragged contour into a cloud, and the wind was unbearable in the pines. The driven rain racketed on my bare head and soaked through my woolen coat and laid cold hands on me. I saw the loose rocks and low limbs, and made the right moves, but nothing registered. I was in the same state of ambulatory shock as the big horse.

The world tilted over on a hard slant. Rocks split and rolled underfoot. Trees groaned and seemed about to topple. What held it all together? As we climbed, the clouds dropped toward our heads, and the wind made a low vibration over the ridge. It seemed as if we would never find a level place again. We switched back to the north and west and finally crossed a saddle, and the angle eased. There were green sinks and gulleys, and high knolls crowned with limber pines, and at last a spot just flat enough to camp.

∼

The stove gave its dependable heat, enough to center us in the whirl of storm. Nothing had broken in the kitchen boxes. Beans were heating and I opened a can of peaches. I sat on a box pannier and riveted a leather strap into the burst britchen, trimming the torn leather, drilling holes with the awl on my pocketknife, and tapping the copper harness rivets snug with the heel of the axehead. To shelter the dogs we'd strung a pack cover over a downed pine next to the tent, and I could hear them crunching their food and growling as they jostled, trying to avoid the drips. I dipped thick amber dubbing out of a tin and rubbed it in, feeling it melt into the leather.

Mitch went out to check the horses and came in muttering about the lack of feed. It had looked green from the ridge to the east, but there wasn't as much here as he'd thought. But the sheep were started. Even with the storm they'd want to come up, so we'd hurry them around the leafy pockets and then push them down and cross them above the burn. "I guess the horses will stick," he said, "with Tubby on picket. Tom's dead on his feet. And Elhon's not going anywhere. Hope that wound stuff does the trick."

"She didn't even flinch when you put it on."

"Shock. She's strong, but she'll never be a saddle horse."

"I rode her once, when you were tepeed out. A weasel ran under her feet and she bucked right off the trail. I didn't tell you."

"I remember," he said. "You looked funny around the eyes. We've been lucky so far."

"I'm sort of spooked. Knocked myself out, and now this. Things don't seem real."

"Yeah. Bad luck. A streak. We'll have to watch things close."

"Too bad the rope locked up on your saddle horn."

He gave me a sidewise look. "It didn't. Elhon was balking so bad I thought she was going to dislocate my shoulder. So I got mad and I dallied up."

I nodded. "Yeah. I've taken some wraps when you weren't looking. Won't do it again."

"They call it a dead man's hitch."

That closed off talk. We sat in the candlelight, each in a world apart, listening to the wind.

I was numb. We were a long way out, and it would be a longer one to get back. I fed the fire and left the stove door open for light. I can't remember the taste of food, but only sounds: wind and rain on the tent, and horse bells near camp. And how the flames, like gold birds, softly beat against the walls of the iron box.

AUGUST 22

We descended on foot and got the sheep up without a struggle. They climbed eagerly, rounding the ridge and spreading out in the high pockets where the summer flowers had gone to seed and the dense-grown leaves of bluebell and sunflower showed the faintest yellow. The high country was changing its green for pale gold.

The rain had stopped, but there was thick mist below in Bear Canyon. I had to see if we could get down some other way besides the trail, so I ranged the contours and was disappointed. The ways I found were at least as awful as the canyon trail, and most were worse. On the likeliest one we'd have to jump each horse from a rock shelf onto loose scree just above a cliff band. There were more outcrops below. That was why the trail existed: it was the easiest way.

I'd never felt so cut off, at the end of a faint and risky trail, ringed by gaunt peaks, where sparse green yielded up to stone and space. And my sense of cause and effect had run wild: a misstep in the tent, or anywhere, would cause me to fall much later in a dangerous place, because a pattern had been laid. I saw omens everywhere: a lightning-split pine, deer bones clutched in the rocks, claw marks on a bleached stump. Fear colored the day. That morning as I'd climbed a narrow ridge, I imagined myself having to descend in the dark, or after hard rain, or during a snowstorm. Each step had been a distinct and perilous effort.

This wasn't a story. If Mitch had taken a hoof in his guts, and the fleeing horse had shouldered me off the edge, it would have been a long time before anyone came to look for us. And I could imagine, too well, how I would groan awake, and call, to no answer. And then lie there crumpled in the rocks as it began to rain. I could feel those rocks, and that rain.

We would become nothing. And maybe the dogs would nose our empty faces and howl into the gathering dark. And maybe the horses would stay ticd to trees. Night. Day. Night. Day. Under the racing clouds, the ravens would circle and descend.

And then it would become a story, of broken bodies and starved horses, a tale to draw shudders around night fires and haunt the sleep of the living. It could all still happen.

Nothing meant what it had, before. People and circumstance hold us in our accustomed shapes, but all that was gone. Whatever stands between us and the rock, between our souls and raw, speechless event, that was what I had suddenly lost.

Trees fall, streams flood, bears bite: the world is dangerous.

And I felt a profound terror, in which dread and omen were the first two holds I could grasp. This may be romanticized by those who have not felt it, or feel it only slightly. With a full belly, on a marked trail, we call it *the wild*. But it comes from an act of the mind, trying to accord with the land's own pulse. Fear is the fruit of self-consciousness. If the world must have a point, if it must *mean* in order to *be*, then fear is the cost.

What do you do when fear wears your body like a suit of clothes?

I stood and looked at the country, immense under cloud. There was nothing in it.

I went into the tent and got my book, and sat in the pine duff and opened to the *Odyssey*.

> Sing in me, Muse, and through me tell the story
> of that man skilled in all ways of contending,
> the wanderer, harried for years on end,
> after he plundered the stronghold
> on the proud height of Troy.

Soon I was deep in the poem. As I read, I could feel my bones settling in their proper places. As varying depths of cloud flowed over, the light grew and then receded. An hour had passed, by the cloudy sun, when I set the book down.

I had to do what I could do. I got up and walked to the stove, and felt suddenly brittle. So I set the book on the kitchen box, where I could reach it, which gave me a curious calm. I built a fire in the stove and smelled the smoke. I held a bowl between my hands until it warmed. Water, dry milk, eggs, oil, vanilla. I realized I was saying the name of each thing as I added it. *Flour, brown sugar, soda, salt.* I greased the tin and set it aside, then stirred the batter, feeling the bubbles form, dumb chemical reaction, and the sudden ease in the going of the wooden spoon.

There were red currants on a bush outside, not quite ripe, but I picked a handful and mixed them in. The oven door creaked as I put the pan inside. Then I picked up the book again.

Mitch slung his day pack down.

"Muffins. I love that smell," he said. He dropped a piece of wood next to the stack, and I reached over to put it into the stove. It felt heavy.

"Don't. It's pitch."

"Pitch?"

"Pitchwood. These old limber pines die on their feet, and the sap drains down to the roots. The tree rots away, but the pitch keeps the roots sound. Shave it and smell."

The resinous odor rose, sharp and clean. Mitch filled a mug with water and picked up a broad shaving, and we watched it float, turning in a circle. After a minute, he picked it out; the water formed beads on it.

"Water can't soak in, so it always catches fire." He shook the drops off and then opened the stove door and touched it to the fire. It flared, and he held it between his face and mine. I could see black resin bubbling around the base of the flame.

The shaving burned steadily, like a candle, the flame vaporizing the pitch before it consumed the wood. "It's wasted as stove wood. If you use whole chunks in the stove, you can burn a hole in the top, but it's the best kindling in the universe." It gave off a black, sooty smoke. "It's good to carry a piece in your saddlebag," he said. "These ridges where the big, old limber pines grow are the best spots to find it."

"I'll have to hunt some up," I said. I slid the muffins out, and the currants were tart and unpredictable in the warm, sweet matrix as we ate them, with midday coffee.

Between mouthfuls, Mitch told me a story. Last year he had been climbing with his brother Don, in Little Cottonwood Canyon above Salt Lake City. Donnie was a well-known climber, with ascents of big peaks in Alaska, and was taller than Mitch, lanky, and fearless in a joyful way. They'd finished a hard climb and had to traverse a tilted slab to reach the first rappel. The slab wasn't steep, but it was exposed: it gave along the entire edge to what climbers call "big air."

"We weren't roped. Donnie walked across like it was no big deal. I didn't like the exposure, and I started across like a land-crab, as low as I could get, and as far away from the edge.

"Donnie laughed. I looked up and he was hopping back toward me on one foot. He passed between me and the edge, hopped over to the belay ledge, and then turned and hopped across again. On the other foot."

Mitch sighed. "I was really mad, but then I saw he wasn't making fun of me. He was showing me that it was a lot harder to fall off than it seemed. And it was better to just walk across. So I stood up and walked across. And it wasn't a big deal anymore."

"What sounds good for dinner?" I said, opening the book again.

AUGUST 23

> I saw the men of Sidon and Arabia
> and Libya, too, where lambs are horned at birth.
> In every year they have three lambing seasons,
> so no man, chief or shepherd, ever goes
> hungry for want of mutton, cheese, or milk—
> all year at milking time there are fresh ewes.

"I didn't know that was about sheep," Mitch said.

"What? The *Odyssey*? It's not."

"That part sure was. And you're reading it out loud."

"Sorry. I'll start the stove."

"Too damn early. Go to sleep."

I blew the candle out and got into my bag, but couldn't sleep. Still dark. How you gain strength. I could hear Mitch's clock. There's always more to be lost. A thin moon obscured by clouds, and by canvas. A one-eyed man can still lose the other eye. How long can night last? Death, because it ties your body to the landscape. Why doesn't it get light?

Mitch rolled in his quilts. "Do you want to get up and eat?" I said.

"Shut up and sleep while you can. They won't climb scree to the top. And they won't drop off unless we push them. Warren used to feed these bowls. That's how I knew about it. Pancho never tried to come up here. Now I see why."

"I'll start the coffee and check the horses."

"Don't make noise. I'm sleeping in."

Mitch sauntered off an hour after dawn, whistling and throwing sticks for the sheepdogs. I didn't want to go anyplace. When Pookie followed him, I called her back. I kept the fire going in the stove and read on:

> . . . a man whose bones are rotting somewhere now,
> white in the rain on dark earth where they lie
> or tumbling in the groundswell of the sea.

It could still happen. Would. A raven squawked and I started.

Mitch came back, ate, and walked away.

It began to rain.

First, the ewe and the broken lamb, and blood on my hands. Then, the bear, dead and skinned in a field of flowers. The black pelt hanging from a limb. The gold horse and the weasel. The deadwood cage and the rain. Two horses hung from a lonely tree. The density of things. Points and edges.

More yellow in the leaves than yesterday.

Pitch.

I got my pack and called the dog. Some old wood was only dead and some was pitch, holding the secret, the gift of fire. It was easy to tell. You could cut into it and smell what was real. I found it, dark and heavy, full of possibility. One good piece. Two. Four. The straps of my pack tugged at my collarbones. Six. Twelve.

Fire. Fire when I wished for fire.

And my eye would catch a glint, a pebble or a leaf, or even something ominous, like a cracked tooth fallen from a skull, and sense virtue in it, sense protection. And I'd carry it, until the next thing caught my eye.

Time was no longer straight, like a wire, but a series of unswimmable waves. Each one rolled over and buried me in its salty mass. I saw a currant leaf, yellow-edged, pasted to a rock by the rain. A fresh-fallen limber cone. A tiny red pebble. Too much, and not enough. Rain.

"Bear. Killed a lamb. Right over there." He was out of breath, had come running into the camp. He pulled the rifle from its sheath and the box of shells from the kitchen pannier, and they clinked into his vest pocket and he ran back toward the sheep.

Now I can smell blood, like an animal. There's the smell of the wet wool, and of the crushed herbs under our feet, and the dogs, and of Mitch, and my own smell. And blood. Dead lamb in the rain. So sad. Blood runs out of the mouth, out of the open throat. Into a boot print. Not the bear. He cut the throat. I circle away, and the smell of blood follows.

"Never even had a shot. It's not that sow with the cubs. Looks like a young one. Pure black pelt. Maybe we should night-herd." He looked at me as if I was supposed to say something.

"Okay. Sounds good."

"We could butcher this one for camp meat. It's fresh."

"Sounds good."

"Just hindquarters. The front looks bloodshot."

"Okay."

"You have a knife." He was looking at me. I was going to cut off the legs.

I took hold of the leg and rolled the thing over on its back. Every foul word I knew leapt out of my mouth.

"Can't you do anything without swearing?"

I kept up the stream of curses, unable to stop as I made the first cuts and peeled the skin back.

"Things couldn't get much worse, huh?" I could feel his eyes.

Wet wool. Blood. Leaves squeaked under my boots as I moved, and mud rose between. I cut through the muscle, then severed the white tendons at the joint of the hip. I twisted the leg and it came off and I set it on the peeled-back hide. Rain beaded on the silky muscle sheath, on flesh which had never seen light before. The hoof looked strange, attached to meat.

"They can always get worse," I said.

"You don't have to like it. But you can keep your damn mouth shut." Mitch stood with a ferocious glower, the rifle under one arm.

I looked him in the face. "Do you get off, watching this?"

The rain seemed to stop.

He threw me an infuriated look and stalked toward the camp.

I hung the quarters in a pine. I cooked the meat, but didn't eat it. I finished off the muffins, and kept the fire hot in the stove, and read the *Odyssey*. Mitch buried his face in Joe Back. At close quarters, avoidance is an art.

He took the battery lantern and the gun, and left to night-herd. I read on and let the stove go out. The candle diminished itself to a glossy pool in a white cup. The wax burned my fingertip, and under my fingernail, and then cooled. Dark. I got into my bag.

Bear tracks. The heart-shaped prints of the lamb. A stream of blood fills each of the tracks in turn, spills, and flows toward the next. I step back and leave a deep print, and the blood finds it. The gouge of the heel grows deeper, and blood fills the hollow. They can smell it. They're coming. One muddy-faced with his wounds showing through a torn uniform. And her with long hair, before the wreck, and the touch of it in the smoke. And then black patent shoes with bows, dry ivory lace, and tiny white hairs at the cheekbone. They kneel, all three, and raise their faces. Their mouths open and close, but no words come out.

They can't speak because they don't breathe.

The ashes in the stove are faintly warm, like a dry cloud in my palm. I pour them over my head. So much needs mourning. I go out naked to the rain. So cold. The ashes sting my eyes. And it takes so long to wash away.

Moon in the tent. Rifle barrel. *No.*

"Your turn." It was Mitch with the lantern.

"My turn for what?"

"Night guard. I need some sleep. You watch till dawn."

I'm against a tree, crosslegged, my dog asleep, her head on my thigh. The rifle leans on the other side. It's heavy, for a thing so long and thin. If a bear comes, I'll yell, run toward it, throw rocks, and guard the sheep with all I have, except the power of death.

The clouds have shapes, like bodies, soft and light. Now they open in the west. Now the moon is like a white hand, palm down, pouring darkness on the earth.

Life is all we have. And a bear can kill so easily.

I'm not a bear.

It's a lonely thing to know.

AUGUST 24

I came in at dawn, when it was too cold to sit and walking no longer kept me warm. I slipped the rifle into its sheath and started a fire, and poured grounds over water in the coffeepot. Mitch woke and fumbled into his clothes. We didn't talk. He took the rifle and left. I fumbled out of my clothes and got into my sleeping bag.

I lay there on the edge of sleep, as light rose up around the tent. Mea culpa: I am lazy and difficult, mean and resentful, especially in the grip of misery or deprivation or fear. I say ugly things. Mitch dislikes me: more my doing than his. One of me could not stand another.

And I fall short. That's clear. He's better somehow, whether he learned it or is that way without thinking. He does his duty, I thought. He's tough and clever. He knows how to take a risk gracefully, and how to laugh.

We may not come out of this friends, I thought, but he's the finest companion I've ever had. Even though our partnership is enforced by our situation, it isn't forced in him. He listens intently and won't be distracted by flies or hunger, or even his own thoughts. And he responds. It may be with a reflective judgment, or a joke, or a spur-of-the-moment fandango. But he gives as much as he gets, or more, and that's rare.

But I have this life to live, alone. It's hard. How can you stop your thoughts? Even when you sleep, you dream. And then I slept, and don't remember what I dreamed.

Mitch and I were like two particles with the same charge, and it was time to let him have the camp. There were the two quarters of lamb, hanging from a pine. The day was cool, so I didn't wrap it and stow it next to the ground, but I thought of the bear and pulled the rope to raise it. I washed potatoes and set them on the kitchen box, and took an apple for myself, and left a note: *Took a hike, north and west. Don't wait for me.*

It took an effort for me to leave the camp, but right away it felt better to move than to sit and brood. With Pookie for company I walked west, looking back to see the sheep bedded on the rocky slopes. Then we passed under the eave of the forest, thick spruce and fir, where the rain's moisture lingered and the trees breathed a clean, resinous scent. Beyond the brushy margin the forest floor was open, except where rock outcroppings fostered currants and shrub juniper, and gave me the sense of both enclosure and space.

The gallery forest ended abruptly in a slide, recent enough that a line could be drawn between vegetation and bare, shattered rock. The gray swath extended to the top of a spur. An outcrop of solid limestone had dammed the landslide at the east end, but to the west it spilled farther down. There were pinnacles below and a few big pines standing crookedly among heaped boulders, which formed a rough trench across the slope. One whole side of the mountain had fallen, all at once: a quick gust of fear chilled me. The earth was filled with fire, they said, and the continents floated like chips on the molten, invisible currents. I knelt on the needled ground and then brushed away the needles and put my ear to the soil. I don't know what I thought I'd hear, rumblings or cracks, but instead there was a mineral silence.

I looked around at the rocks that would fall, at the trees that would topple or burn, and I was the only thing afraid. So I stood up again and picked my way across, stopping to watch the dog make her way through the rocks. Her buff-and-black fur was beautiful against the unmoving grays.

We crossed the last shaky runs of talus and entered the forest again, big trees in deep soil. The woods opened, and there was a sloping run of bluebells and sunflowers, then another belt of conifers. The slope leveled for a hundred yards, then formed a curving, flat-topped dike, and I saw the lake.

It was the shape of an egg. The lake had once spilled to the east through a gentle notch, but it had been centuries since it was high enough to overflow. The old channel made a clear path to the water, except for a big, flat-faced boulder that lay precisely in its center, higher than my head. There were other boulders tumbled around the shore to the left, cracked off the cliff above, but none even half so large as this. I put my right hand on its flank. Cold and finely abrasive. I felt as if there should be something chiseled in it, some sign. But there was no carving, no red oxide, not even a scrawl in charcoal. I put my ear to the rock: silence. The world wasn't lost, could never be lost, but I could lose my way.

And then I hear a faint rush, and a ringing that seems to come from inside the rock, hear my own blood following the paths of my body, around and around. And I straighten up and walk around the gray boulder, tapping it with my right hand, *skiff, skiff, skiff, skiff.* Four faces, each with a distinct edge.

I go around again, still touching the rock. I feel something waiting inside it. Some animal I've never seen.

Again. *Skiff. Brush. Touch. Tag.* There are little points on the surface, like the ones that form when you raise a roller quickly from fresh paint, arrested in space. They hurt.

Again. This is where I began. The dog is sitting on her haunches, head cocked, watching me, so I stop and lean on the rock. Then I take my hand away. There's a spot of fresh blood on the rock, and a matching one in my palm. I watch it drying.

The chill is gone. I'm cool, but terribly thirsty. I forgot to bring a canteen. No, it's in the pack, but I don't want a drink. Apple. No, wait. I walk down to the edge of the lake. The water's not clear. It has a fine, green murk that turns the low sun back. The bottom's bedded in sediment fine enough to seal the cracks. There's bare mud at the water's edge, with angular cobbles like a shattered pavement up to the high-water line. I remember this lake, the green porcelain color. I saw it from the ridge, when my brother and I looked down into the Double Heart. And I wanted to be here.

Along the shore the slope is gentle. To swim I'd have to wade a long way out, raising clouds of silt. But I don't want to swim. I squat and put my right hand into the silt. It's soft, like liquid ash. And black, under the tan surface, like powdered iron. I swirl my hand in the lake and then stand and let the water drip back into it, and then start around.

There's almost a path. It weaves through the fallen boulders under the cliff. Through the willows at the inlet, where a thread of water comes down and unravels in a little delta. Across the west on wet sand, stippled by raindrops in endlessly overlapping rings, like a map of time. Across a shallow gully, where spring snowmelt flows, among dark rushes quilled up through the fresh silt. Along the stone dike, gray, black, tan, each color laid in the water's curve. And back to the rock where I started out.

I decide to circle the lake again. It feels as if something is unwinding, as if some constricting hurt, like barbed wire around a bare arm, is being uncoiled. And at the same time as if something else is being gathered, strong like new rope in a gleaming spiral around a belaying pin: stress finding a center, a point for the wind to pull.

Then again. I make it a game. The dog follows and I skip. My hands fly up and she leaps into the air. I lower them and she dashes ahead on the wet sand. I greet the big gray rock like an old companion.

And one time more, as I think of my grandfather Tork winding his gold pocket watch, I know what I'll see, but there's always something else: How water makes its own sky, then loses it to the wind. How a furtive brown bird is submerged in the willows. How reflected pines all point to the center of the lake. How a deer skull, aged fine as ivory, trails sand from an empty eye.

I touch the rock. Then I sit with my back against it, facing the lake. I close my eyes and see red circles, innumerable, like raindrops in a pond, and feel distant heat on my skin. I open my eyes and the lake is a silver disc in the low sun. I find the water in my pack and drink.

And take out the apple and bite into it: cold.

Cold and sweet.

7 ～

Murphy Lake

Between Bear Canyon and the Double Heart the high bowls were picked bare. The sheep started down almost on their own, and we packed the high camp. Coming down the canyon seemed to take no time at all, and except for my first breath-stealing look, after we crossed the saddle, it didn't come close to my apprehensions. It wasn't the Gates of Hell but only a canyon, steep and narrow, and full of hazard, which it had a perfect right to be.

I rode Red this time, and Mitch rode Tony. Elhon stopped at the dug-out section of trail but came across without a fight. We rode to our cache by the beaver ponds, and turned the pack string loose, and let our saddle horses drag their lead ropes as they grazed. As we repacked the panniers, Mitch said the next camp should be close to Murphy Lake. Cassandra was coming soon, and I wanted a semiprivate place to camp. I mentioned the presence of Boy Scouts, fishermen, and *turistas*. On my coffee quest, I'd seen a spot across the creek, at the end of the barely visible track that started above the ford. Why not take a look? The packhorses needed to fill their bellies before we moved camp, and it would be nice to ride without dragging them around.

We caught our horses and trotted off toward the narrows. Below where the beaver ponds drained into the main creek, the canyon was choked on the north by a fan of debris and on the south by a tangle of pine trunks and jagged blocks spilling from an avalanche track. The road held the slope uneasily, southwest of the stream. We came to the ford and I pointed out the side road, but Mitch wanted to see the old camp first, so we rode on. Just above Murphy Lake, he reined up a two-track that wandered east through big pines and crossed a tiny stream.

"This is the usual spot. Good water and a meadow for the horses not far off. But it's close to the lake. You can almost see it through the woods."

"The Boy Scouts'll be all over us."

"Yeah. That's true.. What about those Girl Scouts?"

"Wrong goddesses, I guess. Next time I'll try Athena or Artemis. Besides, with Cassy here, Girl Scouts would be superfluous."

"Yeah. For you, maybe. But my folks are driving up, too, so we have to be on some kind of road. Let's ford the creek and look at your ideal spot."

There was a good ford, and a thick screen of willows and brush along the creek. We rode through it, up onto the stream terrace and along the edge of open lodgepole woods. "Anyplace in here," I said. "Prime residential sites, on Barely Visible Road."

"Hah! The Boy Scouts'll have to wade the crick," he said. "I'll give you that."

"They'll be too bloated on hot dogs and orange pop."

"And it's right below the pass to North Murphy. We take the sheep right up there."

"A road, of sorts. Firewood. Running water. Privacy. Under the pass. What else?"

"Roger might not be able to find us. But we can always leave a note in a plastic bag at the old place. Okay. Let's bring the gear."

Our horses were peevish and unruly. Tony kept breaking into a trot, and Mitch kept reining him in. Then Red started doing the same. Then Red nipped at Tony and got kicked in return. As we came abreast of the ford both horses were waltzing and juggling their bits. "They need a good run," Mitch said. He slacked rein and drove forward with his hips, and Tony went into a stretched-out canter.

"Red. Follow that cab." He didn't need to be pushed. The big horse broke straight into a run, and I had to grab the horn. Letting it go, I rolled forward in the stirrups, flexing my knees, getting my weight over his glossy shoulders, and liking the clatter of hooves and the rush of air.

We seemed to fly, and the world drew out into long streaks of color. The body of the horse seemed to resound until the beat was no longer just hoof to earth but a drumming in my spine, a twofold presence bursting through the air.

Hearing us come up, Tony put on speed and Red strained to catch him. The two horses were racing, as if they had urged us into this. Red had the longer stride, and we passed on a straightaway, then were caught and passed where the road swerved up a hill through pines. I saw Mitch's grin as he thundered by, flipping the reins.

We flew around the last long curve, the road streaming underneath, the horses pounding an arm's length apart toward the bright ponds. A beaver slapped the water and dove. Startled, Red lost his stride, and Tony spurted away as dark-maned heads sprang up from the willows. Tubby bugled, and both geldings answered as we gathered rein, slowing to a canter, then a dancing trot, and splashing through the spring flow that puddled across the road.

"We win," Mitch crowed. "You long-legged bastards just can't keep up."

"Youth craves noise and speed," I said.

"Hah! I'll take speed," Mitch said. "You've got the other part nailed down."

He helped pack up and then rode west to check on the sheep. The right fork was like a big rock-walled pen, and there was leafy stuff in the rockslides, good sheep forage, so we could let them work up toward the steep foreslope under the Double Heart. He'd tie up at the edge of the burn and hike, if he couldn't ride around it. I'd take the pack string down and put up the tent. Then, I'd ride back up. But he didn't think he'd need much help.

Visitors would see this camp. It had to be good. I swept branches
and litter away, and stretched the tent till each corner was a crisp right
angle, then dug a firepit and edged it with clean stone. Instead of
stomping on branches or breaking them over stumps, I actually sawed
firewood and split it, and drove four stakes to keep the woodpile neat.
As shadows climbed the facing slope, Mitch rode in. He whistled: "It
looks like that drawing in Joe Back's book: 'A Good Camp.' Guess what
I found."

"A Girl Scout?"

"No, your hat." He unbuckled his saddlebag. It was flattened and
moist, but there weren't any holes. "A critter set up housekeeping underneath: pack rat or something. But it smells okay."

And it did.

AUGUST 26

Clear and hot. Mitch rode south to look for strays, and I picketed Tom
in the shade and climbed up to the little spring and drank. Then Pookie
and I contoured along the north slope above the burn, looking down on
the sheep. They were so absorbed in the burn's new growth that they
scarcely moved as we passed. How would it be if they liked us? If we
had names for them? But they were too many for that.

The sheep hadn't moved far, but I walked beyond the last ones to be
sure. Above the burn the canyon floor was covered in bluebells,
raspberries, geranium, thimbleberry, and cow parsnip, plants that hid
the treacherous earth. I stepped into holes and swiveled on unseen
branches, as the dog swam through the broken shadows, harvesting
burrs with her coat.

At the edge of the big rockslide we turned back. The herd was already bedded in patches of shade. They seemed content, so I sat on the
slope and finished the *Odyssey*.

There was something about it that went with the way we lived up
here: not just the fact that the Greeks were basically cowboys and
sheepherders, but the way the story moved. Our outfit, pack string and

tent, was our ship in this rocky ocean, and each new camp was an island.

The monsters were gorgeous, and I liked Odysseus for his sharp-eyed, sneaky tactics. But when the hero came home, I liked him less, and when he slaughtered the suitors and hung the slave women, it made me sick. How could he ever live in that bloodstained house again? Scrubbing might erase the blood, but how could his memory ever be cleansed?

And he didn't settle in. He lit out. At the end he was hiding out at a cow camp with his dad Laertes and his son Telemakhos, waiting for the bereaved relations to come and have their turn at revenge. By then even Athena was sick of it, and she asked Zeus:

> O Father of us all and king of kings,
> enlighten me. What is your secret will?
> War and battle, worse and more of it,
> or can you not impose a pact on both?

Good question. Zeus tells her, truly, that the only way is to cause them all to forget. So, with good intentions she flies down and lands next to Arkeisiades, but unable to resist a little gore, she tells him to let fly. He spears Eupeithes in the face, which gets his attention and at the same time cancels it, and then Odysseus and the gang start to hack and chop and stab, yet again.

Recalling why she came, Athena finally hollers out "Whoa, boys!" But ol' Odious doesn't even skip a beat. So, like the county judge with a shotgun, Zeus fires off a thunderbolt—ex machina *ka-boom!* And then with glad hearts, *they all shake hands*?

They forgot. I guess it had to end somehow.

The sheep were still bedded down. I went back to the spring for a drink and moved Tom to a better patch of shade. Mitch was still out of sight. I checked the road for horse tracks, but there was only one departing set, pointed south. East of the road was a gravelly flat of sage and grass that buzzed and clacked with grasshoppers in the day's heat.

The ending still bothered me, but maybe it was true: life's a hacking

match⌐ Truth is a wound, given and received, and memory is fa
only healing, or freedom, is to forget. ⌐

I caught a few grasshoppers and let them go. Among the usual
brown-with-yellow kind were black ones with deep red wings. Forget
grasshoppers. I sat on the ground, leaning against a lodgepole pine.
Forget pine. A raven quarked. Forget.

Next in my book were Aeschylus and Sophocles. While I felt tragic,
I didn't feel much like tragedy. The sheep were quiet. The camp was
already insanely perfect: nothing to do there. The day stretched out,
blond and dazed.

I started on *The Clouds,* an alleged comedy by Aristophanes: "Mine
in the country was the pleasantest life, / Untidy, easygoing, unre-
strained, / Brimming with olives, sheepfolds, honeybees." Horseshit.
Then came some lines I liked, that reminded me of Cass: "I rank with
wine-lees, fig-boards, greasy woolpacks;/ She with all scents, and saf-
fron, and tongue-kissings." Nice.

But then he started in on Socrates, one cheap shot after another. I
decided Aristophanes was a tight-assed, reactionary little son of a bitch.
If he hated Socrates so much, then I'd probably like him. But Socrates
didn't write anything. So I found what Plato wrote about him: *The
Dialogues.* All I remembered about Plato was that after reading *The
Republic* I hated logic and reason. But I tried out the dialogue in which
Crito wants Socrates to escape Athens after being condemned. Socrates
argues that he has to submit to judgment.

> SOCRATES: . . . Tell us, Socrates, they say, what are you about?
> Are you not going by an act of yours to overturn us—the laws,
> and the whole State, as far as in you lies? Do you imagine that a
> State can subsist and not be overthrown, in which the decisions
> of law have no power, but are set aside and trampled by individ-
> uals?

I remembered how I felt after I got my draft notice, when I thought
about going to Canada. Instead, I decided to stay and take the physical
exam, and then tell the draft board that I wouldn't enlist. The board

met in Las Vegas, where my parents lived, and the board turned me down. My father said I should let them draft me, then refuse to ship out to Vietnam.

That didn't make sense to me, to submit to the military and then immediately defy them on their ground: jump into the blades, so to speak. After one of our fights, he said he didn't want me in his house. So I left. But to leave the country seemed wrong.

So I read the dialogue again, following Socrates' argument. You had to obey your conscience first. But to live in a *polis*, you also had to concede the power of others over you, right or wrong. *Politics.* Check. "Whether in battle or in a court of law, or in any other place he must do what his city and his country order him; or he must change their view of what is just."

But our war wasn't just one city against another, with swords. It was tons of napalm, thousands of dead, billions of dollars. And it wasn't as if Jackie Kennedy had run off with Ho Chi Minh. It wasn't a war of revenge but one of illusion. What exactly had they done to us, before we'd beached our black ships and burned their towns? What were we defending? Maybe Dean Rusk really believed that domino stuff: it was a tidy little metaphor. But I'd read that the Vietnamese feared the Chinese worse than we did, with greater cause. And as time went on our reasons sounded more and more like excuses.

Did there have to be a reason? Maybe not. Maybe there'd always be a thousand hackers, ready and willing, for every Socrates. And more vain old men, drunk with power and anger. What could you do about it? Escape? How many countries could you learn to love? Resist? How many times can you leap into the blades? Wait? How many cups of hemlock can you drink?

I had a vision of Socrates, sitting on a stone bench in his own tired flesh. Waiting.

You could join the killers, or be their victim.

Or change their view of what is just. There was hope in that. I turned my knee out and looked at the sole of my boot. The cream-colored rubber was soft; in just over a month it had lost half its thickness. It wouldn't outlast the rocks, but it would last long enough to get me down. And there was hope in that, too.

Just beyond my boot, a butterfly rested on a stem. The wings v___
like faded curtains in a hearse, with a white-rimmed eye on each one.
With the wings edge-on, it disappeared. Maybe fear came and went,
like weather. Or like a butterfly, visiting each flower in turn. I had
more life in me than death. The butterfly rose, and tipped into the
breeze, and was gone.

Pookie nosed me and I sat up. The sun was nearer the ridge. I staggered up and yawned. Then I walked over to the road. There were
horse tracks, headed back down. So Mitch rode past, I thought. He'll
tease me when I get to camp.

But when I got back, Mitch was asleep. It was still too hot to cook,
so I went wading. Down here the rock had worn to rounder shapes,
gravel and cobble, with an occasional boulder, easier on bare feet. But
the waterworn stone was magically slick, as if carved of soap, so hopping on exposed rocks was chancy. But while it was easy to fall into the
creek, I thought, it wouldn't be easy to fall out. So I plunged in.

That night, I sat on a box pannier and read by candle from a long poem
by Lucretius. The introduction called it "natural philosophy," which
sounded like a prelude to sleep. I was prepared for something pompous
and ungainly, but it wasn't. Instead, I felt more awake than I had all
day, and some passages were edged with flame:

> This terror, then, this darkness of the mind,
> Not sunrise with its flaring spokes of light,
> Nor glittering arrows of morning can disperse,
> But only Nature's aspect, and her law,
> Which, teaching us, hath this exordium:
> *Nothing from nothing ever yet was born.*
> Fear holds dominion over mortality
> Only because, seeing in land and sky,
> So much the cause whereof no wise they know,
> Men think Divinities are working there.

Did we fear God, or was that the name we gave to fear? A spider was crossing the ceiling of the tent, suspended from its own candled shadow. It was warm up there from the stove. Maybe warmth was enough.

The spider moved to the rear of the tent, over Mitch's head, and over the foot of my sleeping bag, where it was cooler. If it roosted above my face I'd haze it away. Herding spiders through shadows— that was a poet's game.

AUGUST 27

She had glossy hair with a soft undercoat, like a mink. My fur was coarse, like a seal's, with a metallic sheen. But we were the same kind. We were deep under roots or earth, in a buried place, overgrown and hidden from the eye: that was our home. It was dark but we could see.

Her face was covered in fur, and so was mine. We rubbed against each other, and our coats sparked, sending tiny charges through our bones. She nipped me and I growled. I nosed her and took her loose ruff in my teeth. She cried out. And her scent grew and changed: that was our speech.

I couldn't bear to trade my dream for the day. What I had dreamed, I had done. That's how it felt: the fur, the sparks. And I wanted her again.

Instead, I breathed cold air drawn under the flaps by the draft of the stove, and opened my eyes reluctantly. Mitch had started the stove and gone outside. Cold clothes. Stiff boots. I looked out of the flaps. Frost had given the leaves of cinquefoil edges of white, like fur, I thought, but it wasn't at all like fur. I bent and breathed out and one leaf turned green again.

I smelled coffee, and heard it start to boil, and stood up to move the pot. Under a pine with a feedbag in his hand, Mitch was studying me. I stood up, ducked into the tent, and poured two mugs of coffee; sliced some bread, buttered it, and laid it in the frying pan.

"Come and eat. I'll get two horses caught."

"Got 'em already. We'll eat and then saddle up. Have to shove the *putas* over this way."

"Is there much feed on that dry slope?"

"Not much. What's there is cured out, but there are pockets where they can shade up."

It took all morning to roust the sheep through the burn. We led our horses or tethered them, as the dogs slithered through the down timber, doing the hardest part. The sheep bawled constantly, but at last they lined up along the north shoulder and went. Though I tried to keep them away from the little spring, they fouled it where it met the canyon floor.

I herded high, on foot, and Mitch led my horse and worked along the road. The balsamroot leaves were yellowing, and the highest ones were hemmed in a dead brown. We traversed through sage and sharp-awned grasses until my socks were full of prongs and hooks. Pookie kept flopping onto her side to chew burrs out of her dusty coat, or to gnaw at the pads of her feet. The south-facing slopes had an oppressive, dry scratchiness, and I kept hearing a sound like a chisel against a spinning metal wheel: cicada. Mitch let the herd down to water at the creek below the beaver ponds, and then they climbed up to bed as I watched from above.

This landscape was different from the upper canyons with their rounded glacial bowls and sinks above fast-cutting stream gorges. Down here, gravity heaped up more than the water could carry away: while the canyon broadened from one ridge to the other, the stream itself was confined, forced first to one side and then the other by tongues of debris. Between the roaring, slide-choked stretches were wet meadows where the creek meandered easily. From on high I could see the meadows weren't broad places so much as narrow ones filled in, with the largest and flattest at the joining of tributary streams.

Looking into the sun, I could see the east ridge of Murphy, and a big, exposed face of yellowish white rock, chalky-looking stuff, like a vertical badland. Below it, a huge slide fanned out, forested in some places and flood-scoured in others. Above it to the right was another slip face, harder and grayer, lightly patched with green. I could see the severed piece of mountain, a tilted oval, resting below.

This canyon certainly had its faults, I thought, and also its landslides, headcuts, blowdowns, burns, deadfalls, rootwads, slumps, clearcuts, washouts, and thistles. Compared to Jackson Hole, where I'd spent a summer cutting hay, that glamorous vale with its huge and gleaming Tetons, the Salt River Range was like a narrow-hipped whore, screwed and abandoned, packing a hideout blade. *Don't mess, baby. Do your business and git.*

But I liked the surly, loose, trashy, foxy obscurity of this place. And maybe this was where I belonged. From the slope it looked like a world fast falling apart, but what's good doesn't always look that good. Things happened here, and beauty was unpredictable. And there was freedom. Or, at least, nobody watching.

As we stripped our saddles, Mitch began a tale. Pancho believed in washing dishes, if the dogs hadn't licked them clean enough, and his clothes, if they got to the point where they contained more dirt than their original fibrous mass, but he was dubious about washing himself. Like an anchorite, he shunned not only baths but the idea of baths.

By the time they camped down here, Mitch said, he stank unbearably. After the daily sock-breaking episodes and the fulsome reek that accompanied each morning's Panchovian rise, Mitch had finally had it. But Pancho was impervious to hints and insensitive to bald complaint, so Mitch played on his vanity: Now that they were camped below the ford, there might be visitors. *Mujeres. Chicas. ¿Como no?*

Pancho was a sexual omnivore and complained bitterly of his lack. Mitch emphasized it: *¿Es posible, no? Meseras muy guapas, están de Jackson Hole.* But a pretty waitress wouldn't kiss a dirty neck, or yearn to unbutton a greasy pair of jeans. And here was Murphy Lake, warm and still, the perfect tub.

To prove his sincerity, Mitch actually washed Pancho's extra set of clothes. The next day they rode down to the lake, aromatic knight and hopeful squire, bearing Pancho's clean duds and Mitch's only towel.

Pancho invoked knightly modesty, so Mitch hung the towel on a limb and retreated. But he peeked from the woods, eager to see the great deed done.

Pancho faced the lake. Buck naked with bar of soap in hand, he waded ankle-deep and paused, for eternity. He heaved a great sigh. Then he took each step slowly, as the water lapped around his knees, his thighs, reached almost to his groin.

"*¡Qué mal!*" He shuddered. "*Muy frio por aquí.*" The lakebed was so gently angled that, thigh-deep, the familiar world seemed distant and the water wide. He gazed back at the shore, deep sadness in his face. And then, alarm: What if the women were to drive up now? *Pues.*

He dropped the soap, and caught it. Then he beat a wild retreat, leaving a wake like a motorboat. At the water's edge, he halted to soap his arms and face, and lightly splash the rest. Then he wiped down with Mitch's towel, which darkened to a blend of earthy tones.

He peered up at the woods as he dressed in clean clothes. At last he cupped some water onto his head and completed the towel's ruin, then wielded his broken comb and clamped his hat down tight. *Entereza.*

Renewed, he roared up at the woods: "Hey, Mitch! *¡Mujeres! ¿Como no?* Let's go and eat, my friend."

"He smelled better for a day or two," Mitch said. "But I had to boil the towel."

I thought about that: Mitch was grubbier than I was, but that was like saying a musk ox is hairier than a yak. Cassandra would be here soon, and my wardrobe, owing to damage and dirt, was rather limited. So I filled an empty salt sack with my dirty, ripped clothes, stuffed my plant book in, found the plastic basin and a bar of soap, and trudged off to the creek.

The creek meandered through a willow floodplain, bedded in gravel. Might as well wash everything, I decided, and shucked out of my clothes. I dipped the basin full and rubbed the soap into the cold water. Washing clothes in the small basin was laborious, but Mitch had vehemently objected to my using the dishpan. I'd tried digging a hole and lining it with a trash bag, but it had sprung a leak early in the game, and my exertions served only to pump it full of mud. So I washed one item at a time in the basin, stacking the wet bundles like cannonballs, and flung the cloudy water into the willows, then rinsed. Then I gave each piece a final dip in the creek, letting the cloth trail and spin in the current.

I arranged the wet clothes on the tops of willows to dry in the sun. It was time for some bare-assed botany. I slipped my feet into my boots and put on my hat, and set out, parenthetically clad, with my plant book and journal.

On the gravel bars were dandelion, grasses, willow, yarrow, wild strawberry, and butterweed (mountain and marsh). On the floodplain, the same lot plus a yellow-flowered creeper(?), a wire-leafed blue flowery thing (?), and good old shrubby cinquefoil. On the terraces: willow, shrubby cinquefoil, low penstemon (brilliant blue-violet, wow!), yarrow, fleabane daisy, tall butterweed, rose pussytoes, scattered (bright scarlet) paintbrush, wild strawberry, thistle, and a nice whitish purple vetch.

On the lodgepole fringe grew hellebore, starry Solomon's seal, mountain bluebell, plain cinquefoil and silverweed, russet buffaloberry, wild carrot (yampa? eat the roots?), currant, sweet cicely, cow parsnip, pink geranium, serviceberry, and scattered sapling firs. Whew. Grass in the overflow channels. Fireweed along tire tracks and around campsites. Also lousewort, elephant head, and columbine, with ladies tresses (or bog orchid) by a groundwater pool. The former, I think, from the spiral growth. Northern bedstraw, sulfur-flowered buckwheat, larkspur, lupine.

I wondered why I was doing this and decided that it was my social instinct: the plants were my closest neighbors. But I was tired of writing names. Who cared, anyway? Certainly not the plants themselves. (Did plant have selves?) Stop it!

Let's see: washing done. Plants named. Thinking finished. Time for a wayward wade. I left books, boots, and hat and sloshed off downstream, enjoying the water's suction around my calves and the hollow *clonks* and *crunches* as the streambed accommodated my weight. There was a cutbank over a nice pool. Maybe I could dive, carefully. Yes. Oh yes!

The current rumbled around me, trying to carry me away, and silver bubbles and bits of gravel swirled up where my hands dug into the bed. I surfaced and looked upstream, at the creek waltzing through its tattered landscape, piling water on each grassy bend, braiding clear and cool through the wreck of the world.

The stream gravels were mostly gray limestone, with a flattened, elongated shape. There were pebbles of pure white or straw, gold, orange, or the bricky red I liked best, but they were rare among the predominant grays. I waded back upstream, scooping handfuls, examining, and then letting them wash out of my hands.

Whoops! Time to climb out and lie in the sun. Can't be late for that. I turned to the bank and my big toe slipped into a funny pocket. I reached down and felt around my toe. Couldn't see what it was. Hard and smooth. Wood? Bone? I reached onto the bank for a piece of beaver-cut wood and dug around the thing, clouding the stream. At last I wrenched it from the gravel and raised it into the light.

I'd found a skull. With horns. My big toe had slipped into the eye socket. I placed it on the bank and clambered up. It was dark gold, heavy, slightly polished, maybe a little mineralized, I thought. But it was still bone, not rock.

I sat and looked at it. A buffalo skull. I was sure.

Mitch held the skull for a long time. It was definitely a buffalo, he said. There'd been a kind of bison smaller than the plains variety that favored the mountains. He thought it was extinct by the time settlers filled the surrounding valleys with ranches and livestock. Or maybe that was the cause. He set it down.

The dogs sniffed it, then treated it like a rock. Blasphemers! I rinsed it off and apologized and set it in a pine fork, to dry out in peace and watch over the camp.

AUGUST 28

There's a glint, then a blue dot, far down the road. Cassandra appears in a cloud of dust, or rather her car does, a wholesome Swedish blue Saab 96 in which she is most probably enclosed. I kick the gelding, trying to repeat the savage splendor of my brother's arrival, but he wheels and thunders away from the approaching car. Filthy red assassin.

She speeds up. She's closing. I rein him hard, turn him back, and try again. He goes into a slam-bang trot, and I'm bouncing like a sack of spuds, knees out, as she comes into focus. She's laughing. Some of us are heroes and some are clowns. Just as I relax, Red takes off and almost sheds me, dashing narrowly past the blue car as I blow a stirrup, headed for points east.

"Helloooooooo." Her greeting dopplers down as I catch the stirrup and haul the reins until Red's ears are nearly at my chest. He rears at last. I slack the reins and balance. Hi-yo, *Rojo!*

Did she see it? We lope up behind the car and I bail off.

She steps out smirking. "You almost kicked my rearview mirror off," she says, "you fool." Dark eyes, so dark they seem all pupil, under black bangs, and a rose T-shirt with a catenary fold (the sweetest distance between two points).

Wet lips. Black braid, thicker than a lash rope. Kiss. *Cassata.*

God. The smell of her. She takes my unfamiliar beard between her teeth and growls, in the alto register. I slide my hand up underneath her shirt. *Salamandra.*

"Calluses!" she shrieks, and writhes away, and Red snorts and jerks the reins out of my other hand. Who cares? Run away, Red Horse. She dives a slim hand down my jeans and has me like a hammer handle, ruffles my sun-coarse hair with her other paw and pulls my head down into a second kiss. *Cassoulet.* I cup her back pockets and lift her fairly off the ground.

"Perrin's going blind. Matzoh threw up on the stairs as I was leaving. 'Nushka is a gorgeous, furry little slut. Half the garden came up, and half died. I forgot to water it."

"Fuck the cats. Fuck the cabbages. You came."

"Mmmmm. I think your horse is running away."

Red is trotting up the road toward camp, swinging his head, and stepping on the reins. And then I see the car is rolling the other way down the gentle incline, east. She forgot to set the brake.

I run and fling the blue door back and, falling across the seat, I catch the handbrake lever and jerk it up. *Ka-thunk.* I shut the engine off.

"Good reflexes," she says. "Saved the Saab."

She rolls me in the driver's bucket seat and fights my jeans down over my hips. My feet flat in the road, I feel the sun. *Claviform.* Blue veins.

Black wings. And in their shadow. *Cow eyes.* Io. Innocent?

O, no. Her fat braid curls around my neck, slides across my chest. I grip it and my finger barely meets my thumb. *Candescent. Canteloupe.* The sky burns gold inside the blue. I close my eyes to see.

Midafternoon, lodgepole shade. The forest feels like a Japanese house, she says. I've never been. Where? To Japan. You've never been anyplace, she says. She shakes pine needles from the blue blanket and folds it, and we walk toward the car. I don't think she loves me anymore. She drapes the blanket over my shoulder and takes my hand. It throws our walking off. I barely thought of you, I want to say.

Sitting on the odd, humpbacked car, on the left front fender, she brushes her hair into the sun and braids it again. Black silk. Blue rubber band.

"Your horse probably got back hours ago. Does Mitch care?"

"He's probably asleep. But we'd better go."

"Your turn to cook?"

"I *am* the cook."

"Cavalier *and* chef. Speaking of which, I brought good wine. I hope the bumps didn't ruin it. And beer, to cool in the stream."

"For tonight we've got lamb, with wild mint. Sauces and diversions."

She started the car and I slid into the seat. It felt strange, as if I'd been away for years. And it felt strange, in that posture, to be moving and strange to be shut away from the air. I rolled the window down. Dust.

Red was around the next curve, claiming a meadow, nipping grass and stepping on the reins. So I caught him and rode ahead, trying not to bounce, as she followed. At the ford the water came up to the hubs, but the deepest part wasn't very wide. She made it, and I led her down the track to camp.

Mitch was awake, and spruce. He'd bathed after I rode off, and started a big fire in the pit. "I thought you got bucked off," he said. "Hah! Now I know the truth."

She rose from the car and extended a slim hand. "He got *bucked*," she said.

Mitch blushed like a mountain sunset. "The sheep. I'd better go check," he said.

"A buffalo? How do you know?" She didn't want to touch it.

"The forehead's rounder than a cow, and the horns curve up. You can see from the cores. And it was in the ground before there were cows up here. Or on this continent."

"But you found it in the stream."

"In the bank, where the creek is starting to undercut. I'll show you. It was buried until the creek changed course."

"Maybe that's what we should talk about," she said.

"The creek?"

"Changing course," she said. I really had to decide, she said. She was going to law school, to Salt Lake City. She'd asked me to go with her, but I didn't think she really wanted me to go. And I didn't want to. It was a gesture. A game, reversed. Things had tangled, badly.

"Salt Lake's not all that far," I said.

"To move? Or to drive." She gave me a look. Why couldn't I say it: that it had been a relief to be up here and not to think of her, not to endure her tears and barbs. A year ago we were on the verge of break-ing up. I thought. Or hoped.

She had bad knees, and had decided on tendon grafts. But instead of having them done in Boston, close to her parents, she scheduled them at the University Medical Center in Salt Lake. She'd fly home to recuperate, she said. So I drove her down, parked the blue car, and took a bus back to Logan. And her mother, brilliantly angry, had flown out to stay.

Her family seemed rich to me. Their house was on a hill and looked toward the bay. They had terraced gardens and dwarf trees in terra-cotta pots, and a tiled pool, with a man who came to clean it, and another to do the grounds. "Not enough room for a live-in," her mother said, "but of course we make do." Inside they had an ebony grand, her pride, and many things with names I didn't know: demitasse, armoire, duvet.

Her father was the chief pilot for an airline, jaunty in his blazer. Peter Massey: I liked him, but there was a distance. He told me how they'd saved money on her little car by buying it in Sweden and driving it on a month's vacation there, which was a kind of thrift I'd never tried. His middle name was Ian. Her family wasn't that well off, she insisted. There was some money on her mother's side, but it was tied up. And of course she and her mother didn't get along. My visit was marked by tense pauses and quick, hard looks.

I visited her in the hospital, twice, but she was in pain and so delirious on Percodan that she barely knew me; she kept asking me for things as if I were a nurse. After I got home, she called and berated me for not visiting her. I told her I had, four hours ago, but she wouldn't believe it. I was a liar, like her mother. And her mother was Queen Bitch of Hell, she said.

In the hospital they fought continuously; she remembered that. And when I called again, she told me she was coming to live with me. The insurance would cover her surgery, but she wouldn't take another dime from her mother.

I didn't want her. But she was in pain, more kinds than one, and I couldn't say that. So I rode the bus down and drove her back, bandaged, in her small blue car. And I carried her up the narrow stairs to bed, and across the hall to the toilet, and down the stairs to eat.

It was a college town where part-time jobs didn't pay much. So I started to work on the late shift in a beet-sugar factory, twenty miles away. That carried us into winter, with food and rent at least, but nothing more.

My father and I were talking, with my mother's intercession, but I couldn't ask him for money; maybe tuition, if I reentered school, but nothing else. In the factory I sewed the coarse-filter bags, fifteen feet long, three wide, over steel-mesh frames. There were fresh welds in the big steam lines overhead. On the second day, I asked. Blew up, they said. One dead, one eighty-percent burns. That's how come the job was open.

So I looked up between stitches, which slowed me down. After a week, they sent me on to the cutter floor, to hone the thousands of tiny blades that chopped the sugar beets to oozing strings, and to bolt the cutter bars into the hubs, and then to pull them out, oxidized and dull. I understood, at that point, why there were unions, but of course the sugar factory didn't have one. It was a world of incessant steel shrieks, and hidden fire and steam, and root-mold and burnt-sugar stinks, and grinders spraying sparks onto wet concrete: my nights in America.

Her anger at her mother was unyielding, and so was her pride. No money. Not a dime. When I no longer had to carry her, that helped. One day I came home and found her bathed and naked, except for fresh gauze around both knees, balanced on her two ash crutches with a grin. We spent the whole day making love.

"Do everything," she said. "Get me back."

But just as she began to leave her crutches propped against the bedroom wall, she started having pains. Appendix, she thought, but the doctor said that a fertilized egg had lodged in her left fallopian tube. Left alone it would burst and kill her. They had to cut it out: a ligation. The doctor wasn't sure—there was hope, he said. But she was convinced she'd never have a child.

I'd taken her back, not wanting to, not believing it was right, because she insisted and was in pain, and because I lacked the courage to tell her the truth. And this seemed like retribution. Now I was bound to her by loss and guilt. Even as I tried to comfort her, I would always be the emblem of that loss.

She needed to hold me, as fiercely as she wanted to forget. She and her mother were back on terms, she said, not good, but speaking. She had her finances lined up for school. But seeing me here, like this, she just didn't know. Maybe it wouldn't work. She still loved me, of course. But—

But I had a waking nightmare: she'd be in law school, and I'd be finishing my bachelor's, working part-time. She'd be overworked, anxious, tight, and she'd have another battle with the Queen, and get sick, and I'd be her sole support, and her nurse; I'd be back in the pits, down on the cutter floor, and when her sexual interest flickered up again, her lover: captive on her isle.

I *had* to understand, she said, as if I understood nothing.

I made a spit of green river birch and started cooking the lamb. She didn't try to help or even pay attention to the food. Instead, she paced and fumed, and told me what I should be. Must be. Law school wasn't just school. The first year was an unholy ritual. They'd victimize her. She'd have to fight back, constantly. Law school would be the test of her intellect. It would validate her in the eyes of her parents, and the world. She would do well, she knew. But she was afraid. Sometimes she felt as if her brain were on fire, or as if it were a trap. As if it could ruin her for everything else. And of course there was no way, she said, that I could understand.

She shot questions at me and cut me off after a word. So I bowed my head, turned the spit, mixed flour and water, greased the dutch oven, and fed the fire. I'd been on too many of these wild rides, and they always ended in sobbing, blank despair. The morning's bliss was irretrievable. From the ridge, a shadow poured over us. I felt the drum of my own ears, deeper than the fire and the stream, and felt hardness edging under my skin. I started to sweat.

"Cassandra. I can't—I won't move to Salt Lake," I said.

Then she was sitting on a pannier in the tent, staring away at the tops of the pines, or digging at the kitchen box with the point of a paring knife. I squatted by the firepit, turning the lamb over the red coals, basting it, breathing the rich, burnt fumes. She started to speak. I looked up. She looked away.

Mitch saved us, at the brink. "How about that beer?" he said.

It was almost dark. The lamb was cooling, ready to be carved. Things had eased somehow. I opened the first bottle of wine and filled our cups. Then I stood and recited from the thick green book. First, Li Po.

> If Heaven did not love wine,
> there would be no Wine Star in Heaven.
> If earth did not love wine,
> There would be no Wine Springs on Earth.
> Why should we be ashamed, before Heaven,
> To love wine?

I spilled a few drops on the beaten ground. She started to scold me, then bit her lip. Then I read from Anacreon:

> Fruitful earth drinks up the rain;
> trees from earth drink it again;
> ocean drinks the air, the sun
> drinks up the sea, and him the moon.
> Is there reason, then, d'you think,
> I should be thirsty, when all others drink?

Mitch was patient: all cooks are crazy, and you're crazier than most, said his look. But the food was in sight, and all was in readiness. Don't make me wait much longer, said his eyes. "One more," I said. "Shakespeare." He gave an agonized groan. "But short," I said.

> Who doth ambition shun
> And loves to live in the sun,
> Seeking the food he eats,
> And pleased with what he gets,
> Come hither, come hither, come hither:
> > Here he shall see
> > No enemy
> But winter and rough weather.

"And coyotes," Mitch said. "And poets."

"No grace. Drink up. Eat." I raised my cup, and they leaned in to clink theirs to it. The first sip was so good I didn't want to take another, but of course I did. It was even better. I carved the lamb, and it was pink inside. I opened the lid of the dutch oven, on steaming palomino rolls. It was perfect, in the simplest way. But after emptying one plate,

I was tired. The afternoon had worn me thin. It was an effort to stand. So I started washing up, while they lingered over the fire and the wine, and talked.

"The lamb really was good," she said. "Do the Prestons have a freezer?"

"Yeah," Mitch said, through a mouthful of wine. "Big one. On the mud porch."

"How do you keep it from thawing out?"

He was puzzled. "Plug it in, I guess."

"No, how do you keep the meat from thawing. After they bring it up."

"Here? Well . . . we don't . . . they don't. Bring it. Up."

"You killed the lamb? *Yourselves?*"

"It . . . We didn't. Nope."

"Good." She was visibly relieved.

"A bear killed it. We just cut the hindquarters off."

"A bear *gmrrrfffff?*"

She gained the willows in a bound. It didn't sound like all that much came up, but she made a lot of noise. I followed and she drove me back.

"You bastards, you fed me . . . bear . . . *gmrrrfffff!*"

"It wasn't bear meat, Cass. It was lamb." Consolation and revenge.

"I know it . . . wasn't . . . you bastard . . . bear . . . *gmrrrfffff.*" She wailed and coughed.

"Jesus! Why did I have to *say* that?" Mitch stared desolately into the fire.

"It's the truth," I said. "But the timing wasn't great."

He started to look sick himself and walked off quickly in the opposite direction. I filled a basin with warm water and fetched a clean dishtowel from the tent. After cursing me further, she washed her hands and face, and brushed her teeth. Mitch stayed out of sight, so I left a candle burning and the flaps tied back. He'd come in, once we left.

I carried our two sleeping bags and two pack covers into the trees. She stumbled after, in a dervish fury. She punched me twice on the back as I laid the bedroll out, and tried to kick me as I climbed in, and punched me again once we were lying down.

I told her to sleep in her car. She sobbed and apologized, and we ended up by making tearful, straining love. And sleep fell hard on us, like rain.

AUGUST 29

The canvas was stiff with frost. I heard the stove door squeak. Cassandra murmured and wrapped me tightly with her arms and legs. I waited until her breathing slowed, and quietly disengaged. Beyond the willows, the creek steamed. Smoke from the stovepipe rode the downdraft and spread in the willows along the stream, slower than the water. I decided to let her sleep and went inside. Mitch had coffee on, and it was warm by the stove.

"Trouble," he said. He looked me up and down.

"Maybe so," I said. "She'll get cold and wake up soon."

"That was dumb," he said. "Sorry. Think she'll take off?"

"I don't know. We'll see. It wasn't your fault. But don't mention bears. Christ!"

We filled mugs. "Lord, she's wild," he said. "Little blood-bay mare." He gulped coffee.

"Mitch. She's not a goddamn horse. Okay?"

"Yeah. Sorry." He looked sheepish, and refilled his mug. "That Laurie, the one my brother likes, is beautiful, too. And crazy. You wonder. She left two brand-new sleeping bags in a dryer in a laundromat. Weeks later, Donnie asked her where the bags were, and she just said 'Oh *shit!*'"

"Cassy's . . . She's not crazy. She's . . ." I couldn't think of a word.

"I don't have to worry anyhow. I'm not settled enough for a woman."

"You seem pretty solid to me. You have the patience to herd sheep, when I feel like slaughtering them all with a bazooka or something. And you'd be good with kids."

"Yeah. Maybe I was born to herd the damned things. Sheep, I mean.

When my friends all have kids, I'll be lambin' out and livin' on dry beans."

Mitch rode above the herd and bore down while I pushed the middle. Cassandra, slant-eyed and yawning, took the road. I sent my dog with her to help, but soon Pookie came up the hill, ears flat, eyes round. I could see Cassy down there, like a little black-tailed goblin, flapping her arms and calling vengeance on the sheep. She glanced up and scowled. I gave her a friendly wave, and she dropped both arms to her sides and looked away.

"I don't need it," she said, when I went down to bunch the leaders across. "I really don't. They just run around totally at random, making a racket. They smell terrible. And what they do to the ground— My God! How does it ever grow back? Someday it won't."

"They're pretty disgusting," I said. "Think I'll herd cows next year."

"That's your problem. I'll stick to cats."

"Can't herd a cat. Or shear it. Or milk it. Or ride it."

"They're clean and pretty. You can pet them. You can sleep with them. They purr."

"Once we get the drags across, we'll explore." I saw myself in her sunglasses, huge nose, pumpkin face.

"Ugh. I really need to bathe," she said.

The lake held warmer water than the creek, so I took her there. There were two rafts of logs and weathered boards, poled into the bank. Small trout were rising lazily, and the rushes drew glimmering curves along the mudflats, backed on the west by willow and sedge. Above the wetland were bunches of a tall, lance-leafed sunflower, its small blooms ripening to furry tufts. She asked what it was called. I didn't know.

I gave her other names: wild rose near the waterline, green hips turning red. Above grew the mixed forbs of the forest edge: lupine, coneflower, and fireweed, frosted into pale yellows, peaches, pinks, and scarlets. There was snowberry, still green, with white fruit the size of a pea, and the white froth of birchleaf spiraea, and beyond it thick lodgepoles darkening as the slope rounded north to spruce and fir.

"My God! You *live* here," she said.

"How so?"

"Up here. In the woods. You're not just camping out."

"It's not Japan. But it fits. Don't you think?"

"I think you're both completely nuts. Let's go out on a raft." One floated higher, so we took it. The lakebed cupped a fine gray silt, overgrown with a nondescript water plant. Big dragonflies tilted around us, wings shuffling like cards, and mated in midair. Each male clung to a female, his abdomen curved like a hook and fused to the tip of hers, his head centered over the join of her wings, the two pairs of prismatic eyes giving intricate, parallel twists to the light.

I poled to the center. At each stroke the pole left a gray tornado in the silt. We stripped, sitting on the raft. She hugged her knees and tried to pluck paired dragonflies from the air, but each time she drew back. As she reached, her left breast rose and deepened. The saddest part would be never to see this again. She turned at the waist and spread her yellow towel, and the black tuft of her braid swung across her back and brushed the rise of her hip.

In her sunglasses, she was a stranger. She rolled onto her back and lay there, already tan. In places her skin looked silver in the chasing of the light. She had Christmas stars, white below each kneecap, and a small white scar on her belly that you'd miss, unless you knew it was there.

I lay down opposite. She circled my big toe with her thumb and forefinger. I slid toward her, getting a splinter from the raft, barely recognizing pain, and kissed her belly scar. She drew me up, and her glasses framed two tiny suns.

The raft rocked and sent out a radiant ellipse, then a succession, each ripple hurrying away to kiss, to pet, to slap the dumb, tracked, muddy shore.

A new light had entered the canyon, a dusty, atomic gold. There was smoke in the air—a forest fire somewhere. Far off. I didn't want to mention it. We drifted. The shore was straw-colored. West of the lake, there were clumps of willow, and white ricegrass delicate against the shade, and another tall grass with a plumed seedhead, like a dragon's feather. The little inlet creek beat lightly down a shady draw through low, thick willows and puzzled through white driftwood entering the lake.

"It's better, really, that you don't come to Salt Lake."

"That's how I feel," I said.

"But I want to go away. Semester break."

"To ski?" With those knees, I didn't think she could.

"No. To Fiji."

"Fiji?" Why not Mars, I thought? "What do tickets cost?"

"For me, just tax. But they're strict about immediate family."

"So, for me?"

"Round-trip, about twelve hundred. We might get a break. At least a thousand, though."

"Cass. I'm making all of two-fifty a month up here."

"I know. You should have gotten a real job."

"This isn't real?"

"Not real money. It's an escape. From your fucked-up life."

"Well, maybe it un-fucks me up."

"Riding horsies. Eating meat. Wild animals. Boy stuff. God! Grow up."

"Maybe that's how it helps."

"Why can't you get serious?"

"I am. I might seriously end up in jail. And I took care of you."

"I remember." She pinched her scar, as if she could hold it up, to show.

"Before that."

"You're saying you won't go."

"*Be fair.* I can't ask my folks for money. Not for a South Seas holiday."

"You won't go."

"Can't. I need to finish school. And get the appeal resolved."

"You're not even remotely interested."

Yellowjackets insisted on themselves, drawn to moisture and sweetness. She handed her sunglasses to me. Eyes shut, she tipped over the edge of the raft, into her own shadow. Her braid floated and then sank as the gray silt mushroomed out beneath her pale and wavering shape.

We poled the raft against the bank, and dipped in the creek, going back, and scrubbed with fine sand, then dressed back to back. The smoke was gone. At camp, Mitch had prepared an apology: cubed chicken, from a can, on a bed of rice. Canned peas. Safe. He'd opened a jar of Louise's pickled beets. He was forgiven.

I didn't know about myself, but at least she talked to me without the anguished undertone. We each had an ale, cool, still wet from the creek, and she searched in her car and came out with a narrow paper bag. "I forgot to give you this," she said.

It was a pennywhistle, a Clarke's, of thin, rolled sheet metal, lacquered black and gold, in the key of C. I thanked her and bent to kiss her, and she gave me her cheek. She'd given up. That's why she was relaxed.

And I loved her again, even more, like this, as we ate and then talked around the fire, and she told us all the places she'd seen. I played her a minor tune, slow and full of breathy notes. When the evening star appeared, we joked about wishing on it, about whose turn it was. You could almost see the heat going off the earth, in the deepening colors of the sky.

AUGUST 30

East of the lake the country rose in a milder form of confusion, lifting and dropping into moist pockets and gullies that looked as if they should carry streams but didn't. The woods were thick, and the sight lines were so often interrupted that each place looked vaguely familiar and also vaguely strange. Mitch gave us directions to the herd, turned north, and disappeared.

She sat on a down lodgepole and unraveled her hair. She brushed it hard, counting under her breath. "I'm going when we're done," she said. "Today."

"Mitch's parents are coming up," I said. "This afternoon. Driving from Salt Lake. You'll pass them on the road."

"I have to find an apartment. Now that I know what to look for." She braided her hair and slipped a bright red band above the tuft.

"Will you take the buffalo skull?"

"Shall I leave it with one of your *friends*?"

I ignored the barb. "I'll come. When I'm out of the hills."

"Expecting what?"

There were tears in my eyes, and I hated them, and I could see them in hers as she turned and marched away.

"Cassandra." She didn't answer. "Cass—that's not the way."

The words came back. "I'll go where I please."

"Then *please*. Don't get lost," I said.

She was waiting for us at the ford, and Mitch said he'd go on to the camp.

She took me by the wrist and led me downstream, into thick willows, to a grassy bank above the creek. "I want you to see me, one last time." She turned her back and slipped her blue jeans off. She shrugged her yellow jersey over her head and her braid fell down along her spine. Then she faced me, lips tight.

"You take your clothes off now."

I did. It was sad, and it excited me. She knelt and took me in her mouth. Then she stood up. "I'll miss *that*," she said.

I took her wrists and spread her arms out straight until we touched, the opposite of a hug. She pressed her face against my chest. "I'm seeing someone," she said. I drew back, and she gripped my wrists and forced them out, and kept us in that double cross.

"Don't ask me now," she said. Her voice came through her skull and slipped between my ribs. I looked down at her part, where the shining hair sprang out in opposite directions and then joined in a long, black knot. "And don't be mean." She went limp and pulled me with her whole weight onto the grass.

My feet were in the creek, then out. She wept and struggled, yielded, fought, laughed, and wept again. "Do everything," she said.

Our two aromas mixed and interpenetrated, rough and smooth, the salt, the sour, the sun's bitter milk and the moon's pale tears. The heat was on my back and in my eyes. As we rolled, dry grass blades stuck to her thighs, a willow leaf to her tense and mounded ass. A stub of willow pierced my foot, and I bled into the creek.

And then it was done. She pulled me into the stream and we grappled in the shallows, the gravel sounding with our weight, and then fell, the current shoving hard against our double shape.

Let. *Go.*

Cassium. She brushed her hair and braided it again. She couldn't find the rubber band, so I knelt and cut her a piece of leather from my bootlace. The blade flared in the sun.

"So-o-o primitive," she said, and walked away.

Mitch wasn't at the camp. Or Pookie. She began to load her car.

"I'll write to you," I said. "And I'll come, when I get out. I still . . ."

"Call first. But I'll keep your treasure safe. Your buffalo. Extinct."

I shut the trunk on it as she opened the car door. Arms half out, I took a step.

"No hug," she said. "No kiss. Good-bye."

Mitch's folks drove up an hour after she disappeared. I was drifting about the camp like a ghost when I heard a car and waded the creek in my boots, only noticing that fact halfway across. But it was a different car. Mitch was already there, leading Tony.

They all hugged and smiled. We were introduced. Don and Doris. They were both dark-haired. His father was handsome, like an El Greco nobleman, with a high, firm brow. His mother was pretty and delicately made: I could see her in Mitch's bones and way of moving.

Mitch rode ahead and led them through the ford. I walked across the stream with my boots on. They were already wet. But I guess I looked haggard or even distraught. "His girlfriend was just here," Mitch said. "She's going away to law school."

"How nice," his mother said.

"Well, actually, we just split up."

"That's too bad," she said, touching my wrist.

"Maybe. I don't know yet." I looked up at the ridges.

"Sometimes women know best," she said. Mitch and his father both rolled their eyes up, at the same instant, in the same way. "We brought you some steaks, dear," she said.

"When I went to the dentist, I called 'em and said to bring some beef. Hamburgers. T-bones. A guy gets tired of eating sheep."

"There's beer in the cooler, son. Let's unload the car."

I wish I remembered more, because I liked them. At that time, I took my friends as they offered themselves: a woman who dressed like a gypsy was a gypsy. It didn't matter that she was the daughter of a rug wholesaler from Philadelphia. A man with a guitar was a minstrel, even if he couldn't play. He had the desire and its instrument. And Mitch was a cowboy saint, herding sheep as a penance, dressed in the rough cloth of the century before. That he even had parents had barely entered my head.

I didn't feel like answering, so I asked them things. Don, his dad, came from a gold rush clan: two roving generations dug their prospect holes in Montana, California, and Alaska. But he'd been working in a ballistics lab in West Virginia when he met Doris Hollyfield. I'd have fallen in love with her name alone, I thought.

He was a chemical engineer and she ran the lab. She looked at him, as he told their story, with a fine, sweet gravity, and then she spoke. She came from poor Virginia hill people, stump farmers. They married and lived in the Allegheny Mountains, near the Cumberland Gap. That's where Mitchell was born, she said, after Betsy and Melinda, and before Donnie and Holly.

As they talked, the parallels emerged. He was an engineer who worked with explosives and propellants. My father was an engineer who worked with atomic bombs. Mitch's grandfather chased gold to Nome. My mother's dad, Frank Christian Torkelson, the only child of a

Norwegian immigrant, found his first job in the Nevada goldfields about the same time. We'd moved to Nevada in 1957, as they were building a desert enclave to test the bomb. His family had moved to Utah in 1959, with solid-fuel rockets hot on the drawing boards. Both of us were overkill brats, the spawn of national defense, and both herding sheep.

But I didn't say that aloud. The family talk made me feel better. My dad's family had been ranching and farming in Utah and Wyoming since the 1840s, but a lot of our clan had come from Virginia: Lewises and Crawfords. They may have condescended to those yeoman hill folk, Hollyfields and Blacks, over bolts of calico and pecks of coarse-ground meal.

The sky filled in. Mitch's dad had a weather bump. "Smells like a big, strong change," he said. They were such handsome people. I had no time to learn their faults, if faults they had. After four beers I loved them unrestrainedly, and then began to nod over the ruins of my steak.

Cassandra's gone. The sociometrics bastard. What's his name. *Mercedes-Benz.*

"Hey Pard. Better roll into your sack," Mitch said.

"I'll wash up," his mother added. Doris Dolores Holly Beautyfield Black.

A field black with holly, at the dolorous edge of woods. God shed his grace.

Cassa, in cassum. Thee.

AUGUST 31

The canyon was rich in places where no one wanted to be, full of shadows and sinks where you could slip into the invisible. All morning I'd been wandering thick woods and cloistered glens, looking for strays. I hadn't found any, and there was no place east of the lake where you could take five steps in a straight line. The constant backtracking had ruined my sense of where I was, and I always took two steps to the left where I should have taken four to the right. Was that the same patch of fireweed? Where's the split-trunked spruce?

I wasn't lost, but I had a constant, nagging sense of dislocation. A jackstrawed heap of deadfall, where three falling pines collided, blocked the outlet of the sink. I had to scramble out to the left: another set of directions to recall. The outlet led to a loose, descending gully that looked like a hundred other loose, descending gullies. The only real directions in this mess were up and down. So I sat down and shut my eyes.

There are laws that never change. Once you learn them, everything makes sense. Stars make sense, and the rising sun, and gravity, the implacable need of water to descend, and the way the earth gives way to roots, and the way the roots hold soil, then let it go. It all makes so damned much sense that you feel it pulling at your bones.

Maybe our minds, and our speech, worked in ways that the rest of the world didn't. Maybe a lie was our way of adjusting to that: an invisible hinge.

What would the Prince of Liars say? *I feel nothing. She has no hold on me. Nothing was as I wished. I will not miss her. What she does is all the same to me.*

Mitch and his dad were herding, with all three dogs, and his mother was making a fancy lunch. I didn't want to cloud their visit, so I'd packed my lunch and planned to stay out all day. It was early afternoon, but I wasn't hungry. I wasn't anything.

I felt like some natural thing come unstuck, like a lightning-split pine that had wrenched loose and was walking, puzzled, and staring at its rooted sisters and brothers. Some of them had been killed by beetles and their bark was peeling off. The channels gnawed by the beetles made intricate glyphs in the bleached, dead wood. What did they mean? I got my journal out of the pack and laid a page on the woody bas-relief and rubbed my pencil across. Someday the words might come. Or never.

Uneasily, I stood up. I picked my way through thorny tangles and deadfalls, crouched and balanced across the cutbanks, and skirted the soggy bottoms of sinks. In the few openings the plants had grown up thickly and wrapped my shins, gumming my cuffs with green and stitching my socks with burrs. It was the borders—stream to gravel,

) willow, meadow to forest, or the broken rim where a slope
＿＿ down—that offered safe passage: edges were the best routes.

Some sinks held little ponds, and in their wet margins I saw tracks:
mouse, weasel, elk and deer, a coyote, porcupine. No sheep. In these
chaotic woods, I was the only stray. There was a fresh bear track in the
moist sand. But I didn't feel scared, this time: it was a sign of what
belonged, of what should be.

At last I came out on a logging road and headed back to camp. To
one side of it was a wet slope, eager with willows, bright with little
springs. The water collected in a cluster of ponds, and in one I saw a
beaver and a muskrat swimming circles together. At first I thought the
smaller beast was the beaver's kit, but I crept up and saw the thin,
tapered tail. As I got close, they both stopped to watch me, ready to
dive at any threat. I sat as quietly as I could, and they began again.
They swam double rings in the pool that held the beaver's house. Why?
Maybe because they liked it. Maybe it was pure play.

They let me go without ceasing their game. As I looked back the
ponds gleamed like mercury or molten gold, still and calm, open to
the approaching night. Along a shadowy bank the lupine glowed,
the blooms progressing to furry seeds along each stalk, a violet-touched
white.

Why do some colors stand out at dusk? Why do some objects then
appear to be lit not from the sun or the air, but from their very being,
as they burn on the edge of darkness?

And why do they make us feel this way?

SEPTEMBER 1

While I slept alone in the woods, it snowed. The air smelled different
when I woke, and the canvas was heavy as I raised it. The world had
gone white, by the thickness of a good wool coat.

We needed to move the sheep up toward the pass. I shortened my
stirrups so Mitch's dad could ride, and I slogged, which fit my mood.
Mitch and his dad rode into the snowy woods and disappeared. It was
either a dream or too real. *Cassandra's gone.*

I wished for that, and now it seemed like tragedy. *I want you to see me, one last time. I'm seeing someone.* What could I do? Lie. Get drunk. Embarrass myself. Have bad dreams. Bite my lip. Spit.

Get up and herd the sheep. That never changed.

But in white, the canyon was a place in which everything was changed: each snow-encumbered pine seemed heavy with conse- quence, so beautiful I had to stop and cry. I was supposed to turn the leaders. That was my job. I should find the herd. But instead I tipped back and rested against a pine. Pookie stretched up until her head fit into my hand. When you feel tragic, nothing like a steaming dog. The hard curve of her skull. Pook. Pookie. Pookissima. I rubbed my face with snow.

The clouds lifted and I forgot the sheep. The meadows, pines, talus, firs and spruces, all things were brilliant, defined by snow. I could only look around and try to stuff the white magnificence through the pinholes of my eyes.

The world was speechless with snow.

Then the herd. First, a few high blats.

Then the awful, spreading blather:

> Gobble everything before us.
> *Blah, blah, blah-blah-blah, baaaa, bla-lala.*
> Now rejoice in mindless chorus:
> *Blah, blah, blah-blah-blah, baaaa, bla-lala.*

Cries of the damned. The day would be miserable, I knew. Why go to meet misery? I could wait. I had lots to do. I could lean against a dripping pine and cry.

> Stop crying at everything you see.
> *But I still want to cry.*
> How can you weep, in front of sheep?
> *I've been here since July.*

The sheep were upon me, and I dutifully turned them to the ford as they milled and blatted and festered. They wouldn't cross. Losing my patience, I grabbed a bell-ewe by the wool and dragged her bodily across, kicking and splashing, as her poor lamb floundered after. Then the rest of the humped white mass came blatting, splattering, bleating, shitting, crowding, fouling, pissing, and pocking the clean gravel of the streambed, and crumbling the innocent banks.

My boots were soaked. Again. Or still. Mitch rode up and was surprised that I'd gotten the leaders to cross. His dad appeared and together we pushed the drags—lame ewes, laggards, bums—across and then moved the herd to the slope behind the camp.

Mitch's mother came out of the tent to watch her son and husband, tall in the saddle and overlooking the wealth of nations. We were three men driving a herd of sheep, high in the mountains of the interior, with a woman watching us. O Israel, thine increase: wool and flesh.

Brutal. I can't live like this.

Watching the sheep, I kept wanting to take my knife and push it through my hand. Crazy. I chose the exact spot to rest the point on my palm, and then I thought that maybe it should go through the back of my hand instead. I was going to flip a coin but my pockets were empty.

Part of me stayed calm, and tried to calm the other part: you can imagine things. Okay. You can imagine this. But there's a difference between what you think and what you do.

The clouds receded and the snow disappeared. All was brown and gray and green again. We pushed the sheep up to the aspens under the pass. The first yellow aspen leaf I found, I ate. No good. But I swallowed it. I don't think they were watching. Then they rode back down to camp, talking above the racket of the two horses descending a rocky hill, as I fell behind.

I wanted to throw my knife away. No. Stupid. Can't live without a knife. So I folded my arms, to keep my hands out of sight. I felt like an idiot walking down a steep slope with my arms folded, but I only fell twice. Three times.

Doris Hollyfield Black had cooked something up. Hamburgers. I wasn't hungry, but I think I ate one. Mitch was talking. Roger was supposed to come up the next day, to get the herd over the pass. He was bringing a tepee-tent, to set up in North Murphy. Mitch would sleep there, staying with the sheep, and I'd move the camp around the forks the following day. It was good there hadn't been more snow, since the pass was steep and slick and rocky. Okay.

Mitch would stay with his parents until they left. Then he would ride up to the sheep and hold them near the top. He thought we were out a marker and I should look for strays again. Take some rope. If there was an old ewe hiding out with bums, I'd probably have to rope her.

Okay, I said.

Maybe I did look pretty bad. He wanted me to use a horse, but in that up-and-down jungle the ability to scramble over logs seemed more important than speed. So I got the rope and dropped a canteen and some rain gear into my pack and walked off. I guess I didn't say anything, though. When I got to the creek he realized I wasn't catching a horse and yelled, but I ignored him and walked across in my boots again—the creek washed all the words away.

There were elk trails forking and joining and sneaking through tangly brush, so I decided to use the logging road to get some elevation. From there I could find a vantage point and listen for lonely bleats. Other than my own.

The road switched back and forth, with a landing at each corner where logs had been piled. All that was left were the snags and splits— unsalable stuff—and the disturbed air that hovers over every ill-used place. I got sick of looking at stumps and slash, so I veered off into the woods, up tight little gullies and down into pockets where I could throw stones farther than I could see.

It was all coverts, holes, and sanctuaries, better country for game than for the hunter. There was frequent bear sign: rotten stumps dismantled, heavy rocks turned up and the digs and scrapes of claws. Higher up the woods got rougher and craggier. A big opening in the trees turned out to be a huge rockslide. At the top was the gray face I'd seen from the other side. This whole slope was displaced rock, ceaselessly overlapped and superimposed. I could feel the uncanny rhythm of it, feel how mountains fell apart and then reformed, settling and slowly filling in with pine needles and dust, with the leaves of thistle and fireweed, with twigs and tiny bones and spiderwebs, how the country was making itself up.

But I was supposed to find stray sheep, not stray rocks, so I started down. The snow had already disappeared; meltwater drained so fast up here that few streams came down, and there were innumerable pockets and sinks. Some were floored with broken rock or broken trees, some carpeted with sedges and silt, and in some were small black tarns.

Beyond the toe of the big gray slide I found a larger pond hidden in a ragged forest, mostly lodgepole, half of it dead or dying. Dragon Pond, I called it at first sight. It was set in drifts of rock, curving back on itself like a jade dragon.

It must fill up in spring, I thought, to the watermark on the stained, bare shingle, and overflow briefly down a gully full of splintered trunks, and then sieve out through its rocky banks until it settled to the ring of silt that sealed its bed. Most of it was less than waist-deep, with only two or three spots to swim, and one deep enough for a careful dive. But I didn't go into it at all. I crept down to the water's edge and looked.

Down the iron-colored banks, the boles of fallen pines angled like tusks and then warped through the surface, each white length subdued to ivory, to jade, and then immaterializing under the furry silt. Despite the snow and the melt, the water was dead clear and almost lifeless, with no minnows or fairy shrimp or frogs. It probably froze fast to the bottom.

The receding water drew rings of gray and tan and black. The color shift was repeated, more richly, under the water. At the edge was coarse limestone and shattered wood, with a light filling of pale green silt: ash to bone. Deeper in the pond the wreckage gathered periphytes and silt: sage to olive. At the deepest points the silt was featureless, lending the water the hypnotic aqua of a thermal spring: a clarity you can't see through. I put my hand in. Cold. I had no desire to swim. Or drink.

Or stay. I stood up. Yellowjackets touched down on the surface, one by one, and lifted off. A woodpecker drilled. A gust of wind stroked the pool from sky blue to gold, to white before it settled back into its somnolent green again.

Looking into the pond, I forgot myself: that I'd hurt my love and lost her, that there was always more to lose, that I was weak and filled with doubt, that I would die. I was given to watching. And yet if a yellowjacket landed on my arm, I'd flick it off. This intense heed was new to me: it was like seeing through my skin.

Which scared me a little, because I didn't know what to call it. So I tried to find a word: beholding, outsight, watchery.

Watchery.

That was it: lookery, walkery, waitery, *watchery.*

Having found the word, I had to go. Dragon Pond was beautiful, but it wasn't a place to stay too long. It was one in which you'd lie awake all night, listening for a voice, waiting for evidence that couldn't come.

I could see between the conifers, clear across the canyon to the dry side, where aspen shimmered high above the burlap thatch. As grasses cured and the flowers set seed, the canyon's open ground had changed its greens for parchment, rust, and leather brown.

I found some fresh tracks, a limping ewe and two or three lambs, not feeding. The tracks had been made after the snowmelt, so this little bunch had descended the slope by themselves. I followed them to the logging road, and down it.

On the main road I found a rubber boa, gentlest of snakes. I'd been mystified by one the year before, finding it under leaves in a rattlesnake-filled canyon in Utah, and I'd looked up its name in a book. It was made for tangles and rock gardens layered in duff. In the forest, you'd never see it at all.

It didn't move. It must have been run over by Mitch's folks on their way out. I picked it up, expecting it to be stiff and cold, but it was alive. It coiled in my palm and tucked its head under its coils. The tiny, soft scales were a blend of brown, gray, and green, with a metallic luster. It was nothing like rubber but more like fine silk, braided around a heavy core. It had tiny, polished eyes on a rounded head, which looked otherwise exactly like its blunt tail, and a yellow throat.

I held it, enjoying its soft, deft, neat pliability. Once it got over its fear, it might enjoy my warmth. Since it was a small snake, I talked to it in a small voice, and at last I set it just off the logging road, near a trickle of water where it might find a bug. But it coiled again.

It took more time to get its courage up and look out from underneath itself, and twice as long to move. There were wild strawberries along the road, trying to fling their runners across it. It was in such scarred places, along roads and not in the untouched woods, that they formed the largest, sweetest fruit. I ate berries, one by one by one, as the snake made its escape. I put my finger in its way and it flicked out its fine black fork of a tongue and tasted me. Then it slipped across my knuckle with no sound, only a ribbon of touch.

The limping ewe and the lambs were at the ford. The ewe was lame in her right front leg, barely touching it to the ground. I'd have to tell Mitch. I chased her and grabbed her by the wool and dragged her across, and the three lambs followed. Wet to the waist, I let her go and she shook as the lambs nuzzled her. Then they all headed off in the right direction to rejoin the herd. I remembered the rope in my pack.

I sat down and took off my boots and wrung the water out of my socks, and took off my jeans and wrung out the dripping legs. The sun was no longer warm, but the camp was near. So I tied the wet legs of my pants around my neck and slipped my bare feet into my boots.

I looked back and there were birds flying close to the water, flashing through the last light, swifts catching their tiny prey, much faster than swallows, wilder and more precise in their flight.

SEPTEMBER 2

There was a rustle on the canvas, a thin sound multiplied, like someone trying to rouse us by tapping softly with bundled twigs. "Snow," Mitch said through the dark.

"Snowing," I whispered, and went back to sleep.

At dawn, we rode up toward the pass. The snow, sky, and air were luminous blue, and the high, bare rocks looked black against the sky. We rode up under the belly of a cloud and then into it, silence and blue light.

We found the herd waking up with moans, like recruits on a cold bivouac. They'd drifted around a ridge to the east, and Mitch rode that way, followed by Ansel and Tikki-Lo. When I saw them headed up the ridge, then I'd begin to drive the sheep above me toward the gap. In the cloud I couldn't see it, but Mitch said it was there.

Mitch had sent word out with his folks on the new location of the camp. Roger would drive up, catch a horse, and load it in the pickup rack with a packsaddle and a set of panniers. Then he'd drive back down to the mouth of North Murphy. Our fresh supplies would go on that horse, with the range tepee, and he'd drop them at our next camp. Then he'd climb up the north side of the pass and meet us.

The clouds began to open. The Star Peaks were entirely white, and the long scree slopes and limber pines all covered in snow. A bull elk bugled from that side, and there was an answer from the canyon, a high vibrato sweeping down to end in a grunt. Then there was another, but it wasn't an elk. The bugles had started a coyote howling, its cry making shivery harmonics with the calls of the elk. Then another coyote howled, and more coyotes, a pack, a tribe, a nation.

I imagined the coyotes singing: how their open mouths would steam, how their eyes would close as their song leapt high and far—*the cold is coming.* And how their heads would come down and their eyes open again, steady yellow with a weightless grasp of all that moved. What did they feel, with the approach of cold? It didn't sound like mourning. Did they remember blue moonlight and blood smoking on the snow? Whatever they felt, the coyotes cried long and loud and high: *Always the cold—always the cold-cold-cold.*

Red pricked his ears and Pookie barked, and I saw dark silhouettes along the ridge. The sheep were moving up. Echoes found their way across, Mitch's shouts and the yips of the border collies. The elk stopped bugling. One coyote howled, then none. I led the horse across the steep slope, yelling as Pookie woofed, and we pushed them into the cloud. The herd bawled as one, devouring all other sound.

The slope was clad in tufts of grass and dried sunflowers—mule ears and balsamroot—that bent downhill with the snow's weight. When I stepped on them my foot would slip. Under the snow the bare dirt had become a reddish mud with the properties of grease. The only solid spots were toothy little outcrops. The sheep had no trouble, but Red slipped and went down twice as I led him across. The right stirrup was packed with mud.

Under each spinney of aspen was a belt of snowbush, and each broad three-veined leaf held a heaping tablespoon of snow. When I shouldered through, the snow tipped down my neck, times a hundred. Soon, I was soaked. There wasn't a way to get around. But I could have chosen a spot where the sheep had already knocked the snow off, I thought. The difference between dry and wet was the same as between smart and dumb.

Leading Red, I scrambled up loose chutes and over rattly outcrops. Sometimes the branches would close behind me and slap him in the face, and he'd balk until I pulled on the reins. I was bathed in sweat inside the yellow slicker, but to shed it would be worse. Pookie shook almost constantly as her tail thinned from a brush to a ratlike prong.

The snowy incline rose forever. The aspens had lost a few leaves to the storm but most still hung, gold and vermilion, almost fluorescent in the cloud-filtered light. Clouds filled the canyon and then rose, covering us in a succession of thicknesses and whites.

The fold that I was climbing converged with one to the east, and Mitch appeared, leading Tony. Soon we were in talking range.

"'Bout there," he said. "I didn't see that footsore ewe and those bums. Did you?"

On a slope this steep I'd have noticed her limp. "No," I said. "Didn't pick 'em up."

"Damn. She must be hiding out again. Have to find 'em later."

Suddenly the ridge rolled out from under us, into a cloud that moved in a different current of air. We were on the pass. To the northwest the ridge rose like an island tilted up on end, edged by limber pines and bodied with Douglas fir. The dense canopy sheltered a bright, wet green, a secret exception to the snow.

Since we didn't want the sheep to follow the ridge, we tied our horses, and Mitch scrambled down while I went up. I followed the margin of the woods onto exposed rock at the crest. I kept on until I had to use my hands, and was glad to find no sheep. They'd gone into North Murphy, just as we hoped.

I went down into the slanting woods, in case there was an elk trail that a sheep could strike, and stopped to rest against a fir. A cloud filtered through the limbs, and I felt it on my face. Suddenly, I missed Cassandra.

I opened my pack and took the pennywhistle out. Starting on the D, I played "Shady Grove." And she came out of the cloud laughing, so glad, so fine, so faultless, and so fair that tears came to my eyes. But her airy beauty was a lie. She was dating her former professor, the sociologist with the Mercedes convertible, and she'd waited to tell me until that last cruel act.

What if I'd agreed? Would she weigh up her assets and choose? What if I'd come down from the mountains to find his car parked in her drive? I remembered seeing her once when he gave her a ride, her black hair rippling, as she laughed with her head thrown back. She wasn't a princess of the air. But I missed her, and played on until the tune was done.

"Certes." I'd started reading medieval romances and they said things like that. "Certes, milady. Thine absence rings far truer now to me than ever thy speech or seemly bearing."

It was strange, talking to a cloud, but I'd get used to it.

I scanned the woods for sheep. I could hear them, below and to the east, faintly in one moment and then not at all. Having been driven hard during their usual feeding time they were hungry, and quieted as they fed.

I went deeper into the woods. The foliage shed snow like wet linens to the needled ground. It was wild country: no sign of a resting place, no level bit of ground, nothing but the ridge towering above with the two slopes falling away. The clouds seemed to graze among the cliffs and crags. The woods were a refuge, at once familiar and strange. Light entered the forest from all directions. There were no hard lines and no shadows, only a luminous green shade.

I was faced by a low summit, set off from the main ridge by a declivity that cradled a deeper green. I followed the inner slope and found a sink with an opening to the east, and stopped to look in. Enclosed by looming firs, it was hollowed out from the crag like an old cave fallen in, or a church that had lost its roof. The floor was overgrown with bluebells.

At the other end was an outcrop of limestone draped with bracken fern and moss that looked like an altar. It seemed like a place to kneel, and I did. My knees made two soft dents in the soil. Wetness soaked up through the knees of my jeans. I could feel how well the earth supported me.

"Over here." Mitch's hat brim made a dark halo over his bearded face. Roger was hatless, his blond hair pasted to his sunburned scalp, showing a thin spot at the crown. He was grinning.

"You guys made it over so quick I didn't have a chance to help."

Mitch clapped him on the shoulder. "Hah! Good thing you waited. Might have chased 'em all back, otherwise."

"I herded this before, with Warren. It's good to have someone on the north side to turn the leaders down into North Murphy. Easier than trying to get around 'em on the ridge."

"That'd be hell, in this snow," Mitch said.

Roger nodded. "I guess a guy could head on down to the camp and get some lunch. I'll keep Ansel up here for an hour or so to make sure nothing turns back, and maybe hike over the top to see if I can find that rogue ewe."

"I think they hid out quite a ways down from the top, but maybe they'll get lonesome and mosey up." Mitch looked at me. "You see anything up there?"

"Nothing," I said. "Not a single thing."

The range tepee—square-based and seven feet on a side, like a skinny pyramid—was shockingly clean and bright in the sodden opening. Old Tom, a dirtier white, was tied to a tree. We slipped the bridles and tied the horses and then ducked hungrily into the tent.

Struggling back up the hill with a full belly was hard, leading the horse. The ground was loose under the snow, and at times we slid back until we fetched up at a rock or a root. My soles were worn almost flat. Roger had better boots, and even Red's hooves had more purchase. He stood firm as I slid back and almost went between his forelegs.

"Why don't you ride?" Roger asked.

"I'm not sure I want to ride up this slick shit."

"I sure'n the hell do," he said, and shortened the stirrups. He mounted and got Red going as I floundered, sliding back and scattering the dogs like tenpins. He laughed. "Hold on to the horse's tail," he said.

"You're nuts," I said.

"I've done it before. His hind feet go forward when he climbs, not back. Don't let him drag your whole weight. It just keeps you from sliding back. Try it."

Since neither of us rode with spurs, we'd left Red's tail long to keep the flies away. I caught hold, and the horse looked back at me, puzzled but not upset.

"Gee-*up*," Roger cried. Gripping the horse's tail with both hands, I half-ran and half-skied up the hill, and the weirdness of it gave me a rush of joy.

Roger and I found the herd and pushed them down and then went up to the pass to look for strays. Mitch was supposed to join us after packing salt up to the new camp but hadn't shown up yet. "That old Tom is pretty slow," Roger said. "Or maybe he took two loads. Anyhow, a guy probably ought to head on down to make the main camp. It'll be plumb dark under all this cloud." And he dropped off north toward the tepee camp.

By the time I let the stirrups out and started down the south slope, it had started to snow. I got off to lead the big horse down a rocky pitch, and it seemed that my thighs or ankles would give way. When we reached a better spot and I climbed back on, it was dark. Something spooked up from the brush, and Red jumped and braced. Moose? Elk? The old ewe? Too dark to see.

The snowfall thickened, and the wind began to drive it into my face. I thought we were about halfway down, but I couldn't remember any way to tell. So I gave the horse his head. I was blind in the whirling darkness, as he picked his way. When he'd stop, I'd put my hand on his neck and whisper his name, and he'd fidget and shift his weight and go on.

Aspens ghosted up at us, and we crashed through a hedge of snow-bush and down into aspens again. He dragged my right leg against a tree and almost peeled me off. "Watch it, big horse," I said, and he whuffled in his throat. I thought about getting off, but I was exhausted. I didn't think I could walk. I may have closed my eyes, as he grunted through the nasty parts and kept on, carrying me down the ridge.

I'd just hang on another minute, until the red horse fell and rolled over on me, and then it would be done. No more work, no frozen feet, no suffering. Then he stopped. Stupid horse.

I realized the ground was level.

"Oats, oats at camp. Now *go.*" There were lodgepoles just ahead, and he wove us into the blackness as snowflakes hissed in the needles above, filtering through. There was a blacker shape on the left, huge, and I had a moment of unalloyed terror.

It was the tent. I slid off.

"Red," I said, as he breathed heat into my cold, cupped hands.

8 ～

Noʀth Muʀphy

The low clouds spread out on my heart like soft paws, huge and hiding the mountains. The wind and the heavy, wet snowfall had ceased in the night. At dawn I made a fire and ate, but nothing had a taste. My hands and feet stayed cold, with an numb tingling.

The clouds held low but shifted direction, coming from the south, and early that morning the snow was washed away by rain. I packed the panniers in the tent, where it was warm, and then set out to catch horses. After his oats the night before, Red had trotted up the canyon, so I found his track and followed it, with lead ropes and halters and oats in a coffee can.

I found the horses near the burn, in a spot the sheep had missed. First they tossed their heads and nickered, and then they came to me for oats. Tom was gone: Roger had come and taken him in the truck. I tied the end of Pronto's lead into her halter to ride bareback, and led Tubby, since the others would follow her. It wasn't hard but it took over an hour, and when we returned to camp I was wet again and starting to cough.

I dug dry clothes from a pannier and built a quick, hot fire in the stove. My boots had been wet for days; even with the fire my feet stayed cold. After I changed, I dragged the stove out to sizzle and cool in the rain while I rolled the tent and put the saddles on. I was running late, but my head wasn't working right: I had to stop and ponder every move. Sometimes I'd forget what I was doing and would have to stop and look for a clue: stove. Okay. Dump the ashes out and fill in the firepit. Shovel. Okay.

It stopped raining, but dense clouds streamed across at treetop height. I got the horses saddled and had a hard time deciding which packs should go on what horse. A squirrel raged at me from the needled ground, cheeking and huffing, and I was about to throw a pinecone at it when a hawk stooped down between the pines.

The squirrel made it to a big pine, and hauled itself up in a spiral, yapping with fright. The hawk launched from the earth and beat up after, barely missing branches with its wings. The squirrel gained the crowded foliage near the crown. The hawk fluttered, shrieking, and then settled on a limb. Safe, the squirrel flared and chattered, and the hawk glowered back with agate eyes.

I got the packs on the horses and was ready to set out when the hawk wearied and flew off. The squirrel scritched back down to a fat limb and took up its former grievance with me. Who says animals are wise?

From the saddle I watched the squirrel, now level with my eye: its entire body tensed for a fingersnap as its *cheeert* puffed out and its tail flicked once, a flag above the spine. Dodge death and mock it, and then be angry, to take the fear away. Why not? I tried it, that jerky, hyperventilated *cheerk*. The squirrel gaped and then flew up the trunk.

But it made me cough. Red shifted under me. Good-bye, good camp.

The horses' hooves made sucking noises in the muddy road or knocked on the cobbles. A couple of miles down, the road looped around a hill and I saw North Murphy Creek to the left, flowing from a tight canyon into a flat with beaver ponds and runs. The ranch truck was parked by the bridge.

It started to rain again, and I got off Red to put my slicker on. I had to cough and fight a dizzy spell before I got on again. I led the pack string past the pole fence. The dirt road rose along a gently sloping bench through lodgepole, and then climbed an old slide, overgrown with conifers, that blocked the canyon's mouth. The motion of the horse made my head heavy and then too light. My sense of balance was gone. The road was confined by a jumbled hillscape to the north and a steep, timbered ridge on the south. I felt suddenly feverish, trapped in my body.

But my eyes were free. A beaver pond on the left gathered the flow of a spring that issued from the base of the ancient slide. On top of it among the dark firs and spruces were a few stray aspens, a rootstock waiting for fire or avalanche. The road climbed high above the creek. Hidden in its loose gorge under thick woods, the water could be heard but not seen. And then the creek was almost under the road, under a bare slope that rounded out of sight.

Red jumped as a gray jay flew from the brush, and the packhorses flinched in succession, like boxcars bumping in the yards. The jay lit in a pine and called three times.

Above, to the south, was another big landslip with scarlet on its tongue—frost had changed the leaves. We crossed a seep, mosses and a few rushes in it, and Red nosed down and drank. The road draped over a timbered bench top with a streamlet fringed in currants, and at every pleasant spot I looked for the tepee tent, though I knew it was farther on. The sun wasn't even a patch on the clouds.

I rode past an old rockslide, boulders rounded and covered with lichen. Old? How did I know? By the lichen, which grew slowly. But how slowly? I sensed, without really knowing, how long such growth must take. Broken aspens were scattered on the heap, which meant that snow had avalanched down the gash made by falling rock. Trees coming down with the rockslide would have rotted long before lichens could cover the rocks. Watchery eased my pain.

The road descended to the creek, which was purling over cobbles in the bottom of a V, and neither had quite enough room. The stream wanted to meander; it had taken a big bite out of the disused road. Dead trunks divided the stream into pools, each with a curtain of falling water.

Farther, on the north, was a debris flow, softer soil that was thickly haired with willows, with a seep trickling out at its base. Then, real forest: you could see why the loggers had built this road. Lying along it was the crown of a spruce at least eighty feet long. The still-standing trunk was three feet thick at the break, forty feet up. There wasn't any rot, so it must have been snapped by a gust. Yet smaller, weaker-looking trees were still standing all around the broken one. It had grown tall, with many branches, and claimed too much of the air.

One death, it seemed, was to grow big. And to break and fall, and to lie there until you lost your tremendous shape. But another death might be more like a long ride on which you wanted nothing, and all you did was watch and learn. The mountain ash was in glory, with round scarlet berries and gold leaves, and a comforting symmetry. The dark, glossy leaves of chokecherry, like broad pennons, were sunset yellow. In the shade the coneflower leaves, instead of browning quickly as they did in sunny meadows, had gone a slight, even gold.

A grouse flashed out from gray deadfall, and Red started, and set off soft gongs in my skull. It took a minute to calm him, and my head. Then we went on.

On the left was a huge, flat-topped boulder that must have crashed down from the rim. It was two-and-a-half horses long and wide enough for three couples to dance. The east end was separated by a frost crack deep enough to hide in between dances, and the top had collected enough soil to sprout patches of grass, wild raspberries, and a little currant bush.

The canyon forked to the south. A faint trail peeled off and crossed the creek. That looked right. It climbed two banks and then followed a skid road that was washed out in some places and overgrown in others. The canyon had been cut long before, and young trees hid the stumps. The earth had a beaten look—it had been a deck for logs or maybe the site of a sawmill. In a place this remote, it was smarter to haul a boiler in on a stout wagon and saw the logs into lumber. But the only relic was a rusty bedframe. I stopped to rest the horses in an opening where two stumps stood, about six feet tall and notched in an odd way. There were mortises chiseled into them, the size of a letter slot in a door.

And on facing sides close to the ground the curve had been chopped flat.

The stumps fascinated me. They'd been marked by an axe long before I was born, maybe the century before. Had they borne the weight of a riveted iron boiler, or centered a saw? Or were they hewn and shaped from a passion for hewing and shaping, alone? They were almost black where the rain had wet them, and bright silver where they overhung and stayed dry. Lichen had claimed the wettest spots and daubed them lime green. The pitch in old scars shone like amber against the dull pewter of the barkless wood.

I had a rush of dizziness and closed my eyes. The horse grew restless and started walking, carrying me out of the opening and into the bewildering green. We'd climbed into the layer of cloud by the time I saw the skinny white pyramid of the tent through the sapling woods, with older forest at its back. The camp was empty.

Between spells of weakness and fits of coughing, I got the packhorses unloaded. It took a long time, alone, to get the big tent up, with my boots dragging streaks in the soggy remnant snow. I found dry wood under a spruce and got the stove jointed together and lit.

Mitch and Roger smelled the smoke and came down to eat. But I don't think I cooked or ate anything. I think I went to sleep.

SEPTEMBER 4

The tepee lacked a stove, and three was a crowd in the big tent. They let the dogs in and then it stank. I woke up gagging and had to get out of my sleeping bag and put my head through the flaps to breathe while it snowed into my hair.

The next morning I could barely walk. Mitch and Roger moved the sheep down to a clearing where we could count, and I helped, doing only what I was told: *Stand here. Wave your arms. Wake up.*

Roger wrote it down in a little notebook and grinned, the unquenchable bastard. Out seven more, he said, but there might be some lambs hanging back with the lame ewe. He complimented Mitch on his good herding, and Mitch grinned, and I hated them both. I staggered back to camp, crawled under the dripping trees to gather wood, and hauled water. There was a log hollowed out to channel a little spring. I drank from the end, where it fell into moss, and then wrote a stupid poem:

> Today I'm sick, or sort of sick,
> I can walk and talk,
> but my thoughts are thick,
> like crankcase sludge, or gutter mud,
> or a melting chocolate bar
> in a fat kid's pants.

Mitch said that Roger had taken off. The sheep would come up on their own from the forks. He'd keep them from straying over the pass. Otherwise, there wasn't much to do. But I could look for the old ewe and the rogue lambs. Can't you see I'm sick? I wanted to say. But that was tough shit. "I don't care if you ride or not," he said, "but take some rope."

Pookie kept giving me worried looks as I floundered and pulled myself up using limbs. I finally made it to the pass, wet to the skin again. There was a burning under my ribs and an ache under my shoulder blades that wouldn't rub away. On the other side I found fresh tracks, the old lame ewe and more than one lamb, but I couldn't find them. I wandered up and down, across, around. Then I sat still and tried not to cough, and listened for a bleat or a snapping twig. Nada, null and void.

The sky cleared. The sun had dropped below the ridge and I started to shiver. I smeared my way back down, trying to avoid the trail, which the sheep had chopped into colloidal, shit-raisined slime. Each time I had to step in it, my boot picked up a disgusting pound and I couldn't shake it loose.

I don't remember eating. I think Mitch made me some tea. I remember going out in the dark to pee and falling down, and Pookie licking my face. The night was cold, and the stars looked like ice-pick holes in a black bag.

I was shot. They'd thrown me into a wagon on some barrels, wrapped in a blanket soaked in my own blood. I was hot and then freezing. We were in full retreat. I could hear horses on the rocky ground, and the barrels shifted beneath me. Black powder, I thought, and woke up sweating just before dawn.

You don't look so good, the driver said.

Sleep, he said. The wagon rolled on.

I woke in a damp sleeping bag, feeling cool and weak. Pookie peered between the flaps. I wanted to stroke her ears. I lifted the tent at the back and she ran around to lick my hand. The sky was clear. Cassandra was gone.

I washed my face and drank at the hollow log and built a fire, and made some oatmeal with raisins. It had a taste. Mitch came back. "Nothing to do except watch the wooly buggers eat," he said. "How do you feel?"

"Like a dead snake's butt. Squashed goblin shit. Like a—"

"Better, huh? Let's look for those strays. With us and three dogs, they'll be outnumbered."

I had to stop to rest and mutter things: pig snot, gorilla crotch. The clouds gathered and Mitch and the border collies drifted out of sight. I ran out of enormities, so the next time I stopped I got my journal out and wrote down a poem:

> foggy immense country
> obscure under its shroud,
> trees drip, no sunlight, no sky.
> Snow melts from trees,
> and the day seems to rise
> from wet earth, and the leaves,
> throw directionless light,
> and the day lasts forever.

But the clouds broke, and the sun lofted in the high blue to the west. The snow melted fast at the edge of the woods and was gone from the brush and open ground. There were asters opening, purple with yellow eyes, the season's last bloom. Mitch was waiting on the other side of the pass. He looked up from his seat in the roots of a limber pine. "Feeling better now?"

"Weasel groin," I said.

"Ansel found the strays," he said. He led me down, and I saw them bedded in the sun at the base of an outcrop. Mitch whispered for Ansel to stay and grabbed Tikki-Lo. "Shhhh. Catch Pookie," he said. "Damn dogs'll run 'em off."

We split up to sneak down gullies and get below. Then we tried to run them uphill. One lamb flew past us, but our line held. The old ewe started to limp up the ridge, and four lambs followed her. The one left below us blatted and hurried up to join the tiny band.

We got them almost to the pass when the ewe tried to break around us. The lambs scattered. We let Ansel and Pookie work them into a group, as Tikki-Lo lunged at the end of his rope and almost upset Mitch, drawing a swat and a curse. "Hold the damn dog," he said. "I'm gonna get a rope on that ol' bitch." He threw a loop and she evaded it, almost getting past me and the dogs. He dove and landed on her back, knocking her breath out, both of them tangled in the rope. Her sharp hoof spiked him in the ankle and he howled: "Rat-Whore-Snake!"

"Jesus!" I said. "Now we'll both go to hell."

He looked surprised, then laughed. "As long as there ain't no stinkin' sheep. Just hold this bastard while I get a rope around her neck."

We took turns dragging the ewe. One of us would haul at the rope as she went limp, then jumped up and charged side to side. The other held Tikki-Lo as he barked and strained, and both of us yelled at the other dogs: "Heel, Stay, Shut up."

"Pookie, you son-of-a-bitch, get back," I screamed at twenty-second intervals. The lambs followed, bleating and wobbling: twenty hooves, ten mindless eyes, five quivering tongues. So wretched. I made up a rhyme:

> Ewes, lambs, dogs and thieves—
> How many were going to Saint Yves?

"Saint *What?* Your turn," Mitch snapped. "What'd you say?"

"Nothing. 'Tis brillig," I said. "But it'll be slithy going down the other side."

"*What?* Shut up and grab the damn rope, dammit!"

I did, feeling stronger than I had in days. And, oh how I hated sheep.

SEPTEMBER 6

"Directly above you may now view the rugged westernmost portion of the South Fork of the North Fork," Mitch droned. Over the head of the canyon loomed cliffs banded with brown and dark red and cut by big avalanche chutes. They dipped slightly as they met lighter-colored rock at the crest of the range.

"That's where Chris and I,"—and then I remembered that I hadn't mentioned our trip—". . . thought it would be," I finished. He gave me a diagnostic look.

We let the sheep spread out through the woods and openings and kept our distance. That was fine with me. I rode the north side and Mitch the south, and we met upcanyon in a long meadow that opened under the ragged cliffscape. The soil was deep red, and there were big, squarish, fine-grained blocks of dark red sandstone at the head of the meadow, like a ruined wall. Mitch pointed northwest, where stepped terraces rose to a lower band of cliffs. "Not much feed above this pocket," he said, "so we'll let 'em get here on their own and then push them up those benches."

"What's over that way?"

"North Fork of the North Fork." He laughed. It was gentler over there, he said, not so much rock. He'd scout a way to cross the low divide; I could go back to camp.

I looked for the horses and found them lounging in a green swale. But I felt restless in the camp, so I hiked up toward the pass again. I wanted to climb higher on the ridge and see if there was a way to reach the red pinnacles. The snow was gone from all but the shadiest spots. I came to the opening of the green glade and kept on straight up the ridge, climbing until I found a rocky nest above the pass, against a mountaintop, as if a dragon had scooped out a place to overlook the slow waves of earth.

Some places had a good feeling apart from the weather or circumstance. And it varied with each place. This nest in the rocks had a virtue that would be elusive unless you were alone. It wasn't a place to talk. It was a place to shoulder up into the wind and see the country rolling away in all directions, in ridges, spines, plates, bowls, clefts, folds, gaps, sinks, and shadows, and then to huddle in the calm lee of the rocks.

The country spoke to me. Not in a voice. But there was a rhythm I could follow in the procession of ridges, in the arc of the sun and the weight of the wind. And it was present in the joining of needles to twigs, twigs to limbs, limbs to trunk, and in the way my two legs worked to carry me here. It was a state that I had known before only through love and fear. And I could feel something else, purely and potently other. Standing there I could feel it framing me as undeniably as my bones.

I was *in* the landscape now, and the landscape was coming to life in me. And after forty-seven days of gunfire, blood, lust, gluttony, boredom, hunger, accident, storm, terror, mud, darkness, frost, fever, and snow, I felt as if the Devil himself couldn't kill me, up here in my nest of rocks under the bright blue sky. It was good to sit, good to think, good to stand and shout. And it was good to move.

I made a winding descent of the ridge and struck a trail on the forested northwest. Most recently two or three big bulls had used it, superimposing their sign on the prints of cows and yearlings, all headed up the ridge. They'd moved out ahead of the sheep. Maybe they'd gone over the top and into the Double Heart. I looked that way but kept a course to the east. Where the trail split at the head of the green sink, I saw long bones scattered and found the skull of a great bull elk, weathered but intact, with six tines on each side.

There was a green fuzz in the socket where the spine had fit, and green under the rims of bone where the eyes had been, and seen. I picked it up: heavy from the melting snow. I looked down into the little valley, but something stopped me from going in. Carrying the skull, I rounded it on the north and entered through the gap that faced the pass.

It was the strangest place, not ten steps wide, under columns of fir, filled with such silence that I imagined a tree's heart, or the inside of an egg.

I was kneeling again. I could see the elk trail threaded beyond the gray outcrop. The skull was at my right knee, and I gripped the base of an antler. I rose, measuring each step, and climbed the upper end and set it on the outcrop, bracing it with loose stones so it overlooked the green chapel. And I saw that the inside curve of the antlers matched the cleft of the slope.

But it wasn't finished. I returned to where I'd found the skull and gathered all the bones I could see and carried them into the gap and laid them in no certain order, soft tannin brown, on the cushion of moss beneath the skull. They seemed to float above the green.

I walked back to the entry and turned and looked back at the high-antlered skull, and it seemed to look on me.

I didn't trust my voice, so I dug in my battered pack for the pennywhistle, and wet my lips. Then I breathed in and played an air, as proud and lonely as the old elk's bones.

Wood gathering teaches the age of dead limbs. It teaches how rain penetrates the forest canopy, and how surfaces can deceive. Some fresh-fallen limbs are so wet they're like rubber and can't even be snapped. Bark is an impediment. It scorches on the stove and smolders underneath. If the bark is loose, shuck it. Bare wood is best.

The driest wood I could find was wet to the touch. A hot fire drives the moisture out, but first the hot fire must be devised.

In the absolute wetness of stormbound woods, pitchwood is invaluable for being waterproof and for the immediate blast of heat it yields. A few good splits of pitch will turn a box stove into a forge, and wood that looks sodden may be cribbed over pitchwood kindling to hiss as the steam flees up the pipe, as the fire stays strong on good black resin, boiling out of the heart.

Soon the stove will be whistling with draft, as the base of the pipe turns a glabrous cherry, and you're basking under a layer of canvas, warm and suddenly in bliss.

The rest of your firewood can be fetched in wet, stacked on the stovetop, and once a surplus builds, piled dry for the morning fire.

When Mitch rode in an hour before dark, it was snowing. We let the dogs into the tent, and at their first scuffle over places by the stove Mitch leapt up and looked so fierce that they lay down at once, without a growl. They sniffed and whined as I cut into the ham but otherwise held their hairy peace.

After we ate we worked on the headstalls, cutting off the short reins and replacing them with Roger's bounty: thick new latigo. We set the tin of dubbing on the stove and sealed the new leather. Then we brought our saddles in and tipped them up to dry, to oil in the morning.

And then we were too tired for more. I stepped outside; the night was starless. The sky was damping down again, with no home under it but sleep.

SEPTEMBER 7

Snow chastens the landscape. With a good foot, and days that hold below freezing, the mountain world is both livable and beautiful.

But when snow comes and goes at the season's turn, falling and melting, it makes the broken country far less negotiable. One boot in three steps may light on snowdrift, mud, and ice-slicked rock. Each step requires a set of predictions and each has its own consequence. And your boots stay wet for days on end.

The first snows change the country's tone. In low light, the rocks turn into scabs on white skin, and the spruces sharpen to black daggers aimed at the sky, and each steady job pivots toward risk and accident. Boots slip, hooves flail, and the glazed axe handle flies—out, out—from the frozen glove. This flux from white to sodden brown lends a sense of impending doom that deep winter never seems to fulfill.

The south fork of North Murphy was webbed with trails kept open by elk and deer. We rode up that network through the second-growth

woods in the snow, to move the sheep over the bench land. Mitch rode
Pronto, and the colt followed, bad-tempered, trying to kick the border
collies. Its eye was infected, and we had sulfa powder but could
scarcely catch it. Horses are nervous about their eyes, so the colt was
doubly hard to treat.

I rode Tubby; they were soon out of sight, but she followed their
tracks, and I was free to look around. On the right intermittent gullies
cut deeply into the reddish slopes. Where the trail went into the woods
I saw a long white arrow in the grass, as if chalked on a mottled green
slate. It was a lodgepole pine, three-crowned and fallen dead, holding
the snow. The three tops opened toward me, and going away they
converged to a white point.

We came to a meadow. The tracks of the mare went straight, while
those of the colt and the dogs were looped and braided. Tubby followed
on her own slow time. Maybe time was like tracks, a set of dots that led
someplace. But on all sides of the track the meadow stretched out, not
in any one direction but in all. Maybe the meadow was time.

When I looked closer, it wasn't really a meadow. A meadow had
grass and a variety of flowering plants, but this was filled with brown
coneflowers and thistles still a bilious green. There were no grasses.
And between tall, drooping stalks, the ground was cut with rills.

The sheep hadn't wanted to come here because there was nothing
left to eat. Treeless and fenced with woods, it was a natural pen. It was
grassy once, and it had pastured the skid teams used by the loggers,
Belgians and Percherons like my grandfather's that I loved when I was
small. It would also be ideal to gather and count sheep, and had likely
been used that way, too.

There was no one here to ask. But I had eyes: year by year it had
been ruined, and only thistle could make a home of it now. And if the
meadow was time, then time had been ruined.

By midmorning the snowflakes were small and heavy, and then it
rained. Firs hid their spikes in fog. A woodpecker drilled, unseen, as
the sky shut down and the rain filled the space between the forest
walls. We let the leaders find their way up the benches and rode half
circles behind. Where the snow had melted, the soil was so red-wet it

seemed that the thistles sprouted from raw flesh, and the sheep left a bloody scrape.

Our horses skated down the hills and floundered up, mud balling in the inverted cup of hoof and shoe. You could get off and walk, but you walked on clinging pads of muck that raised your height an inch or two with every step until you tottered, and then came loose and tipped you off balance. With the next step, the cycle began again. Where there was plant life, even thin, tough grass, the soil was firm, but where it was stripped the mud worked its full aggravation. Climbing the benches was like clambering out of a series of greased breadpans.

Every visible surface was wet, even under thick trees. I stopped to watch two mountain chickadees picking the skirts of big spruces. A squirrel yammered. Above scarves of fog, the world was arrayed in stripes of color and a threatening range of whites.

The leaders were already over into the other drainage, and the rest were following. I asked Mitch if he needed me, and he said that he didn't. I told him I wanted to look at the top of the canyon, and he said it was just a bunch of rockslides and a ring of cliffs. I told him I'd be back in an hour.

The woods were full of tracks; I noticed mud scraped in a dirty fan over the snow, and a pungent stink: bull elk in rut. The elk were drifting away from the sheep. I heard shuffles and cracks as they scented me, as they reared up off their beds and melted into the fog. I never saw them, but their tracks were instantly fresh in the snow.

The woods opened on peaks, dark red stone in horizons, with hard layers separated by talus, which held the snow, stark white between swaths of chocolate and burgundy. An avalanche path flooded down to the south, its lower half a heap of bleached pine. Above, I could see the mountain, folded and impassable, grading into the sky. The air smelled clean and full of distance.

I stopped under a dripping tree to write:

> The wind rushes through
> and sings in a winter voice,
> ten winds, a hundred flutes,

and a million pine needles.
Coyotes sing and elk polish their antlers,
burnish each tine on low limbs,
and bugle the first snow down.
And a cold light breaks through pines,
upright and silver on the high ridge:
the mountain's shining horns.

The pages of my notebook were marcelled like spinach leaves, and the tip of the pencil scored the paper. I walked to my horse and rode back and made a fire in the stove. As I dried the journal, I thought about Cassandra. I'd lied to her, out of pity, and we suffered for it, and then her body had betrayed us both. And then she lied to me, and baited me, and reserved the truth until the last. We both suffered, but she wore the scar.

The rain came between the pipe and steel thimble, and hissed on the stove as I wrote a song:

her little cold hands
her long wet hair
woman-going-to-the-sea
makes the world soft

(I imagined a room full of people, holding a ceremony for the rain. Someone made a sound, like a drop touching down, simple, repeated. She touched another, who made a different little sound, who touched another, and so on, until the lodge sheltered a human storm. It would take a whole village to do it right. With Mitch and me it'd be pretty limited.)

While I tried out rain sounds, Mitch stooped into the tent. My lips were pursed, and I was making a muted click with my tongue. I stopped and smiled.

"I don't want to know," he said.

"I was trying to imitate the rain. I was thinking it'd be neat if—"

"Look!" I hadn't noticed what he held: two big gold birds. "Ruffed grouse," he said. "Best goddam eatin' on the planet."

"Wow! How do you cook it—them?"

"Clean and pluck. Then, we'll roast 'em in the stove."

"There're some of those mushrooms down the road. The kind you said were okay."

"Shaggy manes. Go pick some and we'll have a serious fiesta."

Mitch did the cleaning and plucking. He'd hunted grouse and geese and ducks, and knew what he was about. I filled my hat with shaggy manes and sliced them into a pan with butter and wild garlic. I'd never tasted grouse before. After old mutton and beans, it was the stuff of dreams. We each ate a whole bird. It didn't occur to me until afterward that he'd poached them.

"I didn't hear shots."

"Can't shoot grouse with a .30-.30. You'd blow 'em to shreds. Hah! I chucked a couple of rocks. This place is thick with grouse, and they hardly get hunted: too far from the road."

"If it's that easy, I'm surprised there're any left."

"There aren't, close to roads."

"What if you get nailed?"

"How many game wardens have you seen lately?"

"Good point."

"Those boys stick close to the stove and the whiskey barrel. Besides, part of living up here is eating off the woods. It's not like we have fringe benefits. If I was living in town, I wouldn't come clear up here to knock off grouse with rocks."

"True. But why shouldn't you hunt grouse with rocks? It's cheaper than a double-barreled Purdy and a pair of Brittany spaniels. And it's quiet."

"A rock's not sporty. It doesn't cost a cent. You can't brag about the custom-engraved rock you just bought. It's more like picking a feathered cabbage."

"*Cabbages with wings.* The time has come, the Walrus said—"

"To shut up and wash things. Like dishes. And go to bed."

And so, leaving the rest to providence, we did.

The thought of leading the pack string up the slick and viscous trail after the sheep was daunting. Mitch said there was an old wagon road up the North Fork, and that seemed like the best route to move the camp, so we packed up and went our opposite ways.

I led the pack string down the washed-out road, looking at skid trails that snaked up the hill into wet oblivion. An elk bugled from the green wall to the south, and the horses nickered back. The road forked, and I took the way I hadn't been, to the left. It curved above a headcut, where the creek dropped off into a deeply eroded gulch, and then held to the south bank above the streambed.

The rocky channel held pockets and pools, with no visible flow between them. The rocks in the creekbed were either flat gray or dark red, a contrast unpleasant to my eye. A little stream came clattering in from the south through spruce roots and fell into the gorge, only to disappear.

A thin layer of cloud floated halfway between ridgetop and creek, and slow rain ticked on the shoulders of my slicker and dripped from limbs to the soaked ground. Twig tips shivered when hit by drops and made tiny gestures; by the time you could focus they were still again.

The mud was like wheel-bearing grease, and the constant drip from the trees could send you mad. This canyon had been clearcut early; the stumps, almost four feet thick, were pure silver like sea wrack. The second-growth spruces and firs were thirty feet tall. The only spots still dry were near the trunks of the few remaining old spruces and Douglas firs, so shaggy with limbs that the wet took a week to get in.

We reached the fork, and just below the stream crossing was a dry spot under thick trees above the stream. I wasn't tired, but stopped to savor the dryness and let the horses nip wet tufts of grass while I ate wild rosehips, using my teeth to scrape the tart, sticky flesh. At my feet were pellets of scat in two sizes: elk and deer. There was a litter of small bones, toothmarked, so a coyote or a fox had eaten here, out of the rain. And there was a modest firepit, seldom used. This was a place held in common, in which to rest and stay dry.

I thought of cats on rainy days, how they assume a gentle nothingness. And how the dogs loved sleep almost better than waking. Death wasn't the enemy, here in the dry place under the trees, among the broken twigs and bones. Minds went with bodies and could never be separate or pure if bodies were not. And a life could be worn thin, or worn out. It would be good, after hard and difficult being, not to be.

I stepped out into the rain again and mounted, and set off up the wagon road. At the fork there was a beaver pond, heavily silted and vegetated, with no recent sign of use. From bare ground—clearcuts and the road—more soil washed into the creek, so the beaver ponds would fill in more quickly with silt. When the dam couldn't be raised, and the water was no longer deep enough to cover a swimming beaver, they moved on to build in another spot.

Birdcall: *plllea-oooo!* To sing on a day like this. A flicker dashed out of a mistletoed pine and flapped away.

The canyon deepened, in thick firs and understory, a place where the sun never stayed and in winter would not touch at all. On the left a branch trail forded the creek in big cobbles, and I could predict where it went: a secret cutoff between the two forks. The right-hand slope was more open, with wide-spaced pines and brush and wilted sunflowers that rattled gently in the rain. On a bank, one pink geranium and a lavender harebell flowered.

Shaggy manes erupted from the road, from ruts where it seemed impossible that something so soft, breakable at a touch, could force its way. There were aspens on the right, and the road climbed into them; flattened on the ground among the yellow leaves was one that had gone iron black. I reined the horse up and bent over before I recognized the small black heart as an aspen leaf. Then I saw others spotted or halved with gold. And in an aspen fork, revealed by the loss of leaves, an abandoned nest was catching rain.

So much despair in cities and in books. I'd learned to live outside, in weather, under the changing sky, and so my dreams lived, too. Suffering was plentiful, yet despair was scarce. I didn't have to imagine that the mountains loved me. They had changed me. I had a country, and I would live in it.

I rode on, leading the horses. Across the road the rain had washed pine needles into rusty bars and crescents and polished the exposed rock and dirt, making up bright patterns with aspen leaves and the final bloom of asters.

The canyon pinched down to a rubbly gorge, and the road doubled north, up the open slope. A failing outside edge and debris from above narrowed the old wagon tread into a rocky trail. Opposite, dark woods absorbed the view, while the road switched back to the west and gained a bench that led into aspen groves and a rolling hillscape.

Aspen were scarce in the canyon's other fork, but they claimed this soft terrain and graced it. Their clear profusion of yellow and vermilion, seen against the spruce darkness put a sweet catch in my breath. In the needles of a young, solitary spruce the fallen aspen leaves hung bright, like Christmas balls.

This was a new sort of place: easy contours, with lots of timothy. The horses jerked their heads toward the rich grass, so I let them graze. It was set with groves of aspen, uncommonly straight and slim. The larger trees had black scars, Egyptian eyes, where their lower branches had fallen, edged with lichen of a deep orange, like fresh rust on cast iron.

The rain stopped, and a light gust covered us in droplets, then in spinning leaves. The horses raised their heads and we set out again. The rolling bench lands ended, and the trail crossed a steep slope high above the creek and then turned north into a pretty, cupped park.

The old road had log drains to let water underneath: large rocks had been set between logs, leaving space. Then smaller logs were laid in a tighter layer, and over that, thin poles with a covering of gravel and dirt. Most of them had collapsed, but this one still worked where a steel culvert would have rusted out long since.

On the south, the forested ridge lowered to a saddle; that was where the herd had crossed. I checked the pretty park for sheep, stopping to listen, and farther along the road saw muddy sheep tracks and the prints of Mitch's horse: he'd pushed them west. The road narrowed to a trail and then made long switchbacks up through old spruce and fir. Where it gained a notch and leveled, I found the herd.

Coming unexpectedly on the sheep, I could still be surprised: they didn't fit this place. A dog barked above, and Pookie loped out of the woods to greet us. Then Mitch rode toward me, grim-faced and shaking his head.

"We have to hold 'em back," he said. "There's another herd in the way: Carricaburra's."

"That's a name?"

"Carricaburra? He's Basque. Ranches just over the line in Idaho. I figured his herders'd be over the top by now. And there's only one way to get a herd up on the crest."

"Where do we camp?"

"Not far. There's a set of hills, and we'll put the tent on top of one. Nice country, isn't it?"

"Different. A lot gentler than where we've been."

"Yeah. With some trail work, you could herd this part out of a wagon: No cracked sawbucks and busted britchen straps. No cold beds on the ground."

"I like the tent and the pack string."

"You'd change your mind when the snow set in. Let's go and throw the damn tent up. We have to keep the leaders from moving any farther. If they mix with that Basco herd, it'll be hell to sort 'em out. And the herders will probably shoot us."

We rode up and set out the camp. To the south was the ridge that separated the two forks, with rounded slopes on the side that faced us. The spine of the range was due west. Northwest, we could look up the long, bare ridge we'd use to drive the herd up onto the crest. To the north, the country rolled: you could ride anywhere, in circles, in figure eights, eyes closed, drunk or half asleep.

The sheep wanted to go up. Badly. We cursed them and dogged them and finally drove them all the way back to the pretty, cupped park, which they proceeded to chop into muck. By then we were both hungry and mad.

I rode up to cook, while Mitch posted himself in the beleaguered notch, in hopes they'd start to bed down. I made tortillas and heated beans and ate, then walked down with his food in the dutch oven, which I'd warmed on the stove. The *borregas* were restless. He de-

cided to herd past dark. I should go back and rest, he said, in case we
had to take shifts.

With the flaps tied back, I sat by the stove and looked out as sunset
outlined the high ridge. My late reading had taken its toll: we were low
on candles. But there was still enough light to write in my journal:

> I thought that I wanted to disappear, and be unknown. But
> keeping this book runs contrary to that. What I see and feel
> makes me want to write, and writing gives me pleasure. I could
> bury this under a cairn of rocks, or open the door of the stove
> and in seconds it would all be smoke. There's no assurance that
> it has any value, or meaning to anyone beside me. If I had to be
> certain that what I write will be appreciated, or deserved, then
> I'd probably leave nothing.
>
> I can always change my mind. But for now, I'll keep it safe.

Mitch came in and fell exhausted into his bed. I went outside to
herd and watched the moon rise over the folded hills. Our camp was
too dark to be seen, but there was a light moving to the north on a
higher hill, like a star circling close to earth. It was one of the Basque
herders, carrying a gas lantern. The sharp white point dipped and then
changed into a triangle of soft yellow: he'd gone inside their tent. There
seemed to be a faint orange pulse on the hill behind their camp, and I
wondered what it was.

Something in me rose with the moon. And the moon almost frightened me then, with its tilted ellipse, so near it seemed like someone's
face—bone-white and gray. The features were blurred, as if through
silk or gauze, and around it were faint spectral rings of color. To the
west the sky was banded with clouds.

The sheep were quiet. The clouds spread east, sending a translucent
wave across the moon, then deeper waves, until the moon became a
furry disk and then only a spot on a dark and shifting sky. Clouds
poured over the crest and covered it, and the rain began again.

I was tired. Damn the sheep. I couldn't even see them in the rainy
dark.

I stooped into the shelter of the tent. The air was moist with en-closed breath and night's humidity. I slipped into my bag, guiltily, and then I slept.

SEPTEMBER 9

Mitch was still asleep. Barefoot, I stepped outside to a heavy dawn. Clouds lapped over the crest and threatened rain. Below the camp lay dense mist. I listened for the sheep: nothing.

I ducked back in to kindle a fire. Listening to the pop and hiss, I scooped coffee into the pot and—delicious moment—slipped into my still-warm bag to watch the dancing circle of light projected through the open damper.

The rain began, and accelerated. As it absorbed water, the tent's canvas tightened and the pitch of the raindrops increased: first dull *whops*, then sprung *whups*, then a flurry of *whips*, building to a sibilant roar.

I waited, as if for nothing else on earth, for the coffee to turn, for the subtle jet of steam. When it rose, so did I. My clothing was sticky with moisture, cold against my skin. My socks, full of grass awns, had to be worn another day: no time to wash clothes, nor weather to dry them. Spongy boots received my feet ungraciously, as the storm beat a last tattoo and then diminished to idle punctuation. I had a longing for blue sky. I looked out the flap, and the cloud was dwindling to the east.

Instead of walking through rainsoaked woods, I'd make sourdough biscuits.

As I took them out of the oven, Mitch woke. "Oh shitsky," he said. "We better dust some butt. Those damn sheep'll be here any minute." All three dogs barked at once. I heard a *baaaaa*.

The morning was sunny, and we spent all of it running through the damp woods, trying to hold the herd down and turn them north. They were restless and as feral as sheep can be, sneaking around us in fours and fives, creeping in stealthy files, and marching silently up the fir-shadowed slopes. It was like playing soccer against five teams, on five fields, at once. We didn't even try to catch and saddle horses. The horse band had wandered all the way back down to the grassy aspen slope. I could see their tails flirting with the sun, a half mile below the clamoring herd.

It was bright and humid. We finally got them stopped when they got hungry and started to feed. At last they lay down in shady spots. When we got back to camp for lunch, we were thoroughly shagged; the dogs fell on their sides, panting, and quickly went to sleep.

We dozed and then woke up crabbily. Mitch ordered me to go and wrangle the goddam horses up. Should've done it first thing, etc. I scooped oats into a feedbag, took a halter and extra lead, and strode off down the hills. The dogs came after me, and I could hear him yelling: "Tikki-*Lo!* Get back here, you little dried-out piece of *shit!*"

But the sheep were bedded, I could see the horses, and the aspen groves were galleries of white and gold. So I made up a horse-catching song:

> All you pretty horses, circling pretty land,
> fat on rye and timothy, running in a band,
> anywhere you run, you're running
> in my open hand. In my open hand.

The horses saw me coming and nodded their heads. Red snuffled in my direction and then trotted over. He dipped his head to accept the halter, then lifted his whiskery chin and showed me huge teeth. As he crunched the oats, I scratched his withers until he shivered with pleasure.

Then the other horses came. I gave oats to Pronto and waited for the colt. Mitch had discovered that when it was nursing we could dust the antiseptic powder into its half-shut eye without even disturbing it. The trick worked again, and the eye was healing.

I slung the feedbag over my shoulder and clipped the extra lead to Red's halter, so I had two long reins. I leaped onto his glossy back and my thighs gripped the ribs beneath his thickening coat as we circled the little horse tribe and got them started, cantering over the golden hills.

In the afternoon the sun was covered and the sheep began to move. On horseback it was easier to turn them, given some risky riding, but they wouldn't settle and feed. Two hills away, I saw the Basques' herd spreading out on the grassy slope above their camp, dogs and herders close behind. I pointed; Mitch looked over, and swore. The herds were still too close, it seemed.

"¡Cabron! We'll have to herd all damn night long," he said.

"Maybe we should drive 'em down again."

"I hate to run 'em over the same ground. We're tearing it up. But it's damn near a full moon, and that makes 'em crazy."

So we drove them down into aspens, farther north. Mitch worried that we were over the boundary of the Preston lease, but he'd left the map at camp. "Looks like those guys already fed this off," he said, "but there's enough left, I guess." We rode back to camp.

"We oughta go over and visit those Bascos," Mitch said. "Find out what's up."

"Sounds good. I'll bake a cherry pie."

"Let's go," said Mitch. The dutch oven was still hot, so I wrapped it in a burlap sack and wore a leather glove. "Let's ride," he said.

"No way, José. It's not that far."

As we hiked toward their camp, he explained that Basques were horsemen, caballeros, and there was a serious lack of dignity in our arriving on foot. I countered that it would be a far worse loss of face to get bucked off because you scorched your own horse with a dutch oven.

Above their camp they were bedding their herd on the long, grassy slope of the bowl. I counted five dogs and they worked on hand signals alone. "Look," Mitch whispered. "That's how sheepdogs should work. Not this ravening wolf-pack crap."

The herders left a dog posted at each compass point, to contain the sheep. One of them picked up a big, lumpy canvas sack from the ground and took out an object as familiar as it was odd—a highway blinker, one of those orange lamps mounted on a yellow battery box— and set them at intervals around the sheep.

"They bed 'em tight," Mitch muttered. "Helps guard against coyotes, but it's tough on the soil."

One of the herders saw us and hurried down, followed by the remaining dog. It barked, and Ansel and Tiger and Pookie bristled and dashed away, as Mitch swore under his breath: "Makes us look pretty good. Coming in afoot. Dogs running wild like wolves. Son-of-a-rattlesnake!" He felt like a second-rate shepherd.

The Basque's dog stood her ground as ours circled and bumped hips; the four dogs sitting around the herd looked on and whined but never shifted a paw. "Look at that. Those dogs are schooled. Prestons don't spend a lick of time on their dogs. And it comes out of our hide. Oh, dammit anyway!" The man shouted a greeting and then walked toward us and put his hand out to shake.

"¿*Mis amigos. Como están?*"

"¿*Bien, gracias, señor, y usted?*" I was cruising on dialogue one.

"*Muy bien. Están borregueros, tambien?* ¿*Americanos, sí?*"

"*Sí. Estamos del Rancho de los Hermanos Prestón. En la Valle de las Estrellas.*" Valley of the Stars: I was proud of that.

"*Ah. Notabilísimo.*" He said it wryly. "*Una copita?* ¿*Cafe?* ¿*Entiende?*"

"Uhhh, *Sí, grácias.*" I puzzled that out as we all shook hands. Basques had a language all their own, I knew, of staggering difficulty. We exchanged names and his was *Bic-tour:* Victor.

I held up the dutch oven but couldn't remember the word for cherry. Then I did, and blurted it out—*cereza*—but realized I didn't know the word for pie.

"Did you ask for some beer?" Mitch asked.

"No, *cereza*'s cherry. But I can't remember *pie.*"

"Hmmm," Mitch said. "How about pee-ay?"

"No. That means foot. ¿*Uno . . . un dulce de las cerezas?*"

"*Ahhh!—Como no?*" The man laughed. He was young, and had a black beard and bright, intelligent eyes. He and Mitch could have been cousins. "¿*Es una empanada?* ¿*Sí?*"

The other herder came over the brow of the knoll, heavier and older. Victor shouted to him. "*Ay, Juan! ¡A buenas horas, viejo!*"

"*Tarde o temprano,*" he replied, with a sour expression. "¿*Convidados?*"

"*Pásale.*" Victor ushered us into the tent and motioned to the bed.

They had built up a frame of rocks and poles and arranged fir tufts on it, then covered it with canvas and laid out their bedrolls. Mitch and I sat down. It was springy and aromatic.

"How the old-timers made beds," he said. "Tears up the trees, but it smells like heaven."

Juan, the older man, stoked the stove, and we sat and tried to talk while the coffee brewed. When it was done, he poured us mugs and apologized. *"No tenemos vino,"* he said. *"Hay desgraciado. Pero mañana o pasado mañana, tomaremos mucho."* He went on about the wine, but I couldn't make it out. The river of wine?

"Ah, sí," Mitch nodded, *"esta bien, mucho vino."*

I remembered the cherry pie, which I'd set at my feet. I put it on the kitchen box and lifted the lid; it smelled like God's warm breath. After lengthy exclamations in Basque, Juan fetched four metal plates and cut the pie into quarters. We ate it all. *"¡Sabe a la gloria!"* he said, finishing up.

Victor held out a can of tobacco. "Prince Albert," I said. "Hot damn." I rolled a fat cigarette, and so did Mitch, and we smoked until we were dizzy—not long—and drank a second cup of coffee, and tried to converse about horses and sheep, with the four of us in the over-heated tent, each trying to avoid a yawn.

We walked back across the hills toward the moon. When we got to the tent I saw a strange glint on the ground by the firepit. It was my pennywhistle, bent and flattened by the colt. "Evil little shit!"

Mitch walked over and grimaced. "Ouch. Bet he snaffled it out of your pack."

"And brought it here to stomp, where I'd see it. I hope his stupid eye falls out."

"Naw," Mitch said. "Horses aren't evil. He's just a little wild."

He went off with the battery lantern to see if the herd had climbed up, but wasn't gone long. "They're bedded—didn't want to wake 'em up. I'd better get up about two. When the moon gets high, they move. I'll go afoot. The Bascos said they were going over the top tomorrow? For sure?"

"He said tomorrow night they'd be drinking rivers of wine. Or something like that."

"Good. We can't hold these wooly devils back much longer."

SEPTEMBER 10

I rise in the dark without effort, feeling a new toughness, one that is not unkind. The nights are longer and colder, but the mountain dark is not as frightening as it was. I can step out of the tent and not feel as if something is waiting to pounce. I can find the horses and they come to me. Each day I split wood and where my eye goes, the axe strikes. I've learned how to lay a fire that will catch and grow.

Something has happened; I feel stronger, and at the same time, freer. I've learned to endure, but I don't feel *hard:* there's a hardness that I associate with growing up—Royal's face closing as he shot the lamb, or Roger standing over the bear—and I don't feel that way.

Mitch is out with the sheep, and it's good to have the tent quiet, except for the rumble of the fire, writing by candle, waiting for the coffee to turn. Pookie's asleep by the stove. The pencil is dull and I sharpen it with my knife and give the point a final touch-up with a pebble. I feel like I'm opening into the world.

Even with the rain and the snow, wet boots and cold feet, with the ugliness of sheep, with our soreness and sickness and tiredness, even accepting all this just as it is, the beauty is not less, but more. And it is undeniable, like the wetness of rain, or the cold of snow, or the heat of this fire on my skin, and right that this beauty should find me and pass through me like a storm through these pines.

This is the turn of the year. Summer is gone.

Now, the heat of a clear, still day is to be savored. On exposed slopes, except for the crowns of the pines, there is almost no green left. I think about how natural it seems for the plants to die. I spent the whole summer learning the names of flowers, like friends in a strange city, and now they're dying, these friends whose names I know. Some slip out like refugees, in dull browns and blacks, and some go in glory.

Balsamroot covers dry, sun-facing slopes with furry gray-green leaves the length of a child's foot. On the first night of hard frost, whole slopes go yellow and then quickly brown. Then whole hillsides rattle as a cold gust passes and the first driven pellets of snow strike with a fearful clatter, which diminishes as the leaves are weighed down, flattening over the rocks like wet newspaper taking the shape of a curb.

Mule-ear sunflowers grow in moister spots than balsamroot, with rich yellow blooms and a leaf that's long and curved like a stone hunting point. With frost, the leaves in the open turn muddy yellow, with blotches that look like tobacco spit. But in shelter they turn a mild, transparent red and then curl into parchment brown—crackly but not as loud as balsamroot—and laminate along the ground. After a winter under snow they emerge translucent, veined like the wings of bats.

Thimbleberry has leaves vaguely maple-shaped but much larger than a hand, which are first edged in a sickly yellow that moves toward the center. As the yellow claims it, each leaf turns brown and curls in, like a scrap of old leather too brittle for use.

Fireweed has seeds with glossy parachutes that burst from long capsules. I've watched them float by, close enough to catch, over passes far above timberline. True to its name, it takes on molten crimsons and golds, holding its color even as the snow hides it.

Mountain ash, while still green, puts on dense clusters of scarlet-orange berries, and then the long leaves, arrayed so that each side of a branch could be the mirrored image of the other, turn a pale yellow with hints of crimson: the prince on the high hill, an arrow through his breast.

Pearly everlasting has pure white, papery sepals that fluff out from a bread brown center. Green, it captures no one's eye, but now, in death, the sepals have a dense gleam like shredded silk.

The wild carrot turns mustard and blaze orange, then withers in a night, the feathery leaves curling in, as if to grasp their own nonexistence.

Its coarse cousin, the cow parsnip, has huge leaves, which cure evenly to a pleasant straw color, and a bold form, its hollow stems thrusting out multiple stalks, each of which bursts like an arrested firework into umbels. At the tip of each umbel is a large, flattened brown seed. A field of them reminds me of a gospel congregation, hands up in praise. After the seeds fall, each umbel looks like the frame of an umbrella stripped by the wind. As the snow falls, they stand and filter it until only the brown tips show, flowering with frost.

The coffee's done. I pour a cup and divide an orange, and eat a cold biscuit with peanut butter and jam as I write.

Conifers die otherwise, not by season but by storm and rot and fire. Their crowns break off, or their roots lose grip. On ridges, limber pines are gored by lightning, their trunks split by boiling pitch and limbs blown off. Lightning leaves a scar, sometimes a straight path from sky to ground, sometimes a spiral, which weathers as fresh pitch oozes out and ages, to straw and sulfur, rust and umber, stone and soot. A limber pine dies with its roots veined into the rock and can stand for centuries, holding its place in the sky.

In deep woods, in Engelmann spruces, the red rot travels up from the soil, weakening the core, or it carries fire up the heart of a living tree and leaves it hollow. Because they grow tall on unstable earth, spruces are thrown down by wind, or undercut by brawling streams, or scarred and snapped by avalanche. Douglas firs, too, die in great falls, concussions that travel the earth and trouble us as we sleep.

Subalpine firs, which favor north-facing slopes and wet spots, don't grow large here. When the ground is soaked they blow over, but mostly they go yellow, lose needles, and are slowly covered in vivid tufts of moss. By the time they fall, they are so light, so porous, so much reduced that they hardly make a sound.

This is something you learn, if you haven't been taught: the texture and weight of these innumerable deaths, in the forest where so much wood is dead and down and splintered and rotting, where the bones of animals figure the wet brown floor like runes. The forest, though dense and shadowed, hides nothing: it wears death like a coat.

Lie down in the woods, among broken branches and fallen needles and lost leaves, and look close on smoldering fireweed, the brilliant geranium, and wild strawberry fading from rose to black, these last, bright presences: better the leaves than tight faces, white walls, and brushed stainless steel.

The cup's empty, still warm in my hand. Time to go. Catch horses. Ride.

The sky drained to the west, into the white tunnel of the moon. Frost on the grass iced my toes as I saddled up, and the red horse was crazy. He took me on a forward lunge, my arm strained by the horse I led, and ran through the timber, hoofbeats accompanied by the snap of branches on my head and arms. My glasses were opaque with frost, so I ducked my face to the horse's neck and worked my hands up the reins until, without sitting up, I could hold him in.

"What's wrong, Red Man? You smell those Basco horses?" I scratched his neck and he nickered low in his chest. I took my hat off and brushed splinters and bark away, then stood up in the stirrups and swept the saddle.

There was smoke rising from the margin of the woods, and I rode that way. Mitch sat against the base of a pine, leaning over a little fire with his canteen cup in the ashes. Ansel and Tiger were tied. He rose stiffly, suppressed a yawn and then let it come, arching his back until his beard stood straight out.

"You made it," he said. "Cold."

"Got your horse. The sun's not up."

"Didn't you hear all that hell bust loose?"

"No. What?"

"Coyotes in the herd. Killed a lamb. I took a couple shots, but they ran the poor bugger into the shadow of the trees. But I kept shooting— it scared 'em off. The sheep scattered downhill, at least, instead of charging up into the Basco herd. But I thought you'd come roarin' down here."

"I slept right through."

"Lucky. Not much you could've done, I guess. Rough on the lamb. I bled it out and cut the back quarters off. We could take the front for the dogs, since we're low on food, but I don't want 'em eating off the carcass. Help me sling it on Tony and I'll go get some sleep."

With Mitch on his way I rode north of the herd, Pookie trotting behind. They were feeding. If the other herd moved on we could let them go. I thought I heard a shot to the west, not the crack of the .30-.30 but a hollow boom.

I rode up onto a knoll where I could see the crest, and there were sheep moving up the long, bare ridge toward the top. There was another shot and the sheep surged, legs blurring in their own shadows. What was going on? There were two more shots, echoing, and high shouts, and then a wild pealing of bells. A second wave of sheep rushed up the ridge. Sunlight touched the crest and came down, lighting up each sheep in turn, like the dirty sails of a fleet riding the dawn swell. The young herder rode up into sight, his shirt a tarnished red, with a double-barreled shotgun in his hand, held steady as the horse jogged up the slope. *Ka-boom.* That's how they started their sheep.

"Victorrrrrr!" I yelled.

He saw me and raised the shotgun over his head and shook it, and yelled—*"Díos"* was all I could make out. The sheep were bellowing, and the barks of the dogs echoed back from the sandstone cliffs as the old man rode up into hot light leading the pack string, every horse belled and trotting, filling the high bowl with a glorious, brazen racket. And then—it seemed like no time at all—they were gone, sheep, dogs, horses, men, over the rim of the world.

The uproar had roused our herd, and they called back. No matter: our siege was done.

The sun was a gift. I made a quick sweep for strays and granted Pookie a joyous, woofing charge to dig the old ewe and her band of rogues out of the aspens. Then I rode back to the camp.

Mitch was asleep. I caught every horse and let each one eat oats from my cupped hands, checked all the legs and feet, then doctored the colt. After nursing, the colt had taken to sneaking around for a nip. This time I was ready: I flicked a rope and popped him on the ribs. He bucked away, flashing like a hooked trout.

Mitch slept on. I started a fire outside for a pot of beans and, thanking the coyotes—was that heresy?—I cut fresh chops off a quarter before stowing it in the frosty shade. I mixed tortillas, rolled them out, and scorched them on the upturned dutch oven lid.

Once known, all this could be loved in a thoughtless way: the flames invisible in the sun, and tortillas smoking, and beans demanding pepper and molasses, bubbling up a rich steam. I loved holding this modest and flexible house. In the dark, or under storm, the candled warmth of the tent gave me a contentment as pure as anything I'd known. And a tent could be struck and moved and set up once again.

I liked our modest and portable means: the stove's clever shape, the strengths of canvas and latigo, the tricky diamond of a hitch—things knowable, palpable, human. I raked coals to one side and began to broil the slices of lamb.

I could live out here with a string of horses and a tent. And if we had two good women up here, and their arts, and another tent, we could all live well enough. We could camp close sometimes and then move apart. I kept thinking this would be perfect without sheep. But the sheep would give us food and clothes. So a small band would be fine. And good horses, parallel to us in their generations. We would cook up nettles and waterleaf, dig roots, hunt elk and deer, and save the grouse for feasts.

But when summer was gone and the snows came, we'd have to move or die, down to the valley to trade meat and hides for beans and flour. Could we winter on the desert in a canvas tent? It struck me that I was describing the start of our civilization: Levite, Bedu, the hill tribes of Greece. Like them, we would follow our herds, dust and stench the price of our freedom, and mold fresh dung with our hands to build fires. There's something fierce and vivid about the herding tribes, always moving, always armed and suspicious, always taking or trying to take.

If the thought seemed noble, the life could be cruel: I knew that now. And we would know enforced stoicism and learn the hatred of strangers. We could afford only our own truths, and the need for loyalty would soon overwhelm our kindness. And even in that tight little band, pain could still make us strangers.

That rush of insights, like one horse stampeding a band, overwhelmed me. So I stopped imagining and took a deep breath: I didn't have to make the whole world fit into my head at once. The world doesn't have to make sense. The world *is*. And I could live without knowing the beginning and end.

I stirred the beans, turned the chops, and admired the tortillas. It wasn't that hard to live up here, once you learned what had to be learned. The hard part would be to go back.

I whistled and Mitch woke up inside the tent. I realized the flies were gone. They'd lessened when Cassandra was here, but I hadn't noticed. The sun was warm on my back, and on the side of my face as I turned to the heat of the fire. He rattled some papers. "The food's done," I said.

Mitch came out with a map. "Those Bascos must have thought we didn't have good sense."

"How so?"

"I thought maybe we were on Carricaburra's allotment. We never even crossed the line. Those thieving bastards were on our side."

"And we rode up with a deep-dish cherry pie." I laughed.

"They probably expected worse. Stealing feed is a game with those guys."

"Maybe it's sheepmen, period."

"Hah! Those damn Bascos beat everyone."

We stopped arguing to eat.

He went out to catch a horse as I washed up and thought about the whole strange business of livestock. You get the sense, as a herder or cowboy, of being attached to the herd, and the feeling's oppressive. My dad dreaded having to go out when one of the herders quit. And I thought of my granddad complaining that he couldn't keep good help. It struck me that if they could, ranchers would literally *keep* the help. It wouldn't be a big leap from owning sheep and cows to claiming Mitch and me. One reason, I realized, that cowboys and herders will quit a good job for a poor one is to break that psychic enslavement.

I kept getting madder and madder. At thieves who spawned burghers who reared proprietors, a gang for whom possession was the only point of life. I ended up throwing pinecones at a rock.

Odi et amo. Catullus. Me too.

Pookie watched me from the fringe of the woods, head cocked. I stopped throwing cones and looked at her, and she gave a tentative wag and lifted a paw. So I dropped the last pinecone and buried my face in her thick ruff. Then I growled and pushed her over on her side, and held her down. There was pitch on my hand, and I could feel it sticking to her coarse hair. I rolled away, and it was her turn to leap, snarling, and to close her jaws on my wrist until I whined in submission.

Too weird. She sat back and cocked her head again.

"Hey, Pooka-pook. I don't know what to make of it, either."

A birdcall stopped us both. I couldn't see the bird, but the call was a sweet hinge-creak, repeated. It sounded like Grandma's front gate. All I could do was listen, and hope it would come again.

9 ~
Salt River Crest

We'd talked about night herding, but we needed rest. The sheep were all around the camp, and the dogs would warn us if the coyotes came back. They'd been trailing the other herd, Mitch thought, and peeled off when ours, bedded loose and without blinkers, proved easier pickings.

Mitch woke me early. There'd been no sign of coyotes, but he hadn't slept. He was nervous about the move up the ridge and south along the crest. There were three steep drainages they could stray down, so once on top we had to drive fast and hard for about two miles. Then we'd drop them into the Double Heart for three days before trailing out along the ridge.

Our exit from North Murphy was slower than that of the Basques and lacked their style: no explosions or bells. We dogged them at first light up the ridge. There'd been a trail, but the other herd had turned it into a smear of disturbed earth. It was steep, but Red felt good under me, solid and sure. We had the leaders on top by sunup.

Mitch rode through with Anselfrond to turn them south while I worked with Pookie and Tikki-Lo, keeping the pressure on. The limpers and stragglers reached the top a half hour later. I found Mitch just over the crest. "That's Stewart Creek down there, and the leaders are probably in the head of Corral Canyon, so I better get over there quick. They're spread out, so push the drags until they close up some. If it goes okay, I'll be waiting south of that double-top peak, to turn the leaders east. If it doesn't, we'll be hunting sheep for weeks."

He rode off, the herd parting like a bow wave in front of the horse. As the sheep milled in his wake, Ansel jumped up and ran across their heaving backs.

I hadn't been on the crest since crossing Prater Pass, and after a summer in the canyons it felt as if walls had fallen away. The ridge was a rocky archipelago in the sky. If there was any great and measuring eye, you could not escape it here.

Just south of where we gained the ridge, there was a gentle summit, and beyond it rose Stewart Peak, split by a shadow line with an east of bright bronze and a west of snow-patched blue, where a ragged forest rose almost to the top.

We'd driven the herd across ridges but never along one so high and narrow. The continual up-and-down was hard on Red, and his neck was sweaty when I got off to lead. I sent Tikki-Lo high and Pookie low, to nip the laggards. It took an hour to drive the herd into the peak's shadow; in the shade the sheep seemed to gain momentum. When I stopped to rest, they kept going. Halfway around the peak I stepped onto a trail, a relief from sidehilling, and led the horse at a slow walk, following as the herd formed standing waves over down trunks and outcrops, ewes bawling and lambs leaping high into the air.

South of the peak, the trail was just below the narrow crest, so I ground-reined the horse and scrambled up for a look: against the morning glare I could see dark red towers looming over the south fork's broad avalanche paths. To the west was a rocky summit splitting the air between Corral and Birch Creeks, which fell in giant steps toward Star Valley far below. The trail rounded a shadowy cove at the head of Birch Creek and then curved the other way, around the west flank of the double-topped peak. The mountain had a high, pointed summit on the east and a crumbling one to the west. It was cold in the shade of the peak and then gloriously warm in the sun. The air was absolutely still.

Beyond the peak the ridge undulated, surfaced with sharp pebbles cracked from long outcrops of limestone. The stringers of rock were hedged with wild currants, yellow-leaved, the red berries gone dark under frost.

I saw Tony tied to a flagged pine and Anselfrond posted; then I saw Mitch ranging down into the conifer thickets as sheep drained away to the east. I waved and he waved back, and Red bugled to Tony, and the dogs all barked. Then Mitch and I were face to face, as the horses and dogs performed their bumps and nuzzles and growls.

"It worked," he said. "Pretty slick. Perfect weather, too. Probably the only day all year of dead calm on this ridge. Did you get a good sweep?"

"No strays down Birch or Corral. They'd need parachutes to drop off east."

He squinted and looked me up and down. "See any?"

"What?"

"Parachutes!"

We laughed with relief, and roughed up the coats of the dogs. The sheep filtered down until the last wooly rump was gone under the swell of the slope. Below, in the highest bowl, the leaders were already spreading out to feed. We sat in the sun awhile and not one sheep poked its dull head up, so Mitch declared the job done. We'd ride back and pack up and move to the windspill: our last camp in the range.

The two horses grunted and locked their front legs going down into North Murphy, sending loose rocks clattering down. It didn't take long to pack up. We heated coffee on a twig fire and ate tortillas with peanut butter and jam, sitting on the loaded panniers. Then we were off. But as we followed the long arc above the head of North Murphy, Mitch swore and pointed.

"Son-of-a-businessman! It's that old ewe and her rascals."

"I should have noticed she wasn't in the drags," I said.

"Damn! I didn't even think. 'Course she'd have slowed us up so bad that we'd probably have sheep scattered from here to the Tincup Trail."

The Tincup Trail was in the Caribous, clear over in Idaho. I laughed.

Mitch fumed. "Now we have to drag that old skank all the way up and along the ridge to get those lambs. Can't leave 'em in North Murphy, with the coyotes running thicker than fleas. Oh dammit all to hell! You go on. I'd better ride back down."

"I'll set up camp. The flat spot?"

"As if there was more than one. There's a patch of firs for shelter."

"Where do the horses go?"

"Keep Tubby on picket. Lead the others toward the sheep and watch 'em until they're down the steep part. They should start grazing on that cured grass and then get thirsty; the water's down in the bowls. It's a big corral. I'd better go."

"If you aren't back by sunset I'll ride over."

"If I get stuck I'll build a fire." He rode north and disappeared into the ragged woods.

The campsite sloped to the west, the only possible spot. I picketed the old mare. The other horses dropped over the curve of the slope.

To be up here in a storm would be like riding the bow of a ship. The sheltering firs on the west weren't much higher than the ridgepole, and I faced the tent flaps east, over the blue depths of the Double Heart. I set up the stove and kitchen boxes, and laid the bedding out, and gathered such firewood as I could find: dessicated sticks. In the stunted thickets under the camp, broken glass clinked and rusty cans rattled away from my boots. I decided to take a rope and go lower on the slope, where the trees were bigger, and came back up with a bundle—two days' worth.

The air was still and warm for mid-September at 10,000 feet, so mild it made me nervous. So I poled the tent walls and gathered rocks to stack along the hems. I cut fresh meat, then hung the quarters in a scraggly pine and started a fire in the stove, expecting Mitch to return hungry.

An hour later I had a pot of rice and a pan of cubed lamb and onions, red with chili. My tongue was swimming; I stepped out and looked along the ridge. The distant rim of the world was a smoky blue. If I had to go drag sheep through the dark, I didn't want to do it on an empty stomach, so I spooned glistening chili over a heap of rice.

Done. I bagged a couple of tortillas and spooned chili into an empty can. Mitch had his canteen cup and a spoon and matches in his saddle-bag, so we could spend a night out. I puzzled about whether to ride or walk, and decided to go on foot with the battery lantern and some rope in a day pack.

When I set out with Pookie to the north, the sun was gone. The fir jungles were a shaggy, unmoving black, and the great bare faces of the peaks rose to the east like the strokes of a brush. The moon was a disc of flawed glass, backed with gold. And the air was turning cold.

I could hear every step, count each particle of grit that ground under my boots. Flash-frames danced in my head: Mitch rolled under the horse and flowering blood from his mouth. Mitch writhing in the rocks with a splintered femur lanced through his jeans. Mitch staring white at the sky. And always the moon, white and observant, lifting above the broken country. I didn't know prayers for this, so I kept walking and whispering *no sweat, no sweat, no sweat.*

Pookie sniffed. Then she barked. A dog barked back. And Mitch's voice floated out of the tangled woods. "Go up or go down, but get out of the way."

I grabbed Pookie's collar and hauled her up the shingly incline. Lumpy profiles bobbed into sight, two, three—the rogue lambs—four, five, six. They bleated softly to each other. Then came Mitchell leading Tony, and they both limped. I fell in behind. "You got 'em," I said.

"Fuckin' A."

"Six lambs. Where's the old bitch?"

"She's not here." He looked away.

"Did you leave her in North Murphy? For the coyotes?"

"Yeah." He clamped his jaw and stared at the blank side of the peak. I could see the muscles working. Then I could smell tears. I didn't know they had a scent. They do.

"Camp's up and there's food. Probably still hot. Horses are fine. I'll lead Tony."

"No." His hand tightened on the reins. He didn't say anything else.

It's harder to herd six sheep than it is six hundred. It took us a while to get them into the head of the bowl. They finally located the herd and shuffled down in the moonlight. Mitch pulled his saddle off right there on the slope, and slipped the bridle off Tony's head. Then he slapped at the horse's rump and missed. The horse called, got an answer from below, and dropped out of sight. Mitch looked toward the camp, gripped the horn of his saddle, and lifted it; the blankets fell out and he tripped on them. He sat down hard, clutching the saddle horn.

"Fuck," he said in a low voice, not his own.

I lifted the saddle. He stood up, sucking air through his nose, and gathered the blankets and slung the bridle over his shoulder. We tramped back up. I forked the saddle onto our pile of gear and he covered it with blankets. He didn't even look at the food. He shucked his boots and tossed his clothes in the corner of the tent and collapsed.

I made sure he was covered. I sat up with a candle until the moon no longer looked in through the flaps. Then I put the food away and tried to sleep.

SEPTEMBER 12

"Cut her throat."

I touched my face and opened my eyes. Moonlight showed the coarse weave of the tent and the outlines of beaten firs.

"*Mitchell?*"

He rolled in his quilts. "Cut her throat."

"The ewe?"

"She wouldn't climb up."

"Lame. I know."

"Roped her, and she laid on her side and wouldn't walk."

"Yeah."

"So I drug her up. The lambs."

"Yeah."

"Trailing blood. Wool was worn off her ribs and the skin was starting to tear."

"Yeah. Okay."

"*What the fuck do you do?*"

"Don't know."

"*Six lambs.*"

"Yeah."

"She was already dead."

"Okay."

"So I went crazy and kicked her and cut her throat. There was a cliff. I rolled her over the edge and I almost fell." I could hear him moving in his bedroll. "And Tony ran off and the lambs scattered, and I was alone."

I tried to think of words. "You held up longer than I did," I said. But he was asleep again.

And I was alone. Firs inked themselves onto the tent. I fought out of my sleeping bag and went out. The moon burned low on the jags of the Caribous. The shadows of trees cut across the narrow ridge.

O God, goddam. I saw the old, fat, blemished body gaping at the throat, spraying blood as it spun off a broken edge. She. Not *it*. I could barely breathe.

Forget. But the rocks shone hard and blue in the sinking light. The night was as hard as the inside of a rock.

Forget. That flattening sack of wool that even coyotes would abandon to the cold compression of winter, the confessional of snow.

Forget. What would be revealed in June on the streaming talus. Scraped hide, matted wool, and a skull. No message. An arrangement of dead things.

I slipped my knife out of its sheath and imagined an opening between the first two knuckles of my right hand. I imagined the knife, going there. It surprised me how easily the tip came out my palm. In my imagination, it didn't hurt. It felt like the wind, inside my hand. Then I took it away. There wasn't much blood.

I held my hand up to the moon. Pain was a practical matter. I wrapped a bandanna around it, grinding the bones together. And then I imagined the pain.

I don't remember this. The moon was bright.

So I went inside.

～

Heat radiated from the stove. Mitch was gone.

The coffeepot was half full and the kitchen boxes were open. There were crumbs on the flaps. I stepped out into the level sun and it heated the whole length of me.

I walked barefoot to the edge. I had to shift my feet to find a place where I could stand. The old mare was gone, the picket rope trailing over pulverized rock, and my eye followed the twist of the braid all the way to the frayed, wet shag at the end.

The light had barely kindled down in the Double Heart. That was Mitch's name—there was no name on the map. I saw the fat horse shape and the rider dividing it. He was scattering the herd. That was his work. Mine was imagination, or the blade of a knife.

Wide is the grazing land of words.

I untied the bandanna and held my hand up to the sun. Then I tied it tighter and went back to the tent and stirred the coals and stoked the stove. Pookie cried at the flap, and I stroked her. Poor dog. Poor little dog.

I was thirsty. There was no water on the ridge, and we were out. The patches of snow were thin and dirty. It was a long way down to the trickle in the bottom of the Double Heart, and Mitch had taken the horse. I could wait for him, but then there would be nothing to drink and nothing to eat. It was a practical matter.

I didn't really have to think. I got a packsaddle and pad and a halter and put them inside a soft pannier. I added a pot, to scoop water. Then I rolled the matching pannier and stuffed it in. I buckled the straps together so I could carry it as a pack. The top of the slope was steeper than a flight of stairs, and loose, between the tufts of yellow grass.

The horses were at the base, where the grass grew thick. I caught Tom and saddled him and led him down to where I could hear water below. The gully was too steep for a horse. I tied him and scrambled down into the cleft with the empty water bags and the pot. It took a half hour to fill them. In the bottom of the gully there was old, dense avalanche snow, with an arched hole where the trickle appeared. As I drank, I could feel cold air flowing out.

The old horse moaned and wheezed as we climbed, slowly, so slowly, taking long traverses around bulges and concavities. I unloaded Tom and fed him two handfuls of oats. We were almost out of grain. We were low on food, too. We were supposed to use everything up and trail out light. Roger would be up to help. Tomorrow. No. The next day: I'd lost track.

A wind rose out of the west, cool and steady. I sat in the lee of a hedge of wild currants and looked into the Double Heart. It was good to look at the country and think. I could see the summit between the two outlets, the right one, where Chris and I had come up, a sink and the left a plunge. The conical peaks must form, I thought, when the drainage is blocked by a landslide that backs the water up. The old channel might be abandoned, and slowly fill in.

The flowery groove on the right was the original channel. I could picture how it had looked with water flowing that way, and it made sense. The land made sense. Sometimes the water traveled underground, which made it more of a puzzle. But how did that forested dike get there?—a second slide? It wasn't rocky: it looked like a dirt-fill dam. Was the lowest part of the Double Heart once a big sink, like the one that held the high lake? Was it breached first by a headcut in the south fork, then more deeply by the north fork as it undermined the old slide? That would leave a cone of earth in the center.

I didn't know enough to tell. But once I knew enough, I could come back and see what had happened. The land never lied. That was comforting.

Mitch was still down there. He'd spoken out of his sleep; would he remember? I couldn't see him. Maybe he'd come back up to eat. It was a stiff climb. The smart thing would be to hang your saddle in a tree down there, so you could walk down light, catch a horse, and then ride back up.

A hawk dove on me. It seemed to burst out of the air right next to my head, and I felt the pressure of its wings as it veered and then it was past. And it pivoted on the air, *on the air*, like a surfer on a wave, and swung back and hovered without moving its wings at all: they were held in a slight arch, and I could see sunlight through the long feathers and how they adjusted to the flux of the air, and then I looked into its eyes.

And in them was something I couldn't know, cold fire, a mineral brightness. The thing I called beauty could exist without thought, or words. I didn't know male hawks from female. I didn't know their names. But it was big and long-winged and magnificent; it frightened me with its eyes. Then it left. It altered the pitch of its wings and rose straight up, and then swooped west, into the morning shadow at my back.

I opened my journal and drew the hawk in fat, soft pencil, across two pages. When I got back to the camp I found a pen and darkened the slit pupils and outlined the razor opening of the beak. And I will not try to contain this, because it still *is*. We know our lives are changed, and can't explain.

I wanted to go into the Double Heart. So I loaded my day pack and hiked down the slope. The old white horse was halfway down, moving stiffly; this would be his last year in the range. The sheep were in the southwest bowl, which was floored with bluebells and a shallow pond; I could see their tracks like stitches through the tan mud around it. Mitch saw me come down, I thought, but there was no yell of greeting. So I contoured left, away from the sheep, into gullies and over landings with elk beds in the lee of pines, making a long arc, north, then east, then south across bare and sloughing angles patched with grass.

In the foreground the cured grass shone against the near black of spruce and fir on the facing slope. I followed the border of light and shade down to the center, where dusty sunbeams slanted into the depths, looking as if you could climb them.

In a dense grove of spruce there was a fluff of feathers—grouse—but no body: a coyote's good luck? There were coyote prints. The feathers were clean and hadn't been rained or snowed upon. The wing feathers were black with white oval bars scalloped into the margins. Held up to the light they were nearly transparent, and the contrast between the black and the white disappeared: this was something else to know.

I walked east, to look over the dry falls, and stood where the spring snowmelt would fly off into unfinished space. There was no place for the eye to rest, and no path for the foot. Everything had either fallen or was about to fall.

So I walked south along the base of the low summit through the deep spruces and climbed the dike and went down the narrow sink and into the flowery groove. But the flowers were dead and the leaves were brown and matted over the rocks. The underlying shapes were clear now, the rocks under the green.

I looked off the rim and into the great sloping gouge, up which Chris and I had come. Along the braiding channels, thickets of aspen, alders, serviceberries, currants, chokecherries, shrub maples, and mountain ash all overlapped in vibrating pink-shot golds, pointed with scarlet and ember orange. The brightest colors marked avalanche paths.

I turned and wandered back up the sink, bare without its flowers, and over the dike, and through the palisaded grove, and along the rough south slope into spruce and fir. Under the eave of the woods I almost stepped on the bones of a lamb, laid in a bed of wooly hide. It looked as if the animal had simply died here: the leg and shoulder bones were still joined, and the ribs as well. Small bones had been carried off by scavengers, but there was no evidence of butchery— knife marks or greenstick fractures. I knew how a dead sheep came apart.

Agnus Dei. As a lamb knows its mother among the herd, so may the believer recognize God. I couldn't remember where I'd read that. But this was a real lamb. I picked up the skull, and it was about the size and shape of my hands with fingertips overlapped, light as a cardboard box. Maybe it had looked up from here as snow took the high ridge. I tipped it and dust poured out into the air.

There was a ruckus on the wooded slope to the south. Mitch was pushing sheep down toward where I stood, leading Tubby. I circled and came in on the flank, and we put them in the rocky meadow above the outlets. His gaze was turned in. "Get something to eat?" I asked.

His eyes slid off. "I brought some lunch."

"I hauled water. I'll head back up to start dinner. Hungry?"

"I could eat," he said. "Wanted to get this patch."

"Not much to the north. All grass up there. Elk beds."

"Yeah. We'll try to leave it."

"Almost out of grain," I said.

"We're low on everything." He looked at the sheep. Then he shook the reins. He took a different way with the horse than I did on foot, angling south. I came into a narrow grove and a hen grouse flew up, lit, and scuttled off. Her escape led my eye to the cock, his tail fanned out, a velvety, dark-barred walnut, his neck feathers erect, a blue-black ruff. He carried the colors of the fall woods but in deeper shades, more richly embellished. The cock stayed perfectly still, watching me. As my breathing slowed, he folded his tail and retreated, shaking his head. I thought of picking up a rock, but we had a quarter of lamb. So I walked on.

Thinking of Cassandra I walked the bare curves again, looking for my tracks, trying to follow them back. I came to the ridge just north of the camp, and heard the canvas beating in the wind. I could see Mitch in the upper bowl, at the edge of the woods, hanging his saddle from a limb, then pulling a handful of coarse grass to rub the old mare down.

I went into the tent and found my journal and wrote:

> The walls are white;
> the sun shines through,
> tracing each bend of the grass:
> the seeds are ripe and will fall,
> and soon the grass will die.

> There are two cups on the table,
> one green, one red,
> and a small white jar on its side.
> The sun is an afternoon sun;

> even shadows are tossed
> by the wind.
>
> There are spruces
> in the canyon, pines and firs:
> each with a name
> and its own song.
>
> There are seven horses
> on the mountain,
> red, black, and white—
> I must catch them all.

I hefted the quarter of lamb down and cut fresh slices. Then I started the stove and chopped an onion. Once it cooked, I could add the rest of the chili from the day before. I looked into the Double Heart and saw the horses. Mitch was out of sight, climbing the slope, I thought. I had time for another poem.

> From the windspill,
> the mountains are sleeping lions,
> or a lioness, or a woman,
> long and profound, so
> beautiful, lying on her side,
> neck curved like a flowerstem
> or the arc of a deer's leap,
> hair the braided substance of night,
> or a river seen from high peaks,
> that shines like gold or dark blood
> into the calm distance, flowing
> far beyond words—away.

"What are you writing?" Mitch looked into the tent.

"Just stuff. Poems."

He came in. "Did you fall down or something?" He was looking at my hand.

"Slipped. No big deal."

"That handkerchief looks dirty."

"Yeah. I'll change it after we eat."

"Maybe you should soak it." He looked at me again. "Don't let it get infected."

"I won't. You okay?"

"Yeah. Worn out."

"We'll eat and get some sleep."

"Yeah. I'll be fine."

SEPTEMBER 13

I woke up to a coyote, a loud, insistent *gimme* howl. It howled again and I compassed the sound: North Murphy, by the echo, just beyond the narrows in the south fork. How could I tell from inside the tent, wrapped in my sleeping bag? I don't know.

The wind shifted and I got up and tiptoed out to pee. The sky was clear to the north, as the moon rolled down into the west along an arch of cloud. To the south, lightning flickered under a boil of indigo. Then the moon was covered and I heard a gust front sweeping down, the purr of the pines and the thud and shift of the tent.

It came like the wave that tumbled you as a child and filled your mouth with cold salt, wind breaking overhead and the blue rain riding it, and I looked up, and silver spots flew down at me, leaping from one quantum path to the next, darkly bright.

It wasn't the drops that leaped, but my eyes, from one focus to the next.

Fooled again. How much can we accept?

Some. Enough. I raised my face to the rain.

Night rain, high pass

Rain from the southwest
comes as a blue impending dark,
a wind that draws the whole sky down,
a toppling blue, immensely
chill and streaming its water,

blue and silver-blue.
And a joy too quick
for words touches my face
with cold, and
the light's opening.

The tent was a soft shell under the storm. Twenty dollars' worth of canvas, a hundred for sewing it up. A cheap sheet-steel stove, just enough, and a rumbling fire, on top of the broken world with winter bearing down.

If I could be happy with this, then one great problem was solved.

I could be as I wished, without too many burdens: rich in doing and knowing, rich in curiosity and texture, and in thoughts that stood on their own and walked.

Morning. Wind. The tent thunders like a sail and I squint far into the west and see the receding mountain ranges as a blue groundswell.

Facing east, Mitch scans the bowl. The horses are in sight and the sheep are scattered well enough, he thinks, and leaves them to themselves. He cuts tough meat from low on the quarter and chops it to mix with dry dog food. The dogs growl softly as they feed. He scans the bowl again. He wants to bathe in the lake, but the wind's too cold. We sit in the tent, drink coffee, and read books: Thomas à Kempis and Joe Back.

Even though *Horses, Hitches, and Rocky Trails* lacks twenty pages, Mitch has the better deal: the *Imitatio Christi* would grow stiff hairs on a rock. So I try the *Fioretti di San Francesco,* and do better with Saint Francis—poverty, sincerity, etc.—but when he transforms the "very fierce wolf of Agobio" to a meek, bootlicking scrap dog, I give him up, too. Tired of sheep and their champions, I make a bannock in the frying pan and we eat. Then Mitch goes down with clean clothes, hoping for a lull.

I stay and pick currants. Some are a strident red, but most have ripened to garnet and black, gone sweet under their thin skins. Gooseberries. They grow in the shelter of rock outcrops and the leaves are bold yellow, with a few orange, and fewer still spotted with scarlet. As I pick they blow off their twigs and spin down into the lee.

The wind stops. The cookpot is full of berries. I should go swim.

I'm going back to the lake, and I take long, fearless steps down inclines where I wouldn't ride a horse, with the dog running joyful doughnuts around me. The upper bowl reclines under its half circle of tan minarets. On the bench that leads around the end of the ridge, I find a campsite in a fortress grove, sawn stumps and two-by-fours nailed to trees to hold a tabletop. Big rocks tumble around an oversized firepit. It isn't a herders' camp but one made by elk hunters, seldom used.

The lake is lower and the water is murky. Wind has stirred up silt. I'm glad I filled the water bags at the tiny stream: having no outlet, the lake catches runoff and stews it under the summer sun to a rich green broth.

No sign of Mitch. The clouds are sailing overhead but here there's not much wind. I walk around to the big rock. Then I see horse tracks that circle in the opposite direction, and the print of a bare foot in the mud. I walk around to the east shore where the water's deeper. There's a rock I can use for a diving platform. Off with the duds: *Whoosh*.

I was braced for cold, but it's perfect. I open my eyes underneath and it's like being inside a Brazilian tourmaline, sun through smoky green diffusion. I grab a breath and swim out to where it's over my head, and tread water. There are teeny black water bugs, and larger black beetles chasing them. I don't see fish. They couldn't live in a lake like this. I don't see tadpoles either. I swim back to the shallows and my toes raise clouds of silt. Then I swim to the rock.

I lie there, chilled and then warm, watching breezes change the color of the lake. Pookie gets anxious and paddles out to the rock and shakes all over me. I swim to the shore and lie on a rock there, and she repeats the whole thing.

So I put on my clothes and run around the lake, as fast as I can. She chases me. We race through the rushes and along the sand as the lake goes from jade to emerald to black to silver, brushed by the wind.

∼

The last pie of the season, made from wild currants, was cooling on the kitchen box. The last beans bubbled on the stove. A little storm came blustering over and a drop of rain wafted in along the stovepipe and struck the hot iron, gasping into steam. Mitch sat by the stove. "Roger should be up tomorrow afternoon," he said.

"Hope he brings food," I said. "We're down to the last bit."

"He will. We'll gather early and trail out."

"How long does it take?"

"All day. It's about five miles on the map. Probably eight or ten on the ground. But it's rough. Cost you a thousand bucks, if you drive hard and sell your lambs right off the trail."

We ate lamb chops cooked with the last onion, and frybread, and beans, and wedges of gooseberry pie. Mitch lifted a forkful and shut his eyes. I did, too. Then we opened them and smiled. *"Es un empanada,"* I said.

"Es el más mejor en todo el mundo," he said. He stood up and put on his slicker.

"What's up?"

"I'm going to visit the miserable, stinking sheep."

"I thought they didn't need any herding."

"They don't. It's a social call." He left. I had another piece of pie. The berries had an elusive sweetness that hinted at every other fruit on earth. I started to write about that, and put the title down, then changed my mind:

Wild currants

She is asleep who knows
and her dreams distill
the ocean to a droplet,
which, resting in the hand,
is a diamond charm
and a word to open all words,

and a song behind which
all songs lie sleeping.

She breathes quietly, who lives,
and her life infuses the air
with a precious moisture
for which sand is endlessly wept
from eyes of red stone,
a moisture which is a lure
and a cat-footed music,

leaving prints, exquisite
on the dunes,
which the wind carries,
a song like bright dust
swept into the ears of sleepers
calling them to wake, and dance.

Pretty. But it brought Cassandra back. Enough of words. I put the journal down and went out. In the falling light the currants were like drops of blood fixed in the air. I picked a handful—sour and clean—and scratched the brittle thorns from the back of my hand. Then I started walking south.

Air hastened up from the valley to curl over the ridge. Beyond the tracks of sheep, I found the heart-shaped prints of elk crossing from east to west. The air from the valley was rich with the last crop of hay and the lowering rivers, and richer for having risen through pines and firs and meadows of mountain grass.

But it wasn't the smell of the air that played in me so much as the light. The moon and sun lay opposite each other in the sky, exchanging their gleams, and the country was laid out below, all rough and golden.

The ridge was a strong point, the hardest rock in the range. On it you could meet the wind, face it, draw it in and breathe it out. And I felt a desire with no object or reason, except the land and the wild light.

I remembered the hawk, how it breasted the air like a wave, how it turned, riding on nothing I could see, with the light coming through its pinions. And I lifted my arms and began to dance, my hands cleaving the air like small wings, a dance of helplessness, mourning, love, and victory.

There was no one to watch except the dog, and everything I did excited her. She dashed and rolled in the powdered rock and kicked like a fighting cat, then sprang into the air, jaws snapping close to my hands.

It was my dance, that awkward, bold succession of leaps, slides, stomps, and scuffs. Because nothing could be saved, the world would go on, and that was what I had to praise.

I whirled, giving out to the circular forces, hair flying in my face. And I roared, and pivoted on one foot, and dipped low as the dog charged into a strand of storm-beaten firs, and then I ran as hard as I could. I knew nothing of self-preservation or sense, as I flew south over the reefs of gray stone.

My feet seemed to leave the ground. Rock faces dropped away to blue gulfs; the ridge was a gold ribbon leading into the sky. And there was no difference between my eyes and the light, or between my voice and the peaks that echoed, or between my chest and the air that filled it, or between my two hands and the wind.

I reached a point where the east fell away in a great swoop of shadow and the west still sang with light. And I was alone, and glad, and out of breath, at the head of a canyon that led steeply and undeniably down to the valley, and into the dark.

SEPTEMBER 14

Three candles left. We ate the last oatmeal with the last dollop of margarine.

Mitch hiked down, frost splintering from the grass around his boots, as I walked the ridge, wool coat zipped up to my chin. There were clouds in the canyons and valley, and the rising sun extended my shadow across their tops, a gray man-shape miles long. I watched my shadow shorten and then the clouds rose, blowing up formless and visible, encompassing valley, sky, hills, trees, peaks, and sun, all in a thoughtless white.

Mitch returned at midmorning. He thought that coyotes might have scattered the sheep, but he couldn't find any kills. He sat on the brow of the slope and scratched the dogs as he scanned the bowls. There was an itch in the corner of my eye, and I turned and saw Roger walking the ridge from the south, his orange cap burning a hole in the sky.

He carried a frame pack and had a stick. Mitch walked up to him and they shook hands. I tied back the flap of the tent and asked if *El Señor Rogelio* could stand some *café*. "You're early," Mitch said. Roger nodded and set the pack down and unloaded food, and took out a bottle of blackberry brandy.

"Take a swig of this first," he said. It made the round. "Okay. We don't have a buyer yet, and Dad wants to hold off trailing."

"How long?" I asked. Mitch took a longer drink.

"A couple days."

Mitch squinted into the sun. "We're on our fourth day here. I guess there's enough. Two more days, anyhow. But they won't gain weight."

Roger flashed an uneasy grin. "Well, there's no decent feed between here and the valley."

Mitch plucked at his beard. "Six days is pushing it."

"Well, I know. But there's a buyer coming the eighteenth, and the ranger gave us two more days." He passed the brandy again, and my stomach closed on it like a fist. I sat down on a pannier and didn't say anything. He pulled more food out, and I put it into the kitchen box. Cereal. Canned ham and vegetables. Margarine. Five pounds of flour. Coffee. A blue bag of chocolate chip cookies. Peppermint drops. "I brought some extra goodies," he said.

"Dog food? Grain for the horses?" Mitch squinted at the sun.

"Well, no. I couldn't pack a bag of oats up here on my back. They'll survive. Anyhow, since we're not trailing, could we get a count? There's a place we used before."

So we went down and funneled the sheep between two big boulders. I drove, using all three dogs, as they counted. The lambs were almost as big as the ewes; they leaped high when they threaded the gap, even though the ground was flat. I didn't care about the numbers. When they were done, Mitch walked over to me. "I'm ready to get the hell out."

"We're beating it up," I said. "A double heart attack."

He didn't laugh. "Yeah. It's bad, but there's no place else to go."

"Why can't they just pasture 'em at the ranch?"

"If they can sell right off the forest, then they don't have to feed the lambs. Plus Roger said they're still getting their last cut of hay on the north field, and they can't turn the sheep in yet. The baler broke. And their hay hands quit."

"Fourteen-hour days," I said, "and mealy spuds with white-flour gravy. All the rhubarb you can eat. Why in hell would anyone quit?"

Mitch sighed. "Maybe we can try that big slope under the lake again. There's feed left. And then take 'em south of the lake, up in the rocks."

"I walked around that ridge from Bear Canyon. It's rough, but not all that rough."

"We'll just have to hold 'em. Dammit!"

Roger walked over, slipping his notebook into his shirt pocket. "I'd better get a move on."

Mitch turned to face him. "When'll you be up again?"

"Day after tomorrow, about dark."

Mitch gave a harsh laugh. "Bring dinner. No beans, *por favor*. And dog food. And something to munch while we trail out. Cookies. Those butterscotch drops."

Roger blushed and nodded. We watched him climb the slope.

We moved the sheep and held them until they bedded down. As we hiked back up to camp, my ankles hurt, and I made the mistake of saying that. "Arthritis," Mitch said.

"Horseshit!" I shagged a pebble at his boot.

"Hell to get old," he said. As we ate muffins, he said that he'd take his shelter half and night-herd. There'd been coyotes howling the last few nights.

"Over in North Murphy," I said.

"Yeah. Maybe. But they move fast. Let's eat early tonight. You don't need to come."

He wanted to spend the night out with the herd. He'd discovered something—purity in the stoic regime, perhaps in the loneliness. And needed to say good-bye to that.

"Okay," I said. "We'll save the ham for tomorrow night. So what'll it be? Rice and lamb? Or lamb and rice?"

"What are you writing?" My pencil was scratching furiously.

"Bad things about sheep."

"I don't want to hear it, then."

"I won't inflict it on you."

"Maybe we oughta start the food. I'll fire the stove."

"Okay. One more paragraph."

I'll never herd sheep again. My family had owned sheep and cattle, and ranched in Utah and Wyoming since 1850. My great-grandfolks had a ranch in Star Valley, until somebody burned their haystacks one winter and they sold the place. The growing season was too short and they liked Utah better. Irrigation, hay, cattle, wheat, corn, sugar beets, horses, sheep: that was my history, what I had to know. Part of it, not all.

The sheep themselves, as much as I hate them sometimes, are innocent. And we may have been, once, before the frontier. The good part was the steady, stoic, dutiful part. And the trick of making the cotton sacks into curtains and making a joke about the flour gravy and beans. Without that, there'd be no living in this country at all: too harsh, and too much could happen.

If the frontier shaped our character, what was the bad part? That we could claim with perfectly straight faces that God gave us this country. That was the disastrous lie that all the others cover up. That brutal assumption of rights.

The point of the pencil breaks. "Guess I'm done," I say.

"Good. I'm plumb wolfish for lamb and rice. Or rice and lamb."

After we eat he gathers his gear and wraps his shelter half in his yellow slicker and slings it over his shoulder. Then he picks up the rifle. "If it gets weird I'll fire three shots in a row."

"Then I'll come and make it weirder."

"That's about accurate."

"If it gets weird here, I'll write a poem and toss it over the edge. Where's the brandy?"

"I poured some in a hideout jug, but there's more left than you need."

The tent beats in the sunset gusts. I've run out of latigo, and there're only so many rivets that a rotten leather strap can hold. I wander outside, but there's too much wind and space. So I come back in for solace, to sip the brandy and read my book.

I go back to what I've read: that ol' rattlesnake, Homer. But my eye won't rest. Before I finish a line, it jumps ahead to the next, racing as I flip the pages:

I speak of champions among men of earth, who fought with wild things of the mountains, great centaurs whom they broke, and be quiet now beside the long ships, keep your anger bright against the army, quit the war. O Helios, by whom all things are seen! O rivers! O dark earth! O powers underground, we swore an oath and spilt lamb's blood, red wine, and joined our hands, like a dark cloud a shepherd from a hilltop sees a storm, a gloom, more black than pitch it seems with lightning driven along its front. So when these armies closed there came a toiling clamor and far away upon the hills a shepherd hears the roar. Rain-drenched, wind-buffeted, but in his might at ease, with burning eyes— who prowls among the herds . . . Men have twisty tongues . . .

My head was about to split, and I tossed the book onto my sleeping bag and fell on top of it as if my weight could hold it shut.

Wide is the grazing land of words. It frightened me, flying out from the battered green book and spreading its wings, a doom as much as a gift. Over the rush of water, under the roar of wind, or measured with silence, a human voice sounds strange. Words are stranger still, but we are given words. Pain makes us strangers; words can bring us back.

I restacked the firewood and tightened the ropes that held the tent, and heated water, and washed the pots. When I looked out of the tent, Pookie was looking in. So I sat on the ground and ran my hands through her fur, and she licked my ear. Where she licked, the wind was chill.

I put on my coat and hiked north toward the highest peak. The gusts became one gust; the wind blew without pause, then ceased. Small birds called among the stunted firs: goldfinches and mountain chicka-dees. The tallest trees had ripe cones, erect and gleaming with pitch, looking too heavy for the twigs that held them. In the dusk the creamy white froth of yarrow blossoms recalled Cassandra, so strongly that I had to catch my breath.

I stopped. The yellow of the currant leaves was supernatural. It was only a rough walk up to the peak, so I climbed and sat up there among the rocks, east of the setting sun and west of the moon. I gazed down into North Murphy where skirts of talus ended in the country of little hills. It was dark enough that I couldn't recognize our camp. The tops of the hills looked alike, deep blue, and barred with the shadows of pines.

I could see an animal to the north, crossing a meadow. It was a bear, I think, head high, following a scent, traveling fast. It never looked up, or back. Then it was gone.

SEPTEMBER 15

"No coyotes, just howls," he says, stooping into the tent. "I need rest.

"Feels like a storm," he says. He gets into his bedroll and I go to sleep again, and dream of horses: horses running up from the west and through the trees, breaking limbs.

"All hell breaking loose," he says, and gets out of his bag. The wind makes bass-flute notes across the pipe. Now comes hail, little bullets down inside the stovepipe, flying in around it to clink on the granite coffeepot. The wind accelerates and lifts the back of the tent, and the rocks tumble onto my sleeping bag as I grab the steel upright and hold it with my weight. He grips the front pole. The tent tilts east, the back wall rattling like a snare. My hands ache, holding the galvanized steel. Another gust. The tent kicks farther and lower, and I yell to Mitch to hold the stove, so the grip of the thimble on the pipe doesn't jerk it up and strew coals on our beds.

In a lull I get a big rock from the bottom of the tent and set it on the stove. The steel's warm. The dogs come crouching and whimpering into the tent.

When it finally calms, I replace the poles and rocks. The stove is askew, so I straighten it. I'm shivering. I've been standing and holding the tent for an hour without a stitch of clothing. Mitch is half dressed. I put on jeans and a shirt and my wool coat and start a fire. Mitch joins me at the stove. The dogs lick their paws and look sorrowful.

Then it's light.

Stove. Coffee. Cornmeal mush.

In a dutiful fret, Mitch goes down to see where the sheep went during the storm. Most herders come from Spain, or Mexico, or Peru, or from poverty-wracked hamlets in the mountains of New Mexico. True Americans, the beneficiaries of eight or ten thousand years of livestock domestication, won't herd sheep anymore. Why? It's hard work, and you have the nagging sense of being either owned or cheated. It demands sacrifice out of proportion to what it yields. And shepherds are scorned.

Curiously, much of this scorn comes from the ranchers themselves. They cherish their accounts of waywardness, drunkenness, and inhuman passions. But they'd rather hire a drunken scoundrel to herd their sheep badly, while their sons drive dump trucks for the county road crew. Why? It has a mean, diesel-fueled, steel-edged, *Norteamericano* dignity, and it pays.

We love machines: gears and chains, red steel, green steel, black rubber tires. Most of the ranchers bought tractors and sold their draft teams for dog food: efficiency, production, cash flow, industry, wars. *Stop it.*

Mitch comes back. Roger arrives. Did you open the ham? Let's have that. Okay. What about the sheep? Night-herded, coyotes over north. No tracks, just howls. Oh, well they move pretty fast. Yup. No point in gathering tonight. Smells like snow. You think? Upper bowl's hammered. It'll come back.

It rains as we eat, and we watch thin streams blow off the canvas, eating chocolate chip cookies. I put on my slicker and go out.

It clears and I can see the sun setting. There are thick clouds over the Caribous, with a softer look. I look into the valley and see the lights of cars. Then I can hear them, the cry of tires on the wet paved roads. How could I go back?

But they're beautiful, too, that procession of lights rising and falling along the blue-black gleam of the highway. I go back in.

Roger and Mitch are drinking the last of the brandy. Roger brought a quart of peppermint schnapps, to trail out. I can smell it. Ugh. They're talking about being roommates at school, and romantic disasters. So I lie on my sleeping bag at the edge of the candlelight, avoiding the schnapps, and open my grimy book and find myself a romance.

Aucassin and Nicolete, A.D. 1150. *So speak they, say they, tell they the Tale:* Poor Nicolete hails from the wrong side of the Mediterranean. Aucassin is so ragingly in love that he refuses to pursue the family skirmish with the Foul Count, Bougars de Valence. Aucassin's dad Count Garin de Biaucaire—says that if Nicolete is so terribly distracting vis-à-vis the necessary mayhem, well by God he'll burn her at the stake and that'll be that. So they lock Nicolete up for toasting, and deride poor love-struck Aucassin as a rotten patriot and lousy Christian, and tell him he won't go to heaven.

Aucassin retorts that he wouldn't go to their crummy heaven if they paid him in travelers checks, because that's where all the boring, stupid, ugly, nasty, whiny people go:

> These be they that go into Paradise; with them I have naught to make. But into Hell I would fain go; for into Hell fare the goodly clerks, and goodly knights that fall in tourneys and great wars, and stout men-at-arms, and all men noble. With these I would liefly go. And thither pass the sweet ladies and courteous

that have two lovers, or three, and their lords also thereto. And thither goes the gold and the silver, and the cloth of *vair* and cloth of *gris*, and harpers, and makers, and the prince of this world. With these I would gladly go, let me but have with me Nicolete, my sweetest lady.

Bravo! But of course the militaristic ratbastards prevail, so not being a Socrates, Aucassin dutifully goes out and kills hundreds, maims thousands, and captures the Foul Count Bougars. But then he's double-crossed by his perfidious dad, who still wants to do poor Nicolete incendiary harm. *Slam* goeth the door, *click* goeth the key. But instead of languishing, the brave lass spirits herself out of the cell and climbeth over the castle wall:

Here one singeth:

Nicolete, the fair of face,
Climbed upon the coping-stone,
There she made lament and moan . . .
If within the wood I fare,
Lo, the wolves will slay me there,
Boars and lions terrible,
Many in the wild wood dwell,
But if I abide the day,
Surely worse will come of it,
Surely will the fire be lit,
That shall burn my life away . . .

Then, like many a good soul before and since, she hides out in the woods.

It's a *chante-fable*, which means that some parts were spoken and others sung, maybe with a lute, like riding a good horse at a walk, and then a canter. I imagine Nicolete looking a bit like Cassandra, with a sweeter temperament. I can picture the lute, too, and almost hear it, and imagine how the rounded back would feel—well, rather like the swell of Nicolete's fair hip.

She's a Saracen, it turns out, the Princess of Carthage: more than worthy of Aucassin's hand. He discovers her leafy bower in the woods, and her in it. The old ratbastard obligingly dies, but further trials intervene. But at long last, despite shipwreck and other horrendous events, they find each other. And while Aucassin buffs his lance, she bathes herself in a potion called *Esclaire,* and puts on translucent silks, and they enjoy "great gladness and delight," which is as close to explicit sex as medieval romances get.

Slipping at last out of their armor and silks, Aucassin and Nicolete have few regrets. Unlike poor Cassandra and me. But life's not a romance. And she's not gone, really. She's probably sitting in a leather bucket seat.

SEPTEMBER 16

So speak they, say they, tell they the Tale: That night it snowed like a white bitch-kitty.

All three of us slid downhill at first light to gather. Coming back up Mitch's horse fell, but he wasn't hurt. Now the horses are plastered with snow, tied to the stunted firs, and Mitch and Roger are driving the herd along the crest as I pack the frozen camp.

Packing the tent is like folding up a floating dock: eighty pounds of soaked canvas, roll it and force the water out with body weight. Fight with ropes near the freezing point, and spongy leather straps that won't pass through buckles. Soon it will be time to trust the fractious horses, and negotiate all hurt and harm.

Lament and moan. Roger comes back for the cookies and pokes in the kitchen boxes. What's this, he says. The cans—I mashed 'em flat, I say. Oh we bury the cans. I don't—I've been sending them out in a salt sack. Well I don't want the extra load on the horses. Shit, Roger, if you can throw three hundred pounds of salt on a horse then it can carry five pounds of empty cans downhill. Well we bury the cans 'cause it puts iron in the soil. Maybe the soil doesn't need any fucking iron, and they just wash out. No they don't, I'll dig a hole. It's all rock up here. *Watch me!*

Screw you, Roger. I wade into the krummholz and start picking up cans and throwing them at his feet. What about this one, and this, and this. I'm throwing rusty cans at his legs. *Can you dig a hole deep enough?*

He drops the shovel and walks off.

Hey! I'm sorry. It's not your fault.

He comes back but won't look at me and grabs the cookies and stalks off into the blizzard. The snow is blowing straight across, sticking to the west side of everything. I throw more cans out of the stunted firs, two salt sacks full. Then I finish loading the horses.

The trail goes along the backs of the peaks that tower above Murphy Creek, and above the west-dropping canyons, Birch Creek, Call Creek, Lee Creek. The trail is hard to follow in the fast-falling snow, even in the track of the herd. At first I make up spiteful rhymes:

> Tommy Kempis, Agnes Day, prayed their so-called lives away,
> And woke inside the Golden Walls, in Paradise's drafty halls.
> So the pilgrim and the lamb committed their eternities
> creeping, sniffling, shorn of sin, *baaaa*-ing on their bony knees.

I repeat it and laugh. But I'm soaked to the skin and the wind is raw, and then it's too cold to laugh. In the snowstorm, the second canyon is like the first, and I long for chili. Black pepper. Kisses. Whiskey. Salt. Grace. Now we're going down. One for the lead rope, one for the reins. My hand aches all the way up my arm. Death's not the enemy, but pain. I remember thinking I'd never die. But if you think you'll live forever, you can't grow up. Simple. So cold. I can't stand this anymore.

The sun strikes into the torrent of snow, and the world is dizzying and brilliant. Then it quits snowing. I see the shuttling dogs and the soaked asses of the herd.

I ride up behind Roger and try to apologize.

Long old season, he says. Going back to vet school next week. Can't wait.

We're crossing the third ruined cirque. Now that I know sheep, I can see how badly this place is marked. Given sheep and these mountains, I'd probably have done the same. Each year they worried about

getting trapped by early snow, and trailed over the top and then held
their herds on this side: save grass on the home ranch. Get that last
cutting in. Sell 'em off the range. Two more days. It'll come back, they
said.

The wind is whirling big, heavy snowflakes onto the rocks, the
horses, me. God grant us coffee and whiskey and release. I look for a
windbreak, a thick spruce, an overhanging rock, but the bowl is huge
and gray and devoid. Two more days for a hundred years. Now there's
not enough up here to feed a snake.

But it'll come back.

Check-a-roo.

Afternoon. We drive the herd down out of the melting snow and into
red mud. My slicker chafes my neck and my thighs are raw, and my
right hand throbs, so I lead the pack string with my left one. Hey
Roger. Cookies?

Guess we ate them up. Sorry. Won't be long.

The noise is terrible, all these dirty, soaked, suffering beasts bleating
and bellowing, and the dogs barking. And the three of us yelling at the
top of our lungs.

"Rotten stinking devilbastard scum of hell. Git-git-git, *yeeeeeeeeee—
owwww!*"

Coming into the foothills we lose a month, and it's late summer. We
ride through green thickets, look out on the patchwork fields, the pleasant land of Counterpane. The sheep brawl down the aspen hills and
along the opening valley of a stream, through cottonwood, chokecherry,
serviceberry. The cottonwoods are a wonderful gold, the common maple scarlet, the aspens pure yellow with a bloody undertone.

We'll camp on the school section, Roger says. Mom's bringing sup-
per out. We'll set up the tent and eat and night-herd in shifts.

We drive the sheep into a sloping meadow where the grass is still
partly green. It's spotted with sage and circled in aspens, with fenced
fields on two sides, late alfalfa and ripe wheat. I tie the horses to trees
and slip the packs and unsaddle. Elhon snapped another britchen, and

Tubby's front cinch is down to five strings. I set up the tent by myself, while Roger and Mitch work to keep the hungry sheep out of the crops. The dogs are shuttling and barking, as Mitch and Roger yell.

"*Booooooorrega! Puta, puta,* git-git-git! Son-of-a-bitch! *Yip-yowwww!*"

I lean against an aspen and slide down until I'm sitting on the ground. I stretch my legs. I get my black book out. I'm too tired. But looking back up at the crest, bright with the new snow, I write an easy sort of poem:

> When I leave the mountains
> they'll get along fine without me.
> I won't need to worry
> about who's going to wake them
> in the morning or who's
> going to feed the squirrels,
> or did I leave the water running?
> When I left, the water
> was running fine.

SEPTEMBER 17

So speak they, say they, tell they the Tale: Mitch wakes me at midnight. I drink a mug of coffee and stoke the stove. There's some of Louise's fried chicken left, good but not ruffed grouse. That doesn't stop me eating it.

Pookie wants to herd, so I tie her up. Then I walk around the sheep. They're bedded, the ewes and lambs lying with their legs tucked underneath, in doubled pools of shadow. There's a thin slice lost from the underside of the moon, and the field of ripe wheat shines, tassels drooped in a million silky curves.

I walk out into the gravel road. *Aaaaaa!* My heart stops.

Scared by the roll of a black cow's eye. The cow is equally unnerved and trots off snorting, her glossy flanks jiggling in the moonlight. Now I breathe sagebrush, dry grass, road dust: valley smells.

A coyote howls from the mouth of the hills.

Here one singeth:

Walking late
you happen on death
unexpectedly—
stars shining through
clouds and it's there,
a white Cadillac stopped
on a one-lane dirt road,
tough to get by
without looking in.

Or driving home,
to visit family or a friend,
passing late through towns
where the store closes
at sunset and none of the houses
shows light, you see
a black horse standing alone
in a field of ripe wheat
under a moon past full,
and ahead on the road
a dark place under the trees.

Wake Roger. Dirty old sleeping bag. Have to wash it sometime.

Red's hooves sound funny on pavement: *clunk, clunk, clunk, clink.* We drive the sheep down lanes of asphalt, fenced, at the world's end:

"*Borrega! Boo-booooorrega! Yowwww!*"

The ewes go to fall pasture, lambs to the knife. "Y'know," Mitch says, riding alongside, "I really envy those Bascos. They ship their lambs at the trailhead, and pick up a wagon and head straight west. I don't even know if they go back to the ranch. It's an open range herd. They put the bucks in and trail out onto the Snake River Desert. Big country. And it's plumb empty." He shakes his head and rides off.

Now, if you say the word *lonely* I think first of a city, the long, hard streets and doors to be closed and locked. Curtains, hedges, fences, gates. Loneliness lives in the turning away. More fear in that than in lightning, blizzard, hail, rockslide, buck-off, wolf bite, fracture, fever, freeze, or dark of night. We've known the natural dangers for a million years. It's the symbolic fears that are unexplored.

Midafternoon. We turn the sheep into a pasture to the north of the house, through a wire gate. We put the horses in the south pasture and heave the saddles and gear into the shed. Mitch and I talk bravely about going to the Pines Bar and stirring up a fight. We take the old black Chevy pickup. He drives. I'm clutching the edge of the seat. I ask how fast he's going. "Thirty," he says.

"Feels like a hundred and thirty."

So we zoom into town at twenty-five miles per hour. He parks and I go into the tack shop and pick out a couple of new cinches and two rolls of latigo, and some good thong. The man looks up from the sum. "Charge it to Prestons?"

I realize that we both have bushy beards. Mitch has tied his hair back and stuffed it into his collar, but mine brushes my shoulders. "Sure." He wraps it in brown paper and ties it with string. I sign the bill. We walk out to the truck.

"Did you ask Royal?" Mitch frowns.

"If he balks, I'll pay for it. I'm going to fix all the saddles before I go."

We eat big T-bones and go to the Pines, but there's no one worth fighting. So we have two double shots of whiskey each, and almost pass out with our heads on the bar.

"Prestons' herders," someone says as we stagger out the door.

I try to sleep in a bed for the first time since July, and I can't. Too much on top, too much underneath. The door shuts. The walls creak. And the air is stale and doesn't move.

After breakfast, Royal says we'd better go buck bales. I don't say any-thing. Roger starts the tractor and Mitch climbs up on the hayrack.

"No," I say, over the rumble. "Sorry. I'm fixing the saddles and then packing up my stuff."

Roger shrugs and engages the gears. "Whatever. Just let Dad know," he says. The tractor chugs out of the yard. Mitch looks at me from the jouncing rack and doesn't wave, and then he punches the air and whoops as they go around the curve, out of sight.

I go to the shed and lay the tent and panniers out to dry and work the stove over with a steel brush and oil. Then I work on the saddles, one by one, until there's a pile of rotten leather on the dirt floor, clink-ing with tarnished rivets, and the sawbucks are lined up along the harness pole, rigged with stout new latigo. Amen.

How does the world work? Snow melts. Horses will be horses. You can find an animal by its track. Sourdough's no good unless you use it. Gravity wants us to lie down. You can be miserable and not die. Or you can die, too. And in September, rain turns to snow.

I walk out into the yard and scratch Pookie behind the ears and then go into the house. Louise looks up from the stove.

"I got the saddles fixed and the camping gear cleaned up and put away."

She gives me a pacific smile. "That's good. Sometimes we just don't get things finished like we should. There's always something crying for attention."

Royal looks in. "Well. We better go and settle up," he says.

In the parlor, with the door closed, he gets his checkbook out and squints. "Well. Roger thinks you did a pretty fair job. We're out some sheep, but it's a rough old country."

"It is. Beautiful country."

"I figure about two months, rounded off. So what'd we say? Two twenty-five?"

"Two-*fifty*?"

But he's already written the check. He tears it out and looks embarrassed for a moment, but then he looks away through the window. He's done this before. So I take it and fold it, with a twinge between my knuckles, and put it in my shirt pocket.

"A fellow could do a whole lot worse," he says.

Wide is the grazing land of words.

That cuts both ways, but I don't think Royal would get the point. And besides, he just gypped me out of fifty bucks. So I nod and start to go.

He holds his hand out again, and I look down at it and take a breath. And then I shake his hand. Why not? It's softer than I'd have imagined, and his grip is gentle, almost one of regret.

As I turn the doorknob, my right hand aches. I can't forget.

But every summer has to end, they say.

And so the tale.